Front cover: Beef Wellington, page 17;
Caesar Salad, page 125.
Back cover: Strawberry Shortcake,
page 84. Opposite: Toffee
Crisps, page 107.

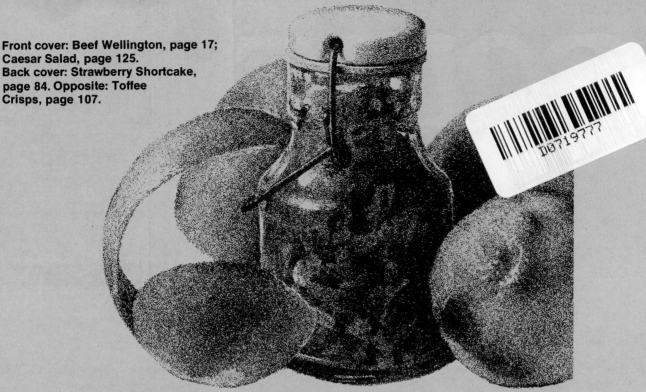

COOKING CLASS COOKBOOK

Fully illustrated, easy-to-follow instructions
for popular recipes from
the Australian Women's Weekly Cooking Classes.
Selected by food editor ELLEN SINCLAIR

Photographs by Gary Isaacs

Contents

Published by Australian Consolidated Press Ltd, 54 Park Street, Sydney, Australia.
Distributed by Network Distribution Company, 54 Park Street, Sydney

POULTRY

Beggar's Chicken

THIS is one of the renowned dishes of the Orient. The chicken was originally wrapped in lotus leaves, then in clay, then thrown into a hot fire to cook. Supply chopsticks to four lucky people.

YOU WILL NEED:
1.5kg (3lb) chicken
3 shallots
2.5cm (1in) piece green ginger
1 teaspoon sugar
3 tablespoons soy sauce
2 tablespoons dry sherry
1 tablespoon water
¼ teaspoon five spice powder
2 tablespoons soy sauce, extra
2 tablespoons oil
extra oil

CLAY DOUGH
1kg (2lb) cooking salt
4 cups plain flour
1½ cups water, approx.

1. Place unsifted flour and salt into bowl; mix well. Gradually mix in water, mixing to a firm dough. Use hands to mix dough; a little extra water may be needed. Do not have dough too soft or it will be hard to handle.

2. Place two very large sheets of aluminium foil on to table, brush top sheet of aluminium foil well with extra oil. Place chicken in middle of aluminium foil. Place roughly chopped shallots, sugar, peeled and sliced ginger, soy sauce, sherry, water and five spice powder into bowl; mix well. Rub chicken all over with extra soy sauce, then rub with the 2 tablespoons of oil, rubbing well into skin. Pull skin at neck end down under chicken, tuck wing tips under chicken and over neck skin. Carefully pour soy sauce mixture into chicken cavity, holding chicken up slightly so that no sauce runs out. Secure end of chicken with small skewer. Wrap aluminium foil around chicken, securing like a parcel.

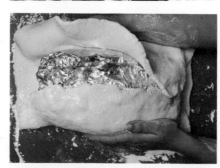

3. Roll out dough to approximately 1cm (½in) in thickness, so that it will completely encase chicken. Fold dough over chicken, pressing edges together; press ends together.

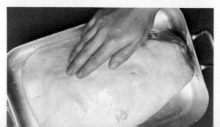

4. Place chicken into lightly oiled baking dish. With wet fingers, smooth out all joins, making sure that there are no holes in pastry, or steam will escape. Bake in hot oven for 1 hour. Reduce heat to moderately slow, cook further 3 hours. Remove chicken from oven, break open pastry clay with mallet or hammer, remove from around chicken. Lift foil-wrapped chicken on to serving plate, carefully remove foil.

How to joint a chicken

WHEN a recipe calls for chicken pieces you can usually buy them, already cut up, in most large food stores or supermarkets. However, if you are only able to buy a whole chicken, you will have to cut it into serving pieces. There's an art to doing this, but it's an art that's easily acquired. Here's how it's done.

1. Cut through skin connecting leg to body, bend leg out, away from body, find the joint where leg hinges, cut through this (there's no need to cut through bone.)

2. Cut each leg into two pieces at joint, as shown; this gives thigh and drumstick. Or the leg can be left in one complete piece.

4. Separate breast and back by cutting through rib bones along each side of body; cut as close as possible to backbone.

3. Cut a slice of breast meat with the wing to make a better serving portion, then bend wing away from body to find joint where wing joins body, cut through this.

5. Cut along edge of breastbone, to divide breast in two; trim away any excess skin and fat. Back portion is not considered as an individual serving piece but can accompany another portion such as the wing, or be used to make soup.

How to roast a chicken

CHICKEN, golden brown and glistening, perhaps with a savoury stuffing added, is one of the most popular of all meals. Here's how to make sure it's golden, moist and succulent every time you cook it.

YOU WILL NEED:
1 chicken
prepared stuffing
60g (2oz) butter
1 cup water
1 chicken stock cube
salt, pepper

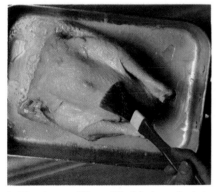

1. If using stuffing, fill this loosely into chicken (stuffing will swell during cooking); secure vent with small skewer. Put chicken in baking dish, rub well with softened butter — particularly over the breast and legs; add salt and pepper.

2. Add water and crumbled stock cube to pan. Roast in moderately hot oven for 30 minutes, then brush chicken well with the pan juices. Move chicken around a little in the pan, so that the skin of the chicken does not stick to the pan during cooking. Add an extra ½ cup water to pan if water evaporates too quickly.

3. Continue cooking in moderately hot oven until chicken is tender; allow approximately 1½ hours for a 1.5kg (3lb) chicken. Brush with pan juices about every 15 minutes. Twice during cooking time (if cooking chicken without stuffing) tilt chicken so that any water inside cavity runs out (this water slows down the cooking time). To test if chicken is cooked, pierce with skewer at the thick second joint; the juices will run clear, not pink. The leg will also move easily to and fro and the skin will start to shrink slightly from the bones. Make gravy from pan drippings.

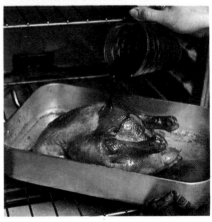

4. Additional flavourings can be added toward the end of cooking time. For Chinese Roast Chicken, add combined ½ cup dry sherry, 1 tablespoon soy sauce, 1 teaspoon grated green ginger and 1 tablespoon honey to pan during the last 15 minutes of cooking time; brush chicken frequently with pan drippings.

POULTRY

"CHASSEUR" means a sauce containing mushrooms and shallots. It can be a sauce for many meats. Here we have allied it to chicken for a dish with rich, superb flavour. Serve with hot rice or mashed potatoes, crusty bread and separate green salad. Serves four.

YOU WILL NEED:
1.5kg (3lb) chicken
30g (1oz) butter
2 tablespoons oil
250g (8oz) small mushrooms
1 large clove garlic
1 cup dry white wine
salt, pepper
½ teaspoon sugar
¼ teaspoon tarragon
2 large ripe tomatoes
6 shallots
2 tablespoons chopped parsley
2 tablespoons tomato paste

BROWN SAUCE
125g (4oz) butter
1 large onion
1 large carrot
¼ cup plain flour
3 cups water
3 chicken stock cubes
salt, pepper

Chicken Chasseur

1. Make Brown Sauce first. Heat butter in frying pan, add peeled and finely chopped onion and peeled and finely chopped carrot. Saute very gently until onion and carrot are dark golden brown. Add flour to pan, stir over low heat until flour is dark golden brown; do not allow to burn. Remove pan from heat, add water, stir until combined. Return pan to heat, stir until sauce boils and thickens. Reduce heat, add crumbled stock cubes, salt and pepper. Cover pan, simmer very gently 1 hour. Strain sauce, retain liquid.

2. Cut chicken into serving-sized pieces. Heat butter and oil in large frying pan. Add half the chicken, fry gently on all sides until golden brown; remove chicken from pan. Repeat with remaining chicken, remove from pan.

3. Add sliced mushrooms and crushed garlic to pan, saute gently until mushrooms are just tender. Add wine, bring to boil, boil uncovered for 3 minutes or until liquid is reduced by half. Add prepared Brown Sauce, sugar, tarragon, and tomato paste. Chop tomatoes roughly, put into electric blender, blend on medium speed until smooth (or mash well), push through sieve; discard pulp and seeds. Add this tomato puree to sauce, add salt and pepper, stir until combined. Add chicken, bring to boil, reduce heat, simmer, covered 45 minutes or until chicken is tender; stir occasionally. Add parsley and chopped shallots.

6

French Herbed Chicken

HERE is chicken cooked in the French style, with herb butter spread between skin and breast.

1. Take 1.5kg (3lb) chicken and using teaspoon with rounded side up, gently ease down and over chicken breast separating skin from meat; be careful not to break skin.

2. Make Herbed Butter: beat 90g (3oz) butter until soft and creamy; add 2 tablespoonfuls chopped parsley, 3 finely chopped shallots, mix well. Beat in 1 teaspoonful french mustard, ½ teaspoonful tarragon, salt and pepper. With small spatula carefully spread butter evenly over whole chicken breast under skin.

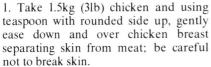

3. Prepare Stuffing: Put 2½ cups fresh breadcrumbs (about ½ loaf bread), 1 egg, ½ teaspoonful thyme, 2 tablespoonfuls chopped parsley in bowl. Heat 60g (2oz) butter in pan, add 2 rashers bacon, chopped, 1 small onion, peeled and chopped; saute gently until onion is soft. Add to crumb mixture with salt and pepper, mix well. Stuff chicken, close cavity.

4. Put chicken in baking dish, add 1 cup dry white wine, ½ cup water, 30g (1oz) butter, 1 crumbled chicken stock cube. Bake uncovered in moderate oven 1½ hours or until cooked, basting frequently with pan juices. Remove from baking dish. Put dish on top of stove, bring liquid to boil, boil 2 minutes; remove from heat. Stir in combined ½ cup cream and 1 tablespoonful cornflour. Return to heat, stir until sauce boils and thickens, add salt and pepper. Serve sauce with chicken. Serves 4.

POULTRY

HERE is a Russian specialty which has become world famous. Butter is wrapped inside a thin cutlet; when cooked and cut into, the hot melted butter spurts out as a sauce. It's traditional for the breast of chicken to be cut with the wing bone attached; this gives the small jutting-out bone shown in the picture. But only two of these can be obtained from one whole chicken. It's cheaper to use chicken breasts only; taste is just the same — but there's no small bone.

YOU WILL NEED:
2 large chicken breasts (or 2 chickens)
flour
salt, pepper
3 eggs
¼ cup milk
white breadcrumbs (from bread about 2 days old)
oil for deep-frying
                    BUTTER FILLING
185g (6oz) butter
salt, pepper
2 tablespoons chopped parsley
1 tablespoon chopped chives
¼ teaspoon grated lemon rind
pinch tarragon

Make butter filling first. Combine softened butter with all ingredients, mix well. Divide mixture into four, shape into four rolls (see step 4 for shape); refrigerate until very firm.

Chicken Kiev

1. If using chicken breasts, remove skin, cut meat away from the bone with sharp knife, giving two chicken fillets from each whole breast. If using whole chickens, remove skin carefully; with sharp knife cut meat from one side of chicken breast, as shown, then continue on and cut wing off, keeping the breast and wing in one piece; repeat with other breast and wing.

2. Cut wing off at first joint, as shown. With sharp knife, scrape meat off wing so that the bone is clean.

3. With meat mallet or rolling pin pound chicken fillets out thinly. There must be no holes or the butter will run out during cooking. However, if flesh does tear while pounding, overlap the torn pieces and pound gently together until firm again. (Meat can be pounded out between sheets of greaseproof paper.)

4. Place the cold butter roll in centre of each chicken breast. Fold end of chicken over on to the butter, then roll up, completely encasing the butter. Coat chicken rolls in flour seasoned with salt and pepper. Dip in combined beaten eggs and milk, then roll in breadcrumbs; repeat the egg-and-breadcrumbing to cover firmly. Place on to tray, refrigerate 1 hour. Lower into deep hot oil, cook for approximately 5 minutes. Do not have oil too hot, or breadcrumbs will brown too quickly before chicken is cooked through. Serves 4.

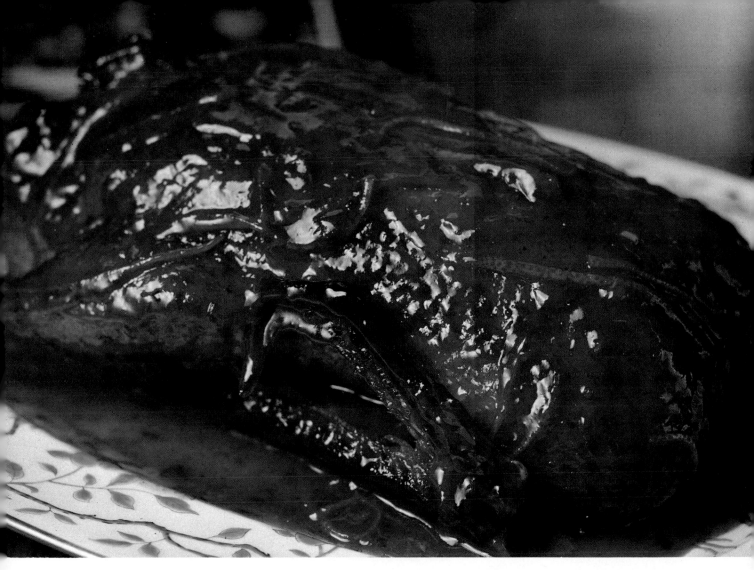

Duck with Orange

YOU WILL NEED:
2kg (4lb) duck
60g (2oz) butter
SAUCE

1 orange
½ cup orange juice
1 tablespoon sugar
2 teaspoons vinegar
2 cups water
2 chicken stock cubes
2 teaspoons lemon juice
3 teaspoons arrowroot
½ cup sweet sherry
¼ cup Grand Marnier
salt, pepper

THIS is for a special occasion — and so good it would make any occasion special. Cook tender duck in a rich orange liqueur sauce until it is glistening and golden. A 2kg duck will serve four people — and they'll love it!

1. If desired, fill duck with any favourite stuffing. Put in baking dish, brush with melted butter. Bake in moderate oven 1 hour, brushing occasionally with the juices in the pan.

2. Remove rind from orange, remove any white pith. Cut rind into thin strips, drop into boiling water, boil three minutes; drain. Put sugar, vinegar, water, crumbled stock cubes, orange and lemon juices and blanched strips of orange rind into saucepan, stir until boiling; boil rapidly until sauce is reduced by half. Blend arrowroot and sherry, stir gradually into sauce, stir until sauce boils and thickens; reduce heat, simmer 2 minutes. Add salt and pepper, stir in Grand Marnier.

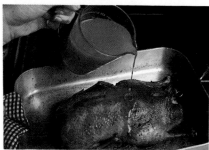

3. Drain pan juices off duck, add prepared sauce to pan; brush duck well with the sauce. Return to oven, bake further 40 to 50 minutes basting frequently with sauce until duck is cooked and well glazed.

1. Chicken Maryland pieces — which can be bought from most large supermarkets — consist of the leg and thigh in one piece. If these are not available, substitute 1.75kg (3½lb) chicken pieces. Coat chicken pieces lightly with flour, seasoned with salt and pepper. Dip into combined beaten eggs and milk, then into dry breadcrumbs, pressing breadcrumbs on firmly. Cut each peeled banana in half, coat with flour, then into egg mixture and coat firmly with breadcrumbs.

2. Place Chicken Maryland pieces one at a time into deep hot oil, fry until very light golden brown, approximately 8 minutes. Do not have oil too hot or chicken will brown too quickly and not cook through. Drain chicken on absorbent paper; repeat with remainder of chicken pieces.

3. Place cobs of corn into large saucepan of boiling water, reduce heat, simmer covered for 20 minutes or until tender; drain, keep warm. Meanwhile, prepare corn fritters: Place sifted flours and salt into bowl. Add egg-yolk, milk, pepper and drained corn; mix well. Beat egg-white until soft peaks form, fold into corn mixture. Drop tablespoonfuls of mixture into hot oil, fry until golden brown and cooked through, approximately 3 minutes; keep warm. Place crumbed bananas into hot oil, fry until golden brown; drain on absorbent paper; keep warm.

Chicken Maryland

THIS golden-crumbed chicken dish is an American favourite; traditional accompaniments are corn fritters, bananas, grilled tomatoes. Colourful extra accompaniments are corn on the cob, bacon curls and pineapple rings, together with green salad.

YOU WILL NEED:
6 Chicken Maryland pieces (see Step 1)
flour
salt, pepper
3 eggs
¼ cup milk
dry breadcrumbs
6 bananas
3 ripe tomatoes
3 rashers bacon

6 pineapple rings
6 cobs corn

CORN FRITTERS
½ cup plain flour
½ cup self-raising flour
salt, pepper
1 egg, separated
¼ cup milk
470g (15oz) can whole kernel corn

4. Return chicken pieces to very hot oil, fry quickly until dark golden brown, approximately 3 minutes; drain on absorbent paper, keep warm. Cut tomatoes in half. Cut each bacon rasher in half, roll up and secure with small wooden stick. Place tomatoes and bacon rolls under hot griller; grill until bacon rolls are crisp, and tomatoes are heated through. Place prepared chicken, bananas, corn, corn fritters, tomatoes, bacon rolls and pineapple slices on to serving plates. Serves six.

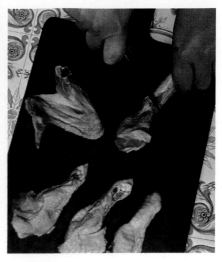

1. Wash and dry wings. Cut off wing tips at joint, as shown. (Use wing tips in another dish, or to make soup.)

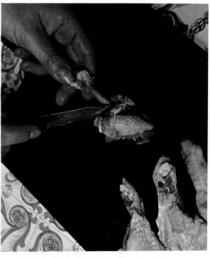

2. Holding small end of bone, trim around bone with sharp knife to cut meat free from bone. Then cut, scrape, and push meat down to large end.

3. Using fingers, pull skin and meat down over end of bone; they will resemble baby drumsticks.

Chinese Chicken Sticks

THEY'RE the greatest novelty nibble you'll ever serve at a party! Perhaps you'd better double quantities they'll go so fast — and everyone will want the recipe. Keep finger napkins handy. Chinese Chicken Sticks are a delicious accompaniment to drinks, and who would guess that they're really chicken wings?

YOU WILL NEED:
1.5kg (3lb) chicken wings
¼ cup soy sauce
1 clove garlic
1 teaspoon grated green ginger
salt, pepper
1 teaspoon sugar
2 tablespoons dry sherry
2 tablespoons oil
1 tablespoon honey

4. In large bowl combine soy sauce, crushed garlic, ginger, salt, pepper, sugar, honey and sherry. Pour over chicken sticks, refrigerate overnight; stir them occasionally. Pour chicken sticks and the marinade in baking dish with oil; spread them out evenly in pan. Bake in moderate oven 35 to 40 minutes or until cooked, basting occasionally with pan juices, stirring occasionally. Remove from oven, quickly brush any remaining marinade over the chicken sticks. Put on plate to serve.
Makes about 24.

1. Joint chickens, cut into large serving-sized pieces. Heat 60g (2oz) of the butter in heavy, shallow pan. Add peeled whole onions and diced bacon. Cook until onions are lightly browned. Remove from pan. Add chicken pieces to pan drippings. Cook until well browned on all sides. Remove from pan. If pan is small, brown chicken pieces a few at a time. Add sliced mushrooms and crushed garlic to pan. Cook gently until mushrooms are wilted. Remove from pan.

2. Add remaining butter to pan drippings. When butter has melted, stir in flour. Stir until golden brown; do not allow to burn. Remove from heat. Add crumbled stock cubes, gradually stir in water. Blend well. Stir over heat until sauce boils and thickens. Add brandy, wine, thyme, herbs and bayleaf.

Coq au Vin

FOUND often on menus of French restaurants, Coq au Vin is easy to prepare in your own kitchen. Ingredients are simple, flavour is superb. An ideal dinner party dish, it can be partly prepared the night before, then with all ingredients combined in a casserole or saucepan, cooked to succulent tenderness just before serving. Quantities given will serve 6.

3. Transfer chicken, all vegetables and sauce to deep pan. Cover, bring to boil. Reduce heat, simmer 30 minutes or until chicken is tender. Season with salt and pepper. Remove bayleaf. Coq au Vin can also be baked in moderate oven, covered, for 40 minutes or until chicken is tender. Serve with hot garlic bread and tossed green salad.

YOU WILL NEED:
2 x 1kg (2lb) chickens, or 2kg (4lb) chicken pieces
125g (4oz) butter
125g (4oz) bacon
12 tiny onions
salt, pepper
250g (8oz) mushrooms
1 clove garlic
½ cup flour
2 chicken stock cubes
2½ cups water
⅓ cup brandy
1½ cups dry red wine
¼ teaspoon thyme
½ teaspoon mixed herbs
1 bayleaf

1. Heat butter in pan, add finely chopped onion, thyme, bayleaf and finely chopped bacon. Saute slowly until very tender but not brown. Add cleaned livers, which have been soaked in salted water for 1 hour, then drained; simmer 7 minutes or until cooked.

2. Put cooked mixture and butter from pan into blender. Add brandy, port, sherry, salt, pepper, cream and finely chopped mushrooms to pan. Stir to combine, bring to boil, simmer gently uncovered until sauce has reduced by half. Pour sauce into blender, blend both together until smooth.

Chicken Liver Pate

THE Australian Women's Weekly has published many recipes for pate over the years, but this has possibly been the outstanding favourite. It can be served on toast or biscuits with drinks or, set in small individual containers, it is a perfect first course for a dinner party. Recipe serves six as a first course. The texture of Chicken Liver Pate is soft and creamy, its taste distinctively different in a delightfully savoury way.

YOU WILL NEED:
500g (1lb) chicken livers
125g (4oz) butter
1 large onion
½ teaspoon thyme
1 bayleaf
6 rashers bacon
3 tablespoons port
3 tablespoons dry sherry
1 tablespoon brandy
salt, pepper
½ cup cream
125g (4oz) mushrooms
60g (2oz) butter, extra
extra bayleaves

3. Push mixture through coarse sieve. Place in individual dishes. Refrigerate until firm.
4. Put extra butter in saucepan, melt over gentle heat until white sediment comes to top; skim off white sediment only. Place a bayleaf on top of each pate, pour the clarified butter over to cover top of pate, refrigerate until set.

MEAT
Wiener Schnitzel

TENDER veal steaks, lightly lemon-flavoured, with a covering of golden crumbs, make a first-rate light meal. If veal is hard to obtain, thin slices of yearling beef can be substituted. Serve with a lemon wedge; hot potato salad also makes a good accompaniment to Wiener Schnitzel. Quantities will serve four to six.

YOU WILL NEED:
750g (1½lb) veal steak
lemon juice
flour
salt, pepper
3 eggs
dry breadcrumbs
60g (2oz) butter
⅓ cup oil

1. Ask butcher to cut the veal steaks very thinly; they should be about 5mm (¼in) thick. If steaks are large, cut each in half. Pound out very thinly with meat mallet or rolling pin.

2. Grind a little black pepper over one side of each steak, pressing pepper well into meat. Sprinkle approximately 1 teaspoon of lemon juice on to one side of each steak. Allow to stand for 15 minutes.

3. Coat steaks lightly in flour seasoned with salt and pepper. Shake off excess flour. Dip steaks into lightly beaten eggs, then into breadcrumbs, pressing breadcrumbs on firmly. If possible, refrigerate 1 hour to set the crumbs.

4. Heat oil and butter in large frying pan, add steaks, cook quickly on both sides until golden brown. Use tongs for turning the steaks — a fork would pierce the meat and allow juices to escape.

MEAT

ALL countries have their food specialties. But this beef dish from Russia has become famous on an international scale. It is excellent food to include in your menu if you're giving a party: noodles or rice are usual accompaniments. Serves 4.

YOU WILL NEED:
750g (1½lb) fillet steak
125g (4oz) butter
1 medium onion
500g (1lb) small mushrooms
salt, pepper
⅔ cup water
2 beef stock cubes
2 tablespoons tomato paste
300ml carton sour cream
1 teaspoon cornflour

Beef Stroganoff

1. Ask butcher to cut fillet in one piece. Carefully remove any fat or sinew from meat. Cut meat into 5mm (¼in) slices. Cut slices into 1cm (½in) strips. (If meat is frozen for one hour beforehand it is easier to cut into thin slices.)

2. Heat 60g (2oz) of the butter in a large frying pan until very hot. Add a quarter of the meat, cook very quickly until golden brown, remove meat from pan immediately. Repeat with remaining meat, a quarter at a time.

3. Add remaining butter to pan. Add peeled and finely chopped onion to pan, saute gently until onion is lightly brown, add sliced mushrooms, saute gently until mushrooms are tender. Return meat to pan with salt, pepper, water, crumbled stock cubes and tomato paste, stir until combined. Bring to boil, reduce heat, simmer, covered for 5 minutes.

4. Put sour cream and cornflour in bowl, stir until well combined. Gradually add to meat mixture, stirring until mixture boils and thickens. Reduce heat, simmer, uncovered for 5 minutes.

TENDER fillet, spread with pate, topped with mushrooms, is encased in pastry and baked until golden. Cut into slices for serving; spoon Madeira Sauce over. Recipe serves four.

YOU WILL NEED:
1.25kg (2½lb) fillet of beef
freshly ground black pepper
60g (2oz) butter
250g (8oz) pate de foie
125g (4oz) small mushrooms
500g (1lb) pkt puff pastry
salt
1 egg-yolk
2 teaspoons water
          MADEIRA SAUCE
2 tablespoons flour
3 cups water
3 beef stock cubes
¼ cup madeira
salt, pepper

Madeira Sauce:
Put baking dish with pan drippings over very high heat until drippings are very dark golden brown; do not allow to burn. Reduce heat, add flour, stir until flour is golden brown, remove pan from heat. Add water, stir until combined. Return pan to heat, stir until sauce boils and thickens. Add crumbled stock cubes and madeira. Season with salt and pepper. Simmer, uncovered 10 minutes. Strain.

Beef Wellington

1. Remove all fat and gristle from meat. Tie securely with string, this holds the fillet in good shape. Grind black pepper over meat, pressing in firmly. Heat butter in baking dish. Add meat, sear meat on all sides until dark golden brown; do this over high heat. Put meat in moderate oven for 10 minutes. Remove meat from pan, allow to become competely cold. Reserve pan drippings for Madeira Sauce.

2. Remove string from meat. Beat pate de foie in bowl until it is just soft enough to spread. Spread a thin layer of pate over entire surface of meat. Sprinkle over a little salt. Press thinly sliced mushrooms on top of meat.

3. Roll out pastry to rectangle approx. 35cm x 25cm (14in x 10in); pastry size needed will depend on length and thickness of meat. Turn meat over and put it top side down in centre of pastry. Fold two outside edges of pastry over meat. Seal with combined beaten egg-yolk and water. Don't have pastry too thick at joins or pastry will not cook through. Press ends together, press with fingers to thin out the joined pastry so it is not thick; trim ends, brush ends with egg-yolk mixture then fold ends towards the centre join, press down firmly. Turn right side up again. Decorate top, if desired, with thin strips of pastry, as shown in picture. Brush with egg-yolk mixture. Bake in very hot oven for 5 minutes. Reduce heat to moderate. Bake further 15 minutes for medium rare; for medium, allow an extra 10 minutes.

MEAT

A CROWN Roast is a special dish for the occasions on which you have extra time to prepare. Order meat a day ahead to give the butcher enough time too. Quantities here will serve six.

YOU WILL NEED:
Crown roast of lamb (16 to 18 cutlets, cut in two separate pieces)
STUFFING:
½ cup long-grain rice
3 cups fresh white breadcrumbs
90g (3oz) butter
3 rashers bacon
1 large onion
1 clove garlic
3 tablespoons chopped parsley
4 shallots
salt, pepper
½ teaspoon rosemary
¼ teaspoon thyme
1 egg
60g (2oz) butter, extra
Stuffing:
Gradually add rice to large quantity of boiling salted water, boil uncovered 12 minutes or until rice is tender; drain. Heat butter in pan, add chopped bacon, peeled and finely chopped onion and crushed garlic, saute gently until onion is tender. Place rice, breadcrumbs, parsley, chopped shallots, salt, pepper, rosemary, thyme and egg into bowl, add onion mixture with butter in pan, mix well.

Crown Roast of Lamb

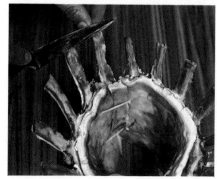

1. Ask butcher to prepare 16 to 18 rib chops, as for cutlets, but without cutting through the sections. Ask to have skin removed, and the chops chined (cut between the bones) for easier carving. Tie ribs together in a circle, bones to outside, to resemble a crown. With sharp knife, carefully remove any skin or fat from bones at top, as shown in picture.

2. Place a large sheet of aluminium foil into large baking dish. Put crown roast in centre of aluminium foil. Gather foil round exposed bones at base, as shown. To keep shape of roast, put a small heatproof bowl or tin into centre of roast.

3. Place a small piece of aluminium foil around each exposed bone at top. Roast in moderately hot oven 40 minutes, brushing frequently with extra melted butter. Remove from oven, remove small bowl or tin from centre. Pack stuffing into centre of roast, pressing down well. Spoon pan drippings over stuffing. Return to oven, cook further 40 to 45 minutes or until meat is tender. Place on serving dish, remove aluminium foil, replace with small cutlet frills for attractive presentation.

FULL of succulence and superb flavour, Veal Cordon Bleu is a dish that's simple to prepare and always appreciated. Slices of ham and cheese are sandwiched between thin slices of tender veal steak which is then crumbed and cooked gently in a butter and oil mixture until beautifully golden. Serve with wedges of lemon, canned asparagus spears, small new parsleyed potatoes. Quantities given serve four.

YOU WILL NEED:
4 large veal steaks (or 8 smaller pieces)
4 small slices leg ham
4 slices swiss cheese
flour
salt, pepper
3 eggs
¼ cup milk
dry breadcrumbs
60g (2oz) butter
¼ cup oil

Veal Cordon Bleu

1. Cut each large veal steak in half. Pound out each piece of veal very thinly. Trim edges to form oval shape. You will need two pieces of veal the same size to make one serving of Veal Cordon Bleu.

2. Put a piece of ham, then a slice of cheese on each of four slices of veal, making sure filling comes to within 1cm (½in) of edge of veal all round. Top with remaining veal slices, pressing edges of veal firmly together.

3. Coat veal lightly with flour seasoned with salt and pepper. Dip into combined beaten eggs and milk, then into breadcrumbs, pressing crumbs on firmly. Repeat egg-and-breadcrumb process. Heat butter and oil in large frying pan. Add veal steaks. Cook gently on both sides until golden brown. Allow approx. 6 minutes each side.

1. Cut eggplant into 1cm (½in) slices. Arrange on tray. Sprinkle with salt, let stand 25 minutes. Rinse under cold running water to remove salt. Pat dry.

2. Trim fat from chops. Mince meat or cut in small pieces. Or order meat in advance and ask butcher to mince it. Heat butter in large pan. Add meat, peeled, finely chopped onion and crushed garlic. Cook until meat browns well. Add undrained tomatoes; mash with fork or potato masher to reduce to puree. Add white wine, salt, pepper, and nutmeg. Bring to boil, reduce heat. Simmer gently, uncovered, until meat is tender and nearly all liquid has evaporated, 45 to 60 minutes.

3. Cook eggplant slices until golden brown; they can be deep-fried or shallow-fried in oil. Drain well. Arrange in base of greased ovenproof dish. Combine grated cheese and breadcrumbs. Sprinkle one-third of mixture over eggplant.

Moussaka

ALMOST every country in the Middle East has a local version of Moussaka, composed of layers of vegetables (usually eggplant), meat and sauce. Lamb is the meat used, but an economical version can be made by substituting minced steak. Cook Moussaka in an oblong dish or tin, such as a lamington tin, to serve easily, cut into squares. Accompany with tossed green salad. Quantities will serve six.

4. Spoon meat sauce over, then spread white sauce evenly. Sprinkle remaining cheese mixture over. Drizzle extra melted butter over. Bake in hot oven 20 to 25 minutes, or until topping is golden brown. Cut into squares to serve.

YOU WILL NEED:
1kg (2lb) lamb leg chops
1 large eggplant
salt
90g (3oz) butter
1 large onion
1 clove garlic
470g (15oz) can whole tomatoes
1 cup dry white wine
salt, pepper
½ teaspoon nutmeg
oil for frying
185g (6oz) cheddar cheese
½ cup packaged dry breadcrumbs
30g (1oz) butter, extra
White Sauce:

Melt 90g (3oz) butter, remove from heat, stir in ½ cup flour, ½ teaspoon nutmeg, salt and pepper. Stir over low heat 1 minute. Add 2 cups milk, stir until sauce boils and thickens. Reduce heat, cook further 1 minute. Remove from heat, add one lightly beaten egg, beat well.

1. Ask butcher to cut rump steak in one piece, approximately 2.5cm (1in) thick. Remove fat from meat. Cut meat into 2.5cm (1in) strips. Cut each strip of meat into 5mm (¼in) pieces, as shown in picture. Cut fat strips into 5mm (¼in) slices. (Fat is put on to the bamboo sate sticks; it helps baste the meat and will keep it moist while cooking.)

2. Place meat and fat into bowl, add soy sauce, honey, chilli powder, cumin, oil and curry powder; mix well. Cover bowl, refrigerate overnight.

3. Thread two pieces of meat on to skewer, as shown; thread a piece of fat on to skewer, then another two pieces of meat. Repeat with remaining skewers until all meat and fat are used. Grill until tender, brushing occasionally with oil.

Sates

SATES are often eaten in the Orient, but the sates of Singapore and Malaysia are perhaps the most famous. Bamboo sticks, used in this dish as skewers to hold pieces of meat, are available at Chinese food stores or large department stores.
A hibachi — Japanese charcoal grill — is ideal for cooking sates. They cost only a few dollars. Make sure the fire is really hot before cooking the sates. Position sticks on hibachi as shown, so that sticks do not burn, or cook sates on a griller. Sate sauce, into which the sticks are dipped, onion rings and chopped cucumber are traditional accompaniments.
The quantities given in this recipe are enough for about 30 sate sticks.
Sates are an ideal choice for serving on outdoor occasions when the mood is pleasantly relaxed. Their taste is excitingly different from the usual fare at barbecues — try them, and watch how quickly they disappear.

YOU WILL NEED:
500g (1lb) rump steak (or chicken, lamb or pork)
2 teaspoons soy sauce
1 teaspoon honey
½ teaspoon chilli powder
1 teaspoon cumin
2 tablespoons oil
½ teaspoon curry powder
extra oil

Sate Sauce:
Heat 2 tablespoons oil in pan, add 1 peeled and finely chopped onion and 2 cloves crushed garlic, saute gently until onion is golden brown. Add ½ teaspoon chilli powder, 2 teaspoons curry powder, 2.5cm (1in) piece peeled and grated green ginger and 125g (4oz) skinned, roasted, very finely chopped peanuts, saute for 2 minutes. Add ½ cup vinegar, ⅓ cup sugar, 1 teaspoon salt, 2 tablespoons peanut butter, ⅓ cup fruit chutney and 1 cup water, stir until combined. Bring to boil; reduce heat, simmer very slowly for 30 minutes or until mixture is thick. Serve hot or cold.

OssoBucco

1. Ask butcher to cut each shank into three equal pieces. Coat with flour seasoned with salt and pepper. Heat 60g (2oz) of the butter in pan with oil. Add shanks a few at a time, brown well on all sides; remove from pan. Repeat with remaining shanks.

2. Add remaining butter to pan, add peeled and chopped carrots, peeled and finely chopped onions, finely chopped celery and one crushed garlic clove. Saute gently until onions are golden brown. Remove from heat. Transfer vegetables to large ovenproof dish. Carefully pack veal shanks on top of vegetables.

3. Drain all fat from pan in which veal was cooked. Add wine, water, crumbled stock cubes, undrained tomatoes, basil, thyme, bayleaf and strip of lemon rind. Bring sauce to boil, mashing tomatoes well, and stirring in brown pieces from pan. Season with salt and pepper. Pour sauce over veal shanks. Cover casserole, bake in moderate oven 1½ hours or until veal is very tender, stirring occasionally. To serve, sprinkle over combined remaining crushed garlic, chopped parsley and grated lemon rind.

OSSO Bucco is one of Italy's most popular dishes. It's made from veal shanks and the name means "hollow bones." It's a meal with great flavour. Quantities will serve six to eight. Saffron-flavoured Risotto Milanese is a traditional accompaniment.

YOU WILL NEED:
6 veal shanks or knuckles
90g (3oz) butter
2 tablespoons oil
flour
salt, pepper
2 medium carrots
2 large onions
3 sticks celery
2 cloves garlic
1 cup dry red wine
1½ cups water
3 beef stock cubes
2 x 470g (15oz) cans whole tomatoes
1 teaspoon basil
1 teaspoon thyme
1 bayleaf
2.5cm (1in) strip lemon rind
1 teaspoon grated lemon rind
3 tablespoons chopped parsley

RISOTTO MILANESE
60g (2oz) butter
1 large onion
500g (1lb) rice
1.25 litres (5 cups) boiling water
3 chicken stock cubes
½ cup dry white wine
¼ teaspoon saffron
30g (1oz) grated parmesan cheese
salt, pepper
30g (1oz) butter, extra

Risotto Milanese:
Heat butter in large saucepan, add peeled and finely chopped onion. Saute gently until onion is transparent. Add rice; cook, stirring, 2 minutes. Dissolve chicken stock cubes and saffron in water. Gradually add stock to rice, about 1 cup at a time; wait until liquid has absorbed before adding next cup. Stir at each addition; add wine. Cover pan for remainder of cooking time. The rice should cook about 20 minutes from the time the first cup of stock is added. When cooked, the rice should be very tender and creamy with all liquid absorbed. Season with salt and pepper. Add extra melted butter and parmesan cheese, mix in carefully with fork.

Boeuf Bourguignonne

1. Trim any surplus fat from meat, cut meat into large cubes. Trim rind and surplus fat from bacon, cut into large pieces. Peel onions, leave them whole, slice mushrooms.

2. Heat butter and oil in pan. Add about a quarter of the steak at a time to pan, brown well on all sides, remove from pan, repeat process with remaining meat. If all meat were added at once, it would not brown correctly. When all meat is well browned, add whole onions, cook until light golden brown, add bacon, cook until crisp, add sliced mushrooms, cook stirring 1 minute. Remove from pan.

IT'S pronounced "Berf Boorg-in-yon," which is the French way of saying "beef in burgundy;" claret, of course, can be substituted for the burgundy. Quantities given will serve 6.

YOU WILL NEED:

1.5kg (3lb) round steak	**1 clove garlic**
30g (1oz) butter	**½ cup flour**
2 tablespoons oil	**2 cups dry red wine**
12 small onions	**3 cups water**
60g (2oz) bacon pieces	**2 beef stock cubes**
250g (8oz) mushrooms	**1 teaspoon sugar**
60g (2oz) butter, extra	**salt, pepper**

3. Heat extra butter in pan, add crushed garlic, cook 1 minute. Add flour, cook until dark golden brown; do not allow to burn. Remove pan from heat, gradually add water and wine, stir until well combined. Return to heat, add sugar, crumbled stock cubes, salt and pepper, stir until sauce boils and thickens. Put meat, and bacon in ovenproof dish, pour sauce over; mix.

4. Cook covered, in moderate oven 1 hour; remove from heat, add onions and mushrooms, stir until combined. Return to oven, cook covered a further 30 minutes or until meat is tender.

1. Place veal knuckle and gravy beef in large pan; add enough water to cover, approximately 2 litres (8 cups). Add salt, allspice, peppercorns, crushed garlic, peeled and chopped onion, whole carrot and bayleaf. Bring to boil, skim surface, reduce heat, simmer, covered, approximately 3 hours or until meat breaks away from bone. Strain through fine sieve and reserve. Remove meat from bones, trim off any fat, dice meat finely.

2. For topping, sprinkle gelatine over water, add crumbled stock cube, stir over low heat until gelatine has dissolved. Remove from heat; cool. Lightly oil 23cm x 12cm (9in x 5in) loaf tin. Pour thin layer of gelatine mixture into base of tin just to cover. Allow to set until jelly-like, but not firm. Arrange sliced stuffed olives and parsley leaves decoratively on gelatine base. Spoon a little of the gelatine mixture over decoration to hold it firm. Refrigerate until set.

3. Pack meat into pan, pressing down lightly. Measure approx. 3½ cups of reserved stock. Dissolve gelatine in this warm stock, allow to become cold. Pour cold stock over meat to cover completely. Refrigerate several hours or overnight. Turn out of tin, cut into slices.

Brawn

THERE'S nothing nicer on a hot day than a slice of old-fashioned Brawn, served with a colourful salad. And you know, with its wholesome ingredients of veal knuckle, gravy beef and vegetables, that it's good for the family. Recipe serves six.

YOU WILL NEED:
1 large veal knuckle
1kg (2lb) gravy beef
salt
5 whole allspice
5 peppercorns
2 cloves garlic
1 small onion
1 small carrot
1 bayleaf
1 teaspoon gelatine

TOPPING
1 teaspoon gelatine
¾ cup water
1 beef stock cube
stuffed olives
parsley

1. Heat 30g (1oz) butter in large frying pan, add meat, brown well on all sides. Remove meat from pan.

2. Add to pan scraped carrots cut into large pieces, scraped parsnips cut into large pieces, peeled whole onions, and peeled potatoes, cut in half. Saute gently until vegetables are golden brown. Remove from pan.

3. Melt remaining butter in pan. Add flour, stir over high heat until flour is dark golden brown; do not allow to brown. Remove pan from heat, add water, stir until combined. Add crumbled stock cubes, tomato paste, worcestershire sauce, mixed herbs, salt, pepper and sugar. Return pan to heat, stir until sauce boils and thickens. Put meat into large saucepan, pour sauce over, bring to boil. Reduce heat, cover, simmer gently 2 hours. Add prepared vegetables, simmer further 30 minutes or until vegetables are tender. Keep meat and vegetables warm on serving plate. Bring sauce in pan to boil, boil uncovered 10 minutes or until of good gravy consistency.

Pot Roast

A GOOD pot roast makes an ideal family meal. Meat, vegetables and sauce cook together in one saucepan. Corner of topside, bolar blade or fresh (ie uncorned) silverside can be used.

A whole chicken can also be pot-roasted in exactly the same way, but needs only 1 hour's cooking time, instead of the 2 hours for the meat, plus a further 30 minutes when the vegetables are added.

The meat pot roast in our recipe will serve six; the chicken serves four.

YOU WILL NEED:

90g (3oz) butter	⅓ cup plain flour
2kg (4lb) piece of corner topside	1¼ litres (5 cups) water
3 large carrots	3 beef stock cubes
3 medium parsnips	3 tablespoons tomato paste
8 small onions	1 teaspoon worcestershire sauce
4 medium potatoes	pinch mixed herbs
	1 teaspoon sugar
	salt, pepper

FISH
Trout with Almonds

TROUT is one of the best-tasting of all fish and, cooked this way it is superb! All the bones are removed before cooking, so there is trouble-free eating. The recipe here could make a light meal for four, or a first course for a dinner party.

YOU WILL NEED:
4 trout
125g (4oz) butter
flour
salt, pepper
¼ cup lemon juice
60g (2oz) flaked almonds
2 tablespoons chopped parsley

1. Wash and scale trout; clean, if necessary; pat dry. Open trout out as flat as possible, skin side up, as shown in picture. Run bottle or rolling pin firmly down back bone, starting from tail.

2. Turn trout over, with sharp knife cut through backbone at each end of fish. Gently lever the backbone out. Remove any side bones that may remain.

3. Coat fish well with flour, seasoned with salt and pepper. Brush off any excess flour. Heat 60g (2oz) of the butter in large frying pan. Add fish, cook quickly on both sides until golden brown; allow approximately 4 minutes on each side (cooking time depends on thickness of fish). Remove fish from pan, place on to serving plate; keep warm.

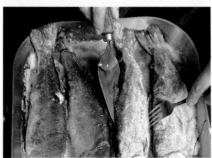

4. Place extra butter in pan, stir until bubbling. Add almonds, saute gently until almonds are light golden brown. Add lemon juice, salt and pepper, stir until nearly all lemon juice has evaporated. Add parsley, stir until combined. Spoon the butter sauce over fish.

FISH

Fish fillets become a really special dish when they're cooked in this light and golden, crisp and crunchy batter. The special flavour of Tartare Sauce is a traditional accompaniment to Fried Fish.

YOU WILL NEED:
6 fish fillets
cornflour
2 cups self-raising flour
salt, pepper
1¼ cups water, approx.
oil for deep-frying

Crisp Fried Fish

1. Place fish skin-side down on board. Work from tail to head. Hold skin at tail firmly. With a sharp knife, held at an angle as a lever, using sawing motion, separate fish from skin. Remove as many bones as possible.

2. Lightly coat fillets in cornflour; shake off the excess. Sift flour, salt and pepper into small bowl. Add water gradually, beating well until batter is smooth and of a good pouring consistency. (Flours differ; you may need to add up to an extra ¼ cup of water for correct consistency.)

3. Using tongs, dip fish into batter to coat fish on all sides. Allow excess batter to drain from fish.

4. Lower fish into deep hot oil. Cook only one or two pieces — depending on size of fish — at a time, so that pan is not overcrowded. Deep-fry for 1 minute, or until pale golden colour. Remove from oil. Allow oil to reheat, re-fry fish until golden brown and cooked through. (This double-frying makes batter beautifully crisp.) Drain well on absorbent paper. Serve with chips and tartare sauce. (See recipe for Tartare Sauce on opposite page.)

How to fillet fish

IF there's an enthusiastic fisherman in the family, or if you are presented with a whole fish, you'll want to know how to fillet fish with a minimum of bother and wastage. (The bones can be cooked with water for 20 minutes to make good stock for fish soup.)

1. First scale fish. With knife or special fish scaler, working from tail to head, remove scales from both sides of fish. Do this under running water, or in a sink or basin of water to prevent scales flying about. When you think all scales have been removed, run your hand over the fish to detect any that may remain.

2. Shown are flat snapper and rounded flathead. To remove snapper head, cut straight across. To remove head of flathead, cut across, then round, following the shape of the head.

3. Turn flathead on its side. With sharp knife cut along backbone from head to tail. For flat fish such as bream or snapper, simply cut along backbone of fish from head to tail.

4. Carefully separate fish from bone. Run knife in across bones keeping as close to bones as possible. Cut across breast bones as shown. Remove fillet completely. Trim off any bones that remain. Turn fish, then fillet other side in same way.

5. If you want to remove skin from fish, rub some salt on your fingers (this makes it easier to grasp the slippery skin). Put fish skin-side down. Work from tail to head. Hold skin at tail firmly. With a sharp knife held at an angle as a lever, using sawing motion, separate fish from skin.

To cook fillets:
Coat fish fillets lightly in flour seasoned with salt and pepper. For four fillets, lightly beat together 1 egg and ¼ cup milk, dip fillets in egg mixture, coat in packaged dry breadcrumbs, or fresh breadcrumbs, pat on to firm. Refrigerate 30 minutes. Heat 60g (2oz) butter and 1 tablespoon oil in pan, shallow fry fillets until golden brown and cooked through. Serve with Tartare Sauce.

Tartare Sauce:
Combine in bowl ¾ cup mayonnaise, 2 tablespoons finely chopped capers, 2 tablespoons finely chopped gherkins, 1 teaspoon chopped chives, 1 tablespoon chopped parsley; season with salt and pepper. Mix well.

1. Shell prawns, leave tail intact. With small, sharp knife make a slit down back of prawn, carefully remove back vein as shown. Wash prawns, pat dry.

2. Put ½ cup of oil into 4 individual heatproof dishes. Add 30g (1oz) butter to each dish. Crush 2 cloves garlic into each dish. Remove seeds from chillies, wash and pat dry. Chop chillies finely, divide evenly among dishes. Season with salt and pepper. Put dishes on oven tray. Put in moderate oven 10 to 15 minutes or until butter has melted and oil is very hot.

3. Remove dishes from oven on tray. Divide prawns between dishes. Return to oven for 8 to 10 minutes or until prawns are cooked. Cooking time depends on prawn size. Serve immediately, sprinkled with chopped parsley.

Garlic Prawns

GARLIC Prawns cooked in the oven or on top of the barbecue have great flavour and gusto. They are currently among the top-pop foods from abroad now enjoyed by Australians. Serve them with crusty bread or crisp rolls. Some people like to dip the bread in the hot garlic-flavoured butter-and-oil mixture.

The quantities given in the recipe here are enough to serve about four people, but of course if you're giving a larger party or barbecue simply increase the ingredients according to numbers.

YOU WILL NEED:
1kg (2lb) green king prawns
2 cups oil
125g (4oz) butter
8 cloves garlic
2 small red chillies
1 tablespoon chopped parsley
salt, pepper

1. Cook rice in boiling salted water 10 minutes or until just tender. Drain. Melt butter in pan, add peeled and finely chopped onion, sliced celery and sliced mushrooms, saute until onions are transparent.

2. Add sauteed vegetables, salt, pepper to rice; mix well. Wash and scale fish, pat dry with absorbent paper. Fill stuffing firmly into fish.

3. Put the fish into a large well-greased baking dish with the water. Brush fish with melted butter, pour lemon juice over. Bake, uncovered in moderate oven 20 minutes; brush occasionally with pan juices.

Baked Snapper

ONE of Australia's most popular fish dishes — firm-textured, good-tasting snapper, filled with a savoury stuffing and baked until deliciously tender. And it is so easy to prepare! Small, new potatoes would make a perfect accompaniment. Recipe serves four.

YOU WILL NEED:
1.5kg (3lb) snapper
¼ cup water
60g (2oz) butter
¼ cup lemon juice
2 tomatoes
2 onions
2 tablespoons chopped parsley
STUFFING
½ cup long grain rice
1 onion
1 stick celery
125g (4oz) mushrooms
60g (2oz) butter
½ teaspoon grated lemon rind
salt, pepper

4. Cut tomatoes into slices, peel and slice onions. Arrange tomato and onion slices alternately on top of fish. Cover, bake further 25 minutes or until tender. Before serving, sprinkle with chopped parsley, serve lemon wedges separately.

Chinese Fish

BREAM is generally used for this dish, a popular item on Chinese menus. It is light, and full of flavour. Serve the fish by itself, or with boiled rice as an accompaniment. The recipe serves two, or four if part of a Chinese meal where there are other dishes.

YOU WILL NEED:

2 x 500g (1lb) whole bream or snapper	3 tablespoons soy sauce
water	6 shallots
salt	5cm (2in) piece green ginger, extra
2.5cm (1in) piece green ginger	3 tablespoons oil

1. Clean and scale fish, remove black vein inside fish. Two-thirds fill shallow pan with water. Add salt and crushed ginger; bring to boil, boil 5 minutes. Reduce heat, put fish in water, cover, cook 10 minutes or until cooked.

2. Remove fish. Drain well, put on heated serving plates. While fish cooks, peel extra ginger, cut in thin slices, then into thin strips. Peel shallots, cut in thin diagonal slices.

3. Pour soy sauce over fish, sprinkle with ginger and shallots. Heat oil until nearly boiling, pour over fish.

Salmon Croquettes

FULL-of flavour croquettes, with a creamy centre and firm golden coating, make an economical light meal everyone will enjoy.

YOU WILL NEED:

220g (7oz) can salmon	dry breadcrumbs
1 teaspoon curry powder	oil for deep-frying
1 small onion	**WHITE SAUCE**
1 tablespoon chopped parsley	90g (3oz) butter or substitute
2 teaspoons lemon juice	¾ cup plain flour
2 eggs for glazing	2 cups milk
	salt, pepper

1. Melt butter over low heat, remove from heat, stir in flour, working until smooth. Return to heat, cook few minutes, remove from heat, gradually stir in milk. Return to heat; stir until boiling. Reduce heat, simmer further 3 minutes, season with salt and pepper.

2. Drain salmon, remove bones and flake; peel onion, chop finely. Add salmon, curry powder, onion, parsley and lemon juice to sauce, mix thoroughly. Spread mixture on to shallow tray, refrigerate until firm.

3. Mould mixture into croquette shapes 2.5cm thick by 5cm long (1in x 2in). Dip in beaten eggs, press breadcrumbs on firmly. Refrigerate 1 hour.

4. Fry in deep hot oil few minutes until golden; drain on absorbent paper. Makes approximately 12.

33

SOUPS
Hot Sour Soup

THIS delicious Chinese soup is of the Szechwan school of cookery and has the traditional spiciness of Szechwan foods.

It has a most superb flavour combination. The bean curd specified as an ingredient is available at Chinese food stores or can be bought in cans at supermarkets. Chinese pickles are available in jars or cans or can be bought in bulk from Chinese food stores. These quantities serve six.

YOU WILL NEED:

250g (8oz) sliced ham
125g (4oz) small mushrooms
250g (8oz) lean pork
30g (1oz) chinese pickles
125g (4oz) bamboo shoots
1¾ litres (7 cups) chicken stock
½ cup dry white wine
½ teaspoon salt
2 tablespoons cornflour
¼ cup water
2 teaspoons white vinegar

1 teaspoon sesame oil
1 egg
6 shallots
250g (8oz) fresh bean curd
soy sauce

1. Cut ham into very fine shreds, slice mushrooms thinly, cut pork, pickles, and bamboo shoots into very fine shreds.

2. Place chicken stock, wine and salt into large pan, bring to boil, boil uncovered for 5 minutes. Remove pan from heat. Place cornflour and water into bowl, stir until combined. Gradually add cornflour mixture to chicken stock, stir until combined. Return pan to heat, stir until soup comes to boil, reduce heat, add ham, mushrooms, pork, pickles and bamboo shoots, stir until combined. Simmer uncovered for 5 minutes.

3. Stir in vinegar and oil. Beat eggs until combined. Gradually add to chicken stock, stirring constantly. Add chopped shallots, add bean curd cut into 1cm (½in) cubes. Simmer 3 minutes. Spoon into individual bowls, top each with a teaspoon of soy sauce.

1. Soak haricot beans overnight in plenty of cold water to cover. Heat butter in large pan, add peeled and chopped onions, chopped bacon pieces and crushed garlic. Saute gently until onions are transparent. Add water, crumbled stock cubes and drained haricot beans, bring to boil, reduce heat, simmer, covered, 2¼ hours.

2. Peel and dice carrots; slice celery; peel and dice potatoes; top, tail and slice beans; slice zucchini; remove skins from tomatoes and chop finely. Add vegetables to simmering stock, bring to boil, reduce heat, simmer, covered, 1 hour.

3. Remove lid from pan, add macaroni, simmer, stirring occasionally, until pasta is cooked, 10 to 15 minutes. Stir in parsley; season with salt and pepper. Serve grated parmesan cheese to sprinkle on top of soup.

Minestrone

THIS is one of Italy's famous soups — rich, hearty, delicious. And economical, too. The recipe will serve six generously. Serve with fresh, crusty bread; offer grated parmesan cheese separately at the table for sprinkling on top of soup.

YOU WILL NEED:

½ cup haricot beans
30g (1oz) butter
2 onions
60g (2oz) bacon pieces
2 cloves garlic
2½ litres (10 cups) water
6 beef stock cubes
3 carrots
2 sticks celery
2 potatoes
125g (4oz) green beans
3 zucchini
4 tomatoes
⅓ cup small macaroni
2 tablespoons chopped parsley
salt, pepper
grated parmesan cheese

1. Heat butter in large pan, add peeled and thinly sliced onions and crushed garlic. Saute gently until onions are golden brown. Add flour, stir until combined.

2. Add sugar, undiluted soup, water, salt, pepper and red wine, stir until combined. Bring to boil, reduce heat, simmer covered for 45 minutes, stirring soup occasionally. Add sherry, simmer for a further 5 minutes.

3. Cut bread into 1cm (½in) slices. You will need 12 slices of bread. Melt extra butter in pan, add crushed garlic, stir until combined. Brush bread slices on both sides with butter mixture. Place bread slices under hot griller until golden brown on one side. Do not brown other side of bread. Pour soup into large flameproof bowl, place bread slices, toasted side down, on to soup. Sprinkle combined grated cheeses over bread. Place soup bowl under hot griller until cheese is melted and golden brown. If you do not have a griller large enough to hold soup bowl, sprinkle grated cheeses on untoasted side of bread, pressing cheese down firmly on to bread slices. Place under hot griller until melted and golden brown. Place bread into soup bowls, pour soup over. Serves 6.

French Onion Soup

SATISFYING enough to be a complete meal in itself, this hot, hearty onion soup from France is a real family favourite.

YOU WILL NEED:

90g (3oz) butter	salt, pepper
4 large onions	⅓ cup dry red wine
1 clove garlic	1 tablespoon dry sherry
1 tablespoon flour	125g (4oz) butter, extra
1 teaspoon sugar	1 clove garlic, extra
2 x 470g (15oz) cans beef consomme	1 stick french bread
3 cups water	250g (8oz) swiss cheese
	60g (2oz) grated parmesan cheese

VEGETABLES

Potato Scallops

EVERYBODY likes Potato Scallops — and these, with their crispy, crunchy batter, are good enough to be a meal in themselves. The recipe makes about 30. Watch them disappear, just like magic!

YOU WILL NEED:
750g (1½lb) large old potatoes
2 cups self-raising flour
1 teaspoon salt
¼ teaspoon pepper
1¾ cups water
oil for deep-frying
extra flour

1. Peel and wash potatoes, cut into thin slices, about 3mm (⅛in) in thickness, dry well. Sift flour, salt, pepper into bowl, make a well in centre, gradually add water, mixing to a fairly thick coating batter; beat until smooth and free of lumps.

2. Coat potato slices lightly with extra flour, shake off excess. Dip each slice into prepared batter, making sure potato slices are well covered. Drain excess batter from each slice before frying.

3. Heat oil in large pan (test heat of oil with a small piece of potato, as for Potato Chips); deep-fry potato slices, a few at a time, until lightly golden. Remove from oil, drain on absorbent paper. Increase heat of oil slightly, add the potato scallops, re-fry until rich golden brown. Drain again, sprinkle with salt.

Chips

FISH and chips, eggs and chips, steak and chips — chips go well with everything and are undoubtedly a national favourite.

Here we show how to cook them well. The double frying ensures that they are golden brown and crisp. For special occasions, the rounded sides, tops and bottoms of the potatoes can be cut off leaving the potato in a neat square, then cut into chips. This ensures that every chip is exactly the same length. The left-over pieces can be added to other potatoes when making mashed potato, or cooked separately as chips for nibbling.

1. Peel and wash potatoes. Cut potatoes into 1cm (½in) slices, then into strips 1cm (½in) wide. Roll chips in a clean tea towel to dry them well.

2. Shoestring potatoes make an attractive accompaniment to grills. Cut potatoes into 5mm (¼in) slices, then into strips 5mm (¼in) wide. For speed, several potato slices can be put on top of one another and cut together.

3. Heat oil in deep pan. Drop one chip into oil, when it rises to the surface surrounded by bubbles, oil is at correct temperature for cooking chips. A frying basket makes it easy to lower and raise a quantity of chips in the hot oil. If not using a frying basket, drop chips gradually into hot oil. Cook 6 minutes, remove, drain well. At this point, chips are only partly cooked, or blanched. They can now be set aside for several hours, ready for final cooking; they will not discolour. Or they can be frozen.

4. Before serving, reheat oil. As before, drop one chip into it to test that it is the right heat. Cook chips quickly for about 3 minutes until golden brown and crisp. Drain well, sprinkle with salt.

French Fried Onions

ONION Rings make a popular extra vegetable with grills of all kinds — and they're so easy and so very economical to make.

YOU WILL NEED:
4 onions
1 cup plain flour
1 cup milk
1 egg
¼ teaspoon salt
oil for deep-frying

1. Peel onions, slice thinly, separate into rings.

2. Put into bowl, add the milk, let stand 1 hour. Drain, reserve milk. This preliminary soaking in milk removes any sharpness from the onions, making them milder in flavour.

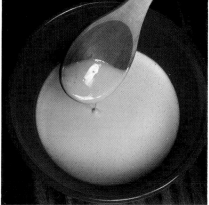

3. Beat egg well, beat in reserved milk, salt and sifted flour.

4. Dip each onion ring into batter, drop into deep hot oil, a few rings at a time so heat of oil does not decrease. Fry until golden brown. Drain well, sprinkle with salt.

RICE and PASTA
Spaghetti Bolognese

WHEN you're hungry, nothing seems to taste as good as spaghetti — and this is one of the world's most famous spaghetti sauces. It comes from Bologna, said to be the centre of fine cooking in Italy. Quantities given here will serve six.

YOU WILL NEED:
2 tablespoons oil
2 onions
750g (1½lb) minced steak
470g (15oz) can whole tomatoes
3 tablespoons tomato paste
1 teaspoon basil
1 teaspoon oregano
½ teaspoon thyme
salt, pepper

1.25 litres (5 cups) water
grated parmesan cheese
500g (1lb) spaghetti
1 tablespoon oil, extra

1. Heat oil in large shallow frying pan or fry pan, add peeled and chopped onions, saute gently until onions are tender. Add steak, stir with fork over high heat until meat is dark golden brown, mashing meat well so there are no lumps.

2. Add undrained tomatoes, tomato paste, basil, oregano, thyme, salt and pepper. Mash tomatoes well, stir over medium heat until all ingredients are combined. Add water; mix well. Bring to boil, reduce heat, simmer gently uncovered, 2 hours or until nearly all liquid has evaporated.

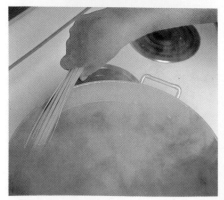

3. Add 1 tablespoon of extra oil to large quantity of boiling salted water. Add spaghetti gradually so water does not go off the boil. Hold long strands of spaghetti at one end and place other ends into the boiling water. The pasta will begin to soften in the hot water and it is then simple to lower strands into saucepan, coiling them neatly inside pan. Cook spaghetti for approximately 10 to 12 minutes or until tender but still firm, drain well. Pile spaghetti into deep bowls, spoon sauce over; offer grated parmesan cheese separately.

THIS is a really good fried rice recipe that you'll want to make over and over again. It combines flavours delicately, yet so deliciously, and makes an excellent light lunch or a tasty part of any meal. Pork, bacon and prawns give it real distinctiveness — the quantities given here will serve six.

YOU WILL NEED:
375g (12oz) long grain rice
3 rashers bacon
250g (8oz) cooked pork
3 eggs
salt, pepper
oil
2 teaspoons grated green ginger
8 shallots
500g (1lb) prawns
2 tablespoons oil, extra
2 teaspoons soy sauce

Fried Rice

1. Put large saucepan of water on to boil, add 2 teaspoons salt. When at full rolling boil, add rice gradually, so that water does not go off boil. Boil rapidly, uncovered, 10 to 12 minutes. When rice is tender, drain immediately. Put colander or strainer under cold running water to remove any starch still clinging to grains; drain well again.

2. Spread rice evenly over two large shallow trays, refrigerate overnight, stirring occasionally; this is to allow rice to dry out completely. Or if you want to serve rice the same day, spread out on shallow trays, put in moderate oven 15 to 20 minutes; stir rice every 5 minutes to bring the moist grains to the top.

3. Finely dice bacon, fry until crisp, drain; slice pork thinly. Beat eggs lightly with fork, season with salt and pepper. Heat a small quantity of oil in pan, pour in enough of egg mixture to make one pancake; turn; cook other side. Remove from pan, repeat with remaining egg mixture. Roll up pancakes, slice into thin strips. Finely chop shallots; shell and devein prawns, if large cut into smaller pieces. Heat extra oil in pan or wok. Saute green ginger 1 minute, stir in rice, stir 5 minutes. Add bacon, pork, shallots, egg strips and prawns, mix lightly. When completely heated through, add soy sauce, mix well.

NOTE: A cooked pork chop, or the Chinese roast pork available from Chinese food stores, is ideal for this dish.

1. Drop noodles gradually into large saucepan of boiling salted water; two saucepans may be needed, as noodles tend to stick together during cooking. Cook approx. 30 minutes or until very tender. Drain noodles well. Return to saucepan. Fill saucepan with cold water, leave noodles in cold water until ready to use; drain well.

2. Heat oil in large shallow pan, add steak. Cook, stirring occasionally, until meat is well browned; pour off any excess fat. Add chopped tomatoes with liquid from cans, peeled and finely chopped onion, sliced mushrooms, crushed garlic, and remaining ingredients. Bring to boil, stirring. Reduce heat; simmer, uncovered, 60 minutes, or until nearly all liquid has evaporated.

3. Place a layer of noodles in shallow ovenproof dish, a 28cm x 18cm (11in x 7in) lamington tin is ideal. Noodles may have to be cut so that they lie flat.

4. Spread half the meat sauce over the noodles then cover with half the cheese sauce. (Both the sauces will be easier to handle if made the day beforehand and refrigerated.) Top evenly with second layer of noodles.

L ASAGNE is a full-flavoured specialty from Italy that makes a good, hearty main meal for the family, an unusual party dish or a distinctive entree. Serve with a colourful salad.

Except for the final baking, Lasagne can be prepared entirely in advance. Lasagne noodles are available in several types: the broad noodles shown in the picture; narrower noodles with a curly edge; green noodles coloured with spinach juice. The broad noodles are easiest to cut when the Lasagne is cooked. Quantities given serve four to six.

Lasagne

YOU WILL NEED:
250g (8oz) lasagne noodles
½ cup grated parmesan cheese
½ cup cream
MEAT SAUCE
1 tablespoon oil
500g (1lb) minced steak
2 x 470g (15oz) cans whole tomatoes
1 small onion
125g (4oz) mushrooms
1 clove garlic

1 teaspoon oregano
¼ teaspoon basil
¼ teaspoon rosemary
1 teaspoon salt
½ teaspoon sugar
CHEESE SAUCE
60g (2oz) butter
4 tablespoons flour
2 cups milk
salt, pepper
pinch nutmeg
125g (4oz) grated processed cheese
1 tablespoon grated parmesan cheese
Cheese Sauce:

Melt butter in saucepan, stir in flour; cook gently, stirring, 1 minute. Gradually add the milk, stir until sauce boils and thickens. Season with salt, pepper, nutmeg. Add cheeses, stir until cheeses melt.

5. Repeat the layers of meat sauce, then cheese sauce, and finally the third layer of noodles to cover top completely.

6. Sprinkle top with grated parmesan cheese. Bake in moderate oven 20 to 25 minutes. Remove from oven, gently pour or spoon cream over the top of cheese. Bake for further 10 to 15 minutes.

Ravioli

ALTHOUGH ingredients and method are simple, Ravioli take a little time and trouble to make. But the effort is worth while — the recipe produces the best Ravioli you've tasted! And there's sufficient for 8 to 10 people. If you don't want to use the full quantity at once, Ravioli can be frozen uncooked.

PASTRY
4 cups plain flour
2 eggs
1 tablespoon oil
pinch salt
¾ cup water, approx.
1 egg-yolk
1 tablespoon water, extra

FILLING
250g (8oz) minced steak
250g (8oz) cooked chicken meat
60g (2oz) salami
2 rashers bacon
125g (4oz) ham
4 cloves garlic
½ cup chopped parsley
½ teaspoon allspice
½ teaspoon salt
2 eggs
½ cup cooked spinach

SAUCE
90g (3oz) butter
1 tablespoon oil
2 x 470g (15oz) cans whole tomatoes
2 cloves garlic
½ teaspoon allspice
½ teaspoon rosemary
½ teaspoon basil
salt, pepper

Sauce:
Place butter and oil into pan, add crushed garlic, saute for 1 minute. Place undrained tomatoes into electric blender, blend on medium speed for 30 seconds or until pureed, or push undrained tomatoes through sieve. Add tomato mixture, with remaining ingredients, to pan, stir until combined. Bring to boil, reduce heat to very low, cover, simmer gently for 60 minutes, stirring sauce occasionally.

Pastry:
Sift flour and salt into bowl. Place eggs and oil into bowl, beat until combined. Add egg mixture to flour, gradually add water, stir until mixture is a firm but pliable dough. If eggs are large, you may not need to use all the water. Do not have dough too soft or it will be hard to handle. Turn dough out on to lightly floured surface, knead for 5 minutes. Place dough into very lightly oiled bowl, cover, stand 30 minutes.

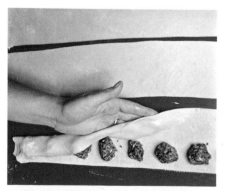

1. To make filling, remove rind from bacon. Put all ingredients except eggs through mincer. Place into bowl, add lightly beaten eggs; mix well.

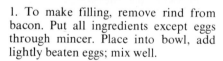

2. Roll out half the dough to 2mm (1/16th in) in thickness. Cut dough into 10cm (4in) strips. Place teaspoonfuls of filling at 5cm (2in) intervals along one edge of pastry strips. Brush along edge of pastry with combined egg-yolk and extra water, lift pastry over filling, as shown in picture. Repeat with remaining pastry.

3. Seal edges of pastry around filling, pressing well together. Cut between mounds of filling with fluted pastry cutter.

4. Place quarter of ravioli into very large pan of boiling salted water, boil uncovered for 20 minutes; remove from pan. Repeat with remaining ravioli in quarter batches. Drain water from pan, add Sauce, bring to boil, add ravioli to Sauce, bring to boil, reduce heat, simmer very gently uncovered for 10 minutes. Serve with grated parmesan cheese.

Gnocchi

PERHAPS not truly a pasta, Gnocchi has been included in the pasta section because it can take the place of pasta in a meal. Indeed, gnocchi is often referred to as a macaroni. If minced veal is not available for the sauce, substitute minced steak.
Quantities given will serve six.

YOU WILL NEED:
500g (1lb) old potatoes
1½ cups self-raising flour
1 egg
½ teaspoon salt
        VEAL AND TOMATO SAUCE
60g (2oz) butter
1 large onion
2 cloves garlic
500g (1lb) minced veal
470g (15oz) can whole tomatoes
2 tablespoons tomato paste
2 cups dry white wine
1 cup water
2 chicken stock cubes
1 teaspoon sugar
1 teaspoon basil
salt, pepper
Sauce:

Heat butter in frying pan, add peeled and chopped onion, crushed garlic and veal, mash veal well. Fry meat until light golden brown. Add undrained mashed tomatoes, tomato paste, wine, water, crumbled stock cubes, sugar, basil, salt and pepper; mix well. Bring to boil, reduce heat, simmer very slowly uncovered for 1½ hours or until sauce is reduced and of a good thick consistency.

2. Take quarter of mixture, roll into sausage shape on floured surface. Roll should be 2.5cm (1in) in diameter. Repeat with remaining dough. Cut rolls in 2.5cm (1in) lengths.

1. Peel and quarter potatoes, boil until very tender; drain well, push potatoes through fine sieve into bowl. Add sifted flour and salt, and lightly beaten egg; mix well. Turn mixture out on to lightly floured surface; knead for 2 minutes.

3. With two fingers, press each gnocchi against cheese grater to roughen the surface on one side; at the same time make a dent in the other where the fingers press; this gives the traditional gnocchi shape. Repeat with remaining gnocchi.

4. Place quarter of the gnocchi into large pan of boiling salted water. Gnocchi will go straight to bottom of pan; when gnocchi rise to top of water, boil for 1 minute, then remove from pan. Repeat with remaining gnocchi in batches. Add gnocchi to prepared Veal and Tomato Sauce: simmer uncovered for 5 minutes. Put gnocchi into serving bowl, spoon over half the sauce. Serve remaining sauce and grated parmesan cheese separately.

BATTERS

Waffles

AMERICANS like waffles for breakfast with honey or maple syrup — perhaps an acquired taste early in the day.
We serve them for a delicious dessert, topped with ice-cream and caramel sauce, bought or home-made. And it is such an easy recipe — everyone can make their own waffles.

YOU WILL NEED:
2 eggs, separated
1½ cups milk
2 cups plain flour
½ teaspoon baking powder
¼ cup sugar
60g (2oz) butter
2 tablespoons cold water

1. Beat egg-yolks and milk lightly together. Add sifted dry ingredients, beat until smooth. Add melted, cooled butter and water; blend well. Fold in firmly beaten egg-whites.

2. Most modern waffle irons are Teflon coated on the inside and waffles do not stick. However they still need to be greased. Brush both Teflon-coated surfaces (for top and bottom of waffle) with oil.

3. Spoon approximately 2 tablespoons of mixture into centre of iron. (With some waffle irons, mixture needs to be spread to cover surface of iron. In the one shown, mixture spreads over whole surface as soon as iron is closed.) Close iron, cook until golden brown, about 1 minute. Makes approximately 10 waffles.

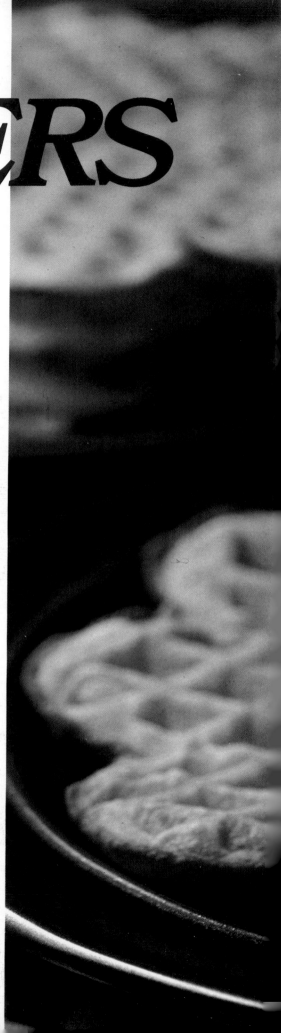

Crumpets

1. Sift flour, baking powder, sugar and salt into large bowl. Dissolve yeast in water, add to dry ingredients, beat until smooth.

IT IS fun to make your own crumpets from a few simple ingredients. The finished crumpet is slightly softer than the commercial variety. After the crumpets are cooked, toast them and serve hot with butter. The recipe makes about 24. Any not eaten can be frozen for later use.

YOU WILL NEED:
4 cups plain flour
2 tablespoons baking powder
1½ teaspoons salt
1½ teaspoons sugar
3 cups lukewarm water
15g (½oz) compressed yeast

2. Crumpets can be cooked in a lightly greased frying pan or electric frypan; if using frypan, preheat to 260 deg F. Lightly grease some egg-rings, put them in pan to heat through. When hot, three-quarters fill the rings with batter.

3. Allow to cook over low heat for approximately 10 minutes or until surface is covered with holes, remove rings. Cover pan, and cook further 2 to 3 minutes or until surface has set. Remove from pan, cool on wire rack. When cold, toast and serve with butter.

(**Note:** 1 teaspoon dry yeast can be used in place of the compressed yeast; sift it with the dry ingredients.)

Yorkshire Pudding

YOU WILL NEED:
1 cup plain flour
½ teaspoon salt
2 eggs
½ cup milk
½ cup water
dripping

Many good things come from Yorkshire in northern England. One of the most famous is this perfect accompaniment to roast beef.

Make Yorkshire Pudding as individual puddings, or as one large pudding cut into squares. Pour over each serving a good gravy made from the roast-pan drippings. Serve as soon as it comes from the oven as its light airiness falls quickly and you'll want it to look its best. The recipe makes 12 individual puddings; the large size serves six.

1. Sift flour and salt into bowl, make a well in centre, add whole eggs. Gradually beat in a little flour from the sides of bowl. Add combined milk and water a little at a time, beating constantly and incorporating more flour from sides of bowl. When all is combined, beat well for 2 minutes; allow mixture to stand for 30 minutes.

2. For individual puddings, put ½ teaspoon of dripping in each of 12 deep patty tins, heat in hot oven for 2 minutes. Fill each patty tin with batter, bake in hot oven 10 minutes or until golden.

3. To make one big Yorkshire Pudding, heat 30g (1oz) dripping in 1½ litre (6 cup) ovenproof dish in hot oven. Pour in batter. Bake 15 to 20 minutes, or until well puffed and golden, as shown in picture 4.

4. This big size makes the more traditional Yorkshire Pudding with a moist centre. The small, individual puddings are lighter in texture; some prefer this, as they're attractive and easy to serve.

1. Sift flour and salt into bowl, add eggs and oil, mix until a very smooth batter, free of all lumps.

2. Gradually add milk, mixing to a smooth batter. Mixture will be quite thin; picture shows correct consistency.

3. Heat pancake pan over medium heat until hot. Add a small knob of butter, and swirl around pan. Pour batter from a jug into centre of pan, gently tip pan so that batter runs from centre around edge. You will use approximately 2 to 3 tablespoons of batter for each pancake.

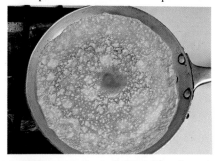

4. When pancake is light golden brown underneath (lift edge of pancake with spatula to check), turn and brown other side. This can be done with spatula, or lift pancake carefully with fingertips and turn quickly. (Watch out for burnt fingers at first, but pancakes are beautifully thin and this method prevents them breaking when being

Pancakes

YOU WILL NEED:
½ cup plain flour
pinch salt
2 eggs
2 teaspoons oil
¾ cup milk
STRAWBERRY LIQUEUR PANCAKES
½ cup orange juice
½ cup water
1 tablespoon Grand Marnier
30g (1oz) butter
3 teaspoons cornflour
1 tablespoon sugar
1 punnet strawberries

turned.) As pancakes cook, spread them out on wire rack — not on top of each other — to cool. Repeat with remaining batter, heating a knob of butter in pan between each pancake.

5. To wrap pancakes for freezing. Place a sheet of aluminium foil on table, lay one pancake on foil, lay a piece of plastic food wrap over pancake, then top with another pancake. Continue layering plastic food wrap and pancakes, ending with food wrap. Fold foil round pancakes, keeping pancakes

flat. Place into freezer bag; freeze. Makes 6 to 8 pancakes.

Strawberry Liqueur Pancakes:

Reserve 4 strawberries for decoration. Place orange juice, water, Grand Marnier, sugar and cornflour in pan, stir until combined. Add butter, stir over heat until sauce boils and thickens, add washed, hulled and halved strawberries to pan, simmer a further 1 minute. Spoon strawberries down centre of four pancakes; roll up, place on to serving plate, spoon sauce over. Decorate with whipped cream and reserved strawberries. Serves 4.

Prawn Cutlets

PRAWN Cutlets make an ideal first course or light meal. This is a particularly light, crisp batter; once the egg-whites are folded in, use the batter immediately. Serve as soon as they are cooked; Tartare Sauce (see recipe on Page 29) is an ideal accompaniment.

YOU WILL NEED:
750g (1½lb) green prawns
1 cup plain flour
2 tablespoons oil
¼ cup dry white wine
⅔ cup beer
salt
3 egg-whites
oil for deep-frying

1. Shell prawns; leave tails on, if desired. Make a slit down back of each prawn, as shown, remove the black vein.

2. Sift flour and salt into bowl, add wine and oil. Beat well until batter is smooth. Gently stir in beer. Beat egg-whites until soft peaks form, fold gently into batter. Dry prawns, dip into batter, drain off excess batter.

3. Deep-fry gently, a few prawns at a time, in deep hot oil until batter is golden and prawns are cooked.

SAUCES

Bearnaise Sauce

BEARNAISE is a perfect sauce to accompany roast beef or steak. The sauce can be prepared ahead of time, covered and left to stand at room temperature until served, or served warm when fresh.

It will keep, covered, several days in the refrigerator. Refrigeration hardens the butter in the sauce and causes the mixture to become firm. Take it from the refrigerator several hours before use to let it return to room temperature. Stir before using to reconstitute to sauce consistency. Bearnaise is not easy to reheat: it's inclined to curdle.

YOU WILL NEED:
½ cup white vinegar
3 shallots
8 peppercorns
1 bayleaf
¼ teaspoon tarragon
4 egg-yolks
250g (8oz) butter
salt, pepper

1. Put vinegar, chopped shallots, peppercorns, bayleaf and tarragon into pan. Bring to boil, reduce heat. Simmer uncovered until mixture is reduced by half. Strain, and reserve.

2. You will need two tablespoons of strained liquid for sauce. Pour it into small jug. Put egg-yolks in top of double saucepan. Stir until combined. Gradually stir in the two tablespoons of liquid. Mix well.

3. Put top of double saucepan in position over barely simmering water, gradually stir in the cooled, melted butter. Stir constantly until mixture has thickened to consistency shown. Remove from water immediately. Season with salt and pepper. Quantities given are enough for six servings.
   (**Note:** Tarragon vinegar can replace the white vinegar and tarragon in recipe.)

SAUCES

A GOOD gravy makes all the difference to the taste of roast meats. Here's the basic recipe. You can vary it by substituting some red or white wine for part of the water; or, for lamb, substituting ½ cup Mint Sauce for ½ cup of water. Any favourite herbs can be added — basil, oregano etc. For extra colour, 1 tablespoon tomato paste can be added with the water. Quantities given are enough for six.

YOU WILL NEED:
4 tablespoons plain flour
3½ cups water
4 beef stock cubes
salt, pepper

A good gravy

1. Remove roast meat from baking dish; keep warm. Place baking dish on top of stove, over medium heat. Bring pan drippings to boil, reduce heat, simmer until all juices in baking dish have evaporated and only fat remains. Pour off excess fat from pan, leaving approximately 6 tablespoons of fat.

2. Leave baking dish over medium heat, add flour, stir until combined with fat.

4. Remove baking dish from heat, add water all at once, stirring constantly. Continue stirring until flour and water are combined; add crumbled stock cubes.

3. Reduce heat to low, continue stirring until flour is of a good brown consistency; do not allow to burn.

5. Return baking dish to medium heat, stir until sauce boils and thickens. Season with salt and pepper. Simmer sauce uncovered for 3 minutes, stirring occasionally.

Caramel Sauce

THIS is a lovely, rich dessert sauce.
Serve it warm or cold over ice-cream or fruit.

YOU WILL NEED:
125g (4oz) butter
1 cup brown sugar, lightly packed
1 cup water
2 tablespoons golden syrup
1½ tablespoons cornflour
¼ cup cream

1. Combine butter and sugar in saucepan, stir over low heat until butter melts and sugar dissolves and mixture turns to thick syrup; bring to boil, reduce heat, simmer 3 minutes.

2. Combine water, golden syrup and cornflour, mix until smooth, add to brown sugar mixture, stir until smooth. Bring to boil, reduce heat, simmer 2 minutes.

3. Remove from heat, stir in cream. Serve warm or cold. Makes approximately 1½ cups.

PASTRY
Pizza

PIZZAS are good for parties, for family meals, for supper. This recipe makes two great pizzas — eat one now, freeze one for later.

YOU WILL NEED:
30g (1oz) compressed yeast
1 teaspoon sugar
1 cup lukewarm water
3 cups plain flour
½ teaspoon salt
4 tablespoons oil

FILLING
1 tablespoon oil
1 onion
2 cloves garlic
470g (15oz) can whole tomatoes
3 tablespoons tomato paste
1 teaspoon oregano
1 teaspoon basil
2 teaspoons sugar
salt, pepper

TOPPING
250g (8oz) mozzarella cheese
4 tablespoons grated parmesan cheese
2 x 60g (2oz) cans anchovy fillets
125g (4oz) black olives
60g (2oz) mushrooms
1 small green pepper
4 tablespoons oil

Make filling first: Heat oil in pan, add peeled, finely chopped onion. Saute until transparent. Add crushed garlic, stir for 1 minute, stirring constantly. Stir in undrained tomatoes and remaining

1. Divide filling in half, spread evenly over each pizza with back of spoon. (The pizza in swiss roll tin can be cut into small squares when cooked and served as a deliciously savoury accompaniment to drinks.)

2. Combine grated mozzarella cheese and grated parmesan cheese, sprinkle over pizzas. Top with well-drained anchovy fillets, finely chopped pepper and finely sliced mushrooms. Sprinkle with halved olives. Spoon 2 tablespoons oil over each pizza to prevent drying out in cooking. Bake in hot oven 10 to 15 minutes until crust is golden brown.

ingredients. Bring sauce to boil, reduce heat. Simmer uncovered stirring occasionally, 20 to 25 minutes or until sauce is thick and smooth; cool.

Cream yeast with sugar, add lukewarm water, let stand 10 minutes or until bubbles appear on surface. Sift flour and salt into bowl, make well in centre, add oil and yeast mixture. Mix to firm dough with hand. Turn on to floured surface, knead for 15 minutes or until dough is smooth and elastic. Place in lightly oiled bowl, cover, stand in warm place 30 minutes or until dough has doubled in bulk. Knock dough down, divide in half, knead each half into a ball. Flatten dough into circle about 2.5cm (1in) thick. Roll out from centre to edge to fit 25cm (10in) pizza pan or 30cm x 25cm (12in x 10in) swiss roll tin. Repeat with remaining dough.

together to keep the smallest chambers closed. After about thirty weeks of fetal life, and trustfully forever after birth, a detergentlike chemical is squirted out inside us in fresh quantities about every two hours, day and night, which cuts down the surface tension by about 85 percent, keeping those lung chambers open. Lying perfectly still, however, breathing as quietly as a certain root vegetable upon a sofa, means that the sudsy molecules begin to slip out of position, sliding away from the very surfaces they're supposed to be holding open.

Without some help, the engrossed viewer would have a serious—and soon terminal—problem. Watch any absorbed TV viewer closely and before too long you'll see the sudden burst of activity—triggered by lung-deep nerve endings in place largely for this purpose—that resets all the alveoli and suds. It's often accompanied by a distinctive jaw rotation, shoulder lift, and chest expansion, but you can tell when it's coming on even with your eyes closed. It's the distinctively audible, inward air-gushing reflex we know as the sigh.

Advertisers have to get their show-interrupting pleas across to human specimens in such positions of utterly minimal alertness, but this isn't as much of a problem as it might seem. A lot of money is spent on studies of what works best for sports show ads, and brain-dulled viewers are ideal. The people most likely to act on Superbowl ads aren't the triumphantly hysterical ones, watching from the winning side's city. They are not viewers from the losing city either. Rather, they are the least involved of all: watchers from cities that have no team in the game, gazes fixed and jaws dropped, who let the messages seep through best.

Back in the sunny hallway upstairs, the baby has been sitting upright, enjoying the fresh air after the assaults of his mother's desktop computer and printer, taking stock and deciding what to do. Far ahead is the distance-blurred door of the bathroom, and that'll do fine as a target.

A carpet is easier for tiny padding hands to grip than the slippery tiles downstairs, but it's also—even if regularly cleaned—a stacked museum of fragments from virtually everything the family's discarded or tracked into the home over the past weeks or months. The largest dust items aren't a problem as this pajama-clad explorer heads out, for they land on the very top of the carpet, and are easily carted away with vacuuming. But others can be so lightweight as to only settle in the ultrastill air which fills this house at night. This means that they're on the top of the carpet fibers just in time for hurrying morning feet to really jam them in so deeply that ordinary vacuuming can't get them. But what—along with the bubbling breakfast chemicals and our ubiquitous skin flakes—are they?

If you have a cat, it's likely that you won't think of it as being especially dirty. Indeed cat lovers are known for thinking of their beasts as clean, in evidence of which they point to all the cats careful grooming, and especially the way cats drag their tongues over their fur. But although many cats truly are far wiser than dogs and would never demean themselves with the embarrassing subservience dogs delight in, there is a type of cat (it must be admitted), which despite its near-mystical origins among the ancient Egyptians, has an IQ approximating that of a noodle and is incapable of stopping this tongue-dragging, even when it's already clean. The consequence is that dried cat saliva in the two micron size range is released into your house in extraordinary amounts. A quarter teaspoon of dribbled cat saliva—which one cat is quite capable of extruding in a single afternoon of this lobotomized auto-cleansing—can contain several billion such fragmentary segments. The dried saliva will stay up in the air for hours, and even in a house that has been free from cats for years, it will still be found coating clothes, chairs, doors, bookshelves, computer screens, windows, and above all, having rained stickily from the sky, it will still be coating every square inch of the carpets. If you're lucky, the surface molecules which survive on this majestic saliva rain won't create later allergies in the deep-inhaling baby.

Pollen fragments will also be wedged deep in the waiting carpet vista, independent of the current state of the pollen season outside. Along with any fresh fragments from this morning's assault, many will have seeped in late last night, after a journey that saw them rise from their grass or other release points in the early morning, to be lofted high in the atmosphere by heat currents at midday, only to sink back earthward at 11 P.M. or later—which is why if you have hay fever there's a good chance you'll suddenly wake up sneezing then. Family members are responsible for some of this pollen, particularly

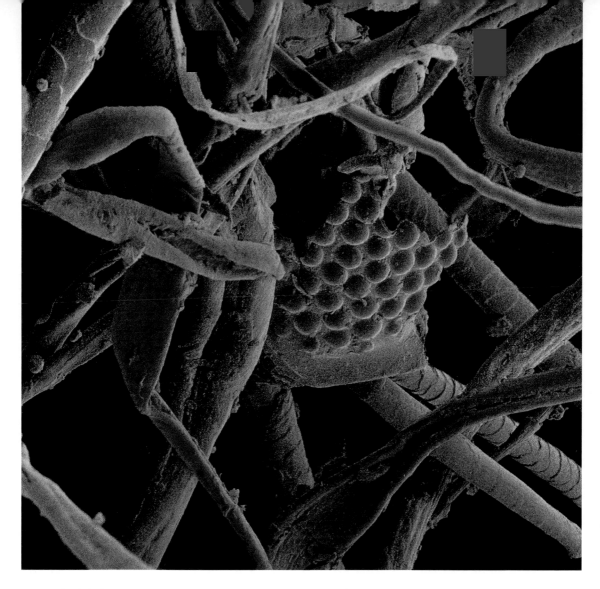

Household dust: nutritiously rich in hairs, skin flakes, clothing fibers, and even—at the center—the intact fragment of an insect's compound eye.

any members that go out a lot, especially in the pollen-rich evenings. It's worst if they have long hair, for that acts as a superb collection net—it's a gauzy filter, just sweeping through great volumes of loaded air—to bring in these treats. (Though, in partial justice, if that family member has hay fever herself, her middle of the night sneezing is made worse when she inhales the pollen from her own draping hair.)

Besides the pollen, cigarette particles, plummeted demodex, food fragments, bacteria, skin flakes, and wedged in deep, all the chunks of shoe-bottom dust that have also been brought in from outside—all this is in the carpet.

When the baby races forward, arms and legs thwacking down, the dust all comes catapulting up, forming a floating haze. Like a great baleen whale, the looming baby monster suctions it all in. The cavernous mouth is filled, and at this point there are two routes of further disposal. Some of it is simply gulped down, sending desperate bacteria, nutrient-rich yeasts, and months-old cat saliva—with only that eight-second delay for all swallows—straight to the huge stomach chamber, with its fatal acid streams. But much of the floating microcargo gets whirlpooled the other way, disappearing down into the lungs.

This could be a problem, for babies breathe through their mouths a lot, which means the dust isn't going to get picked up by the sticky linings inside their noses. They also don't have well-developed tracheal linings further along. What keeps babies from being stuffed with carpet dust and microbes is a population of house-cleaning cells, carted around in vast numbers deep inside their lungs. Grime and rubble come plonking down, soft-landing in the pink inner recesses, and within moments the nearest macrophages start squirming over. These are creatures with all the loving-kindness of Lady Macbeth on a rotten day. They live in the darkened, innermost recesses of our lung tissue, and when the merrily descending bacterium lands, swooping down on what should have been a deserted ideal feeding ground, it's show-time. One bubbling protoplasmic macrophage arm blindly twists forward, then another. A little space opens around the trapped bacterium for a mo-ment, leaving it floating like an astronaut caught in a dimly visible pressure chamber. Then the macrophage starts to digest it alive.

The whole family shares the genetic instructions for creating these armies of marauding defenders, which is why we can inhale so much dust-laden and bacteria-dense air and survive. Sometimes the macrophage un-loads fragments of the acid-ripped bacterium right there in the inner lung cavern; more often the macrophage drags itself forward, out of its cavern, till it reaches the wider openings, the very bottom of the bronchioles, where the sticky lining from so far above extends. It pulls itself on, and simply rides the slow escalator up, an apparently inert microlaundry bag. Usually there's a dead bacterium carried inside, but sometimes a desperate, though weak, tugging can be detected in the microscope: the bacterium hasn't been entirely killed, and is still trying frantically to get out. It won't succeed though. Depending on where the macrophage got on, it has days or weeks before it reaches the top. There's plenty of time for a bit more—punishment?—before the ride is over.

Only with stray asbestos fibers that we suction in does the macrophage meet its match. It grabs, it envelops, it sprays, and tries to gulp. But it has no luck, for asbestos is no soft-membraned bacterium, no easy pushover for inner-lung defenders. Asbestos is a rock, and its needlelike fibers, able to withstand the heat of blast furnaces, are certainly not going to succumb to any pathetic chemical attacks here. The macrophage chokes and dies, there in the hidden pink lung terrain, and the asbestos settles in for a long stay.

Any lead that's inhaled or swallowed by the looming baby is equally hard to clear. Lead enters the blood, and although much settles harmlessly inside the bones, some crosses the body's defensive barriers protecting the brain, pushes in to the growing cells there, and kills them. In large doses, as in a house with old, lead-soldered water pipes or lead paint, this can permanently lower IQ, but even low doses are worrisome. Babies are especially vulnerable, because their brains are still growing. The carpet tramped lead probably got there by the baby's own parents or siblings bringing it there. Metallic lead is too heavy to float more than about thirty feet from a car's exhaust, so anyone walking near a busy road or just in a parking lot will get some on his shoes. Carried home it's jammed into the carpet, for any crawling baby to send bouncing loose again. Even the amounts sequestered away in the bones might not stay harmlessly there forever. If the baby ever gets a strong fever in later life, its body will inadvertently let some out of those bone storehouses and loose into the brain-heading bloodstream. (Girls who grew up near lead-spewing factories in Eastern Europe released the old lead from their bones decades later, even in the safe haven of Australia, when the stress of flu or pregnancy pulled reserves from their bones.) Three thousand years ago there was virtually no lead in human bodies, and even now there's only a little bit in Himalayan farmers, so one way to safeguard your kids is to quit your job, grab a guru, and take your family off to the Himalayas. For the less adventurous, you can just take your shoes off when you come in. It cuts the lead levels at home considerably.

The baby is almost halfway through its journey now, bacteria and most dust defended against, when suddenly something else, something quite different and not at all a typical carpet-borne creature, flutters close. It's the mosquito again, flying up from downstairs; utterly lost in this labyrinthal house, and increasingly desperate to get some iron-soaked water from the very next carbon dioxide generator it finds. Its miniature wings crank faster to lift it up above the landing, for at least a quick view of the terrain up here and to see if there's a clear way outside. Its fertilized eggs are in imminent danger of starvation, there in the tiny pouchlike sacs where they're waiting in its abdomen, unless it can find some blood. At first there's only a view of the carpet edge, but there's some sort of puffing air generation device farther on—which could be the long-sought door to outside?—and the energy-fading mosquito cranks one final level faster, slowly lifting higher in this upstairs air.

And there it sights its food.

The mosquito is suddenly tired no longer. It roars up even higher, to properly survey this wholly unexpected bounty. What fair fate has granted it this waiting baby, nice and plump and succulently available for pump drilling, now on the floor just a few feet below? The mosquito wobbles slightly in the air again, determined to be absolutely sure after its problems with the father, but each time the baby burbles in puzzlement a great draft of carbon dioxide gushes up, and with that perfect course guidance around and no repellent to block its detection, the mosquito—flying Dracula-like, its wings wide out—is ready to swoop down.

A ten-month-old baby is unlikely to protest at all at this point, for how can it know what to expect? Instead it's likely just to watch in delighted amazement; each further burble sending out accurate vector location signals, as this fun, vivid toy circles around, then alights on its pudgy belly. The mosquito glances upward once, but the great watching face is happy as Buddha in the distance above, and there's no sign of danger—there's barely any sign of awareness, from this preposterous protohuman—so the mosquito simply gets to work.

It doesn't hurt, not at first, because two very different nervous systems are at work here. The human baby's pressure receptors, as with those on its parents and brother and sister, are widely spaced. If they were closer together, the human brain could be overloaded with too many signals. The mosquito is so small however, that its first slice can be carefully aimed to slip

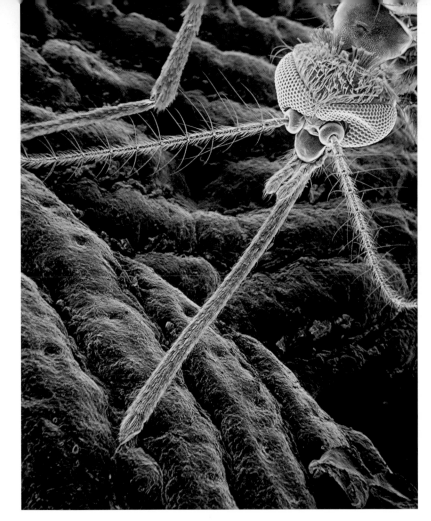

Stretching across the terrain of a human hand, a house mosquito leans in to feed. The tip of the proboscis is sharp enough to slide between our nerve endings, whence the common experience of being attacked without noticing. Only the females bite, needing blood for their fertilized eggs.

between any two pressure receptors on our skin. There might be a slight sensation of tickling, if the mosquito's being clumsy and it tugs on tiny skin hairs as it prepares, but even this is rare.

Once the first slit is made, the mosquito brings down other scalpels, and starts grinding them all into the victim's body in quick rotating motions. To keep the excavation from rebounding closed it starts regurgitating some anti-coagulants into the drilling hole. That would be enough if the mosquito had tapped right into an artery, but even when attacking a simple baby that's not a bright idea. The spurted pressure would be too hard to control. Instead, the mosquito has used its rotary scalpels to ease carefully between blood vessels. Only then will it inject the second chemical which it has carried, waiting for this blessed moment, for the entire duration of its flight inside this home. The chemical turns human flesh into a localized mush—it's something like a powerful detergent—and as soon as that's started bubbling away, the mosquito is finally ready to drink up. The main drinking tube had been started into the top of the hole even as the scalpels were still slicing away at the bottom. Now it's pushed all the way down, output nozzles are hooked up, and pump muscles switched on, quickly pulling up all the dissolved human bits. The procedure is effective and with an impressive pedigree: an expedition from the American Museum of Natural History found 90-million-year-old mosquito fossils with mouthparts strong enough to pierce into dinosaurs.

In theory we shouldn't mind any of this, for even a little baby might have a full pint of blood, and the most assiduously drinking mosquito, pumps powered on high, is only going to take a smidgen, a pinch: the merest drop of our total. And although mosquitoes outside of temperate lands have been estimated as the largest animal killer of humans known—responsible, through malaria, for perhaps a quarter of all infectious deaths since the Stone Age—this one is not likely to be carrying any such dangers. But now, finally, self-preservation takes command. The baby's reflexes might be slow, its pressure receptors wide, but it can detect the itching attack of those injected detergents, and it has enough dignity to keep its own body intact. A sudden pudgy *splat* will end the baby's troubles, the borehole that the now-deceased mosquito left behind jiggles closed, though the anticoagulants and detergents left inside will diffuse a little deeper, to itch for hours to come.

Outside the closed bathroom now, and strange sounds of off-key singing, mixed with intriguing vapors of heated bubble bath, are emanating from under the door. The other family members know that it's more than their lives are worth to disturb the fourteen-year-old sister in her midmorning purification ritual. But the baby tries to haul himself up, to reach that enticingly looming doorknob far above.

Inside this mysteriously guarded chamber, powerful electromagnetic

Opposite: Splash a single drop of water in a bathtub and part of it will rebound up, hovering as the oval in this image, before plummeting down for its second and final landing.

waves from distant radio stations are whipping through the bathtub, lightly electrifying all the salts and metals in the warmed water around the novitiate. They're partly blocked by the mud and crumbled volcanic rock of her face mask—always necessary for The Teenager Taking Her Bath—but a number escape through the glass window across from her, traveling as fast as the TV waves from downstairs, and reach the surface of the moon, skimming low over the craters a bare one-quarter second after whirling past her. A few of the frantic electromagnetic waves stay in this room, scurry into the short antenna strip inside the radio, and from there, after being led through the circuits and intensifying in power they come out as the music—as bonding to her teenage cohorts as the dad's TV sports—she needs to be submerged in.

Why does our exuberant bathtub singing sound so terrible? It's not just a matter of the echoes from steam-moistened tiles, though that's the excuse I use. Few people can pay attention to words and tunes at the same time. Words are generally controlled by the left side of the brain, tunes by the right, and our awareness centers find it hard to deal simultaneously with signals leading up from both areas. This is why lyricists and songwriters usually have to inhabit separate bodies, and why yelps, interpolated hums, and general off-key discordance are the best most mortals can hope for. There's also the problem that most of us are immensely far from having perfect pitch. Skill here was once thought to be something you inherited, but when researchers starting looking into why it cropped up so often in musicians' families, they found that it can often be acquired by practice, at least if you start young enough. The trick seems to be to learn the names of the musical notes at an early age and get used to hearing their sequences. Do that regularly, or have parents who harangue you to do that, and scans will show the result: the parts of the brain that accurately recognize sounds grow extra connections.

This safely solo singer's big toe now reaches with practiced dexterity to rotate the hot-water handle. A teenager taking one bath a day, with forty gallons of water used each time, will destroy the equivalent of several barrels of oil to provide the amount of warmed liquid she requires in one year. The heated water now cascading out was once part of huge, icy meteors that hurtled through the early solar system and slammed into our planet, forming the first oceans in a titanic sequence of impacts concentrated when the earth was just 1 billion years old. The particular splashes of water that enter here have cycled through thousands of sea creatures' bodies, and been returned to the sea from rainstorms of the Jurassic and other eras, before reaching this tub. A little chlorine gas comes out from the faucet with it now, added by the local water-pumping company to kill bacteria. Some gas hovers low over the surface like invisible fog banks and is inhaled, to be broken down in the bather's body sometime tomorrow; much of the rest—chlorine being so volatile—slips out through gaps around the window and quickly tries to rise away from the house. As long as it stays combined with the water the sunlight will destroy it. This is the main reason chlorine is used up in outdoor swimming pools so quickly, especially shallow ones.

A colorful bottle is lifted from the bath's edge and something like a tiny paintbrush removed, while the girl goes back to examining the weird objects emerging from several of her body tips. Fingernails are derived from the flexible armored scales of dinosaurs and other early creatures, and have been decorated for about as long as records are available. Toenails, being the most massively armored, take a year on average to grow their full lengths. Fingernails are less demanding, squirmy little things, and whoosh out of a teen's body at a blistering 100 microns—two hair widths—a day in winter and an even more galloping 125 microns in summer. In four months what was once at the base is now at the tip. Parents are slower, younger brothers are faster, but these are only averages. If someone bites her nails, the nails slide out even faster, at 200 or even 300 microns a day. This is when the bottle is really needed, for the amount of nail substance produced doesn't go up to match. A nail that has been bitten ends up thinner and easily cracked. The effect is enhanced by long, family-escaping tub soaks, for the soaking encourages subterranean fungal arms to twist and grow beneath the surface and that easily cracks what's on top. The molten plastic being painted from the bottle fills up the crevices, as well as easily carrying a bright dye.

Teens love choosing their favorite colors, but these are rarely as original as they think. It's hard for chemists to come up with fundamentally new colors, so fingernail polish dyes—as well as those in hair dyes and lipsticks—are regularly reused. Someone with a good memory might notice that the Cyber-Glow Shocker being so carefully ladled out now looks suspiciously like what was marketed as Executive Bold in the eighties; someone with an even better memory, or consulting old photos, might recognize it as House-wife's Harmony from the fifties.

The faucet is rotated off; the once-mighty meteor water halted by the fourteen-year-old's toe. There's a glance at the backlog of textbooks stacked on the floor, but they are easily passed over. American high school students rank highest in the world on U.N.-sponsored polls asking how confident they are that they're knowledgeable and studying enough. As they also rank near the bottom in how much they actually know, something is amiss. One of the biggest differences is homework time. Studies of immigrants show that when they do well at school it's not because they're living in good neighborhoods or that their parents are well off or speak English well or that there are public role models around: it's simply that they've been piling on the homework. (When the whole family sits around the table and does it together—the older kids helping the younger and the parents nearby even if they can't follow the details—the statistical result is even better.) Girls often do better by high school because they worry and tend to blame themselves when they get bad grades; boys, more likely to blame the teacher or the subject or anything but themselves, are less likely to add on the studying that would help. Admittedly the effort needed for getting into a good university is new. In 1920, the majority of Ivy League universities had almost *never* rejected an applicant, with Harvard continuing that tradition largely into the mid-1930s. Rich children were accepted almost automatically; everyone else—aside from the occasional rare prodigy—knew not to try.

It should be time to get out, as the last digit is now painted, skin-tip wrinkles are assuming lunar proportions, and the next stage of the anointed one's preparations—the final skin lotions and dressing needed before re-entering the outside world—are going to take time. Fingertips and toes are the spots that get especially wrinkly because they have the thickest skin. The swollen skin can't spread sideways, and instead is forced upward. Thinner skin, on the arms or legs, is too taut to absorb much water and so doesn't pucker up. It's good to let the polish dry a little, and anyway, it's always nice to pour in a little more bubble mixture from the squeeze bottle on the bath's edge, the one with the pictures of tender gamboling lambs or their like, and then swoosh it around and watch the bubbles rise. The surface that's produced is one of the thinnest substances visible to the naked eye, for a bubble-bath bubble can remain intact at under a single micron thickness, which is far less than the width of a human hair and even smaller than the baby demodex creatures, now desperately clinging to the bath-steamed openings on the eyelashes of this splashing human.

To keep those precarious bubbles propped up, something strong is needed, a long strutlike molecule, and here is where those bucolic scenes of little lambs or calves take on a little more relevance than is generally appreciated. The substance used is somewhat coyly termed "hydrolyzed animal collagen." It's obtained by herding together such sweet and tender little creatures, then smashing their heads in, skinning their bodies, and using electric saws and hydraulic pliers to yank out their tendons. Mashed, boiled, and then skimmed, the result is a perfect, pliable bubble strut. It's a little less expensive to collect such residues from older animals—unsalable haggard horses or lambs that are so diseased their meat can't be used are especially common—so it's modified fragments of their skimmed and boiled body parts that will often be floating around the tenderly musing girl instead.

The soap on her leg is less spectacularly constructed. Raw soap is heavier than water, but air is lighter. Mix enough air into your soap—as happened, apparently inadvertently, to one now-immortalized batch in 1876—and it will float. If that initial botched batch had been only a few dozen bars it would have been thrown out, but as several thousand of the faulty bars had already been made, they were sold as a reduced-price lot. Customers loved the soap, as did the manufacturer, for wherever zero-cost air was filling up the spaces inside, less soap had to be added. The aerated soaps did have a problem at first, in that they wouldn't lather as much as ordinary ones, because all the extra air cut down the amount of potentially bubbling soap available. The solution for several manufacturers is to add hogs' fat. In its raw state this is a less-than-attractive gray sludge, with an odor that mating pigs find delectable, but which most humans would prefer not to bring into intimate contact with their own bodies. Perfumes and odorants are mixed in to mask the stink though, and some titanium dioxide white paint—the same as in the Danish pastry and coffee creamer—is added to disguise the underlying gray color. Rub such a soap briskly over your hands, and a thick luxuriant foam, white and fresh-smelling now, as if by magic, appears.

One more expensively purchased substance likely to be in this tub should be less disturbing even to the greatest sticklers of purity. A teen's lotions and bubble baths are frequently advertised as being pH balanced. What this means is that they have the same number of free-hydrogen ions as ordinary water. This is an easy chemical result to achieve, for in many cases the manufacturers simply add water, at a notably higher price, it is true, than what's pouring out from the faucet.

A final swish of the hand in the water, and the girl gets out of the tub, to finally engage in the task all teen girls must determinedly face at some point in the day, which is to stand on the scale. The whirling dial briefly holds suspense, till finally it stops and she sees, once again, that she weighs too much.

It's a hard fate to avoid, even though this is an excellent time of day to weigh yourself—our body weight goes down to its lowest point every day around noon, then floats up in the evening, swollen with extra metabolized water. Hormonal controls mean that a girl at puberty is going to be pumped up to perhaps 25 percent fat, compared to the 15 percent that an average boy that age will have. The difference is excellent preparation for a future pregnancy, but society doesn't let her put that weight on and be content. American men are now two inches taller than they were, on average, in 1960, and they weigh twenty-seven pounds more. American women are also two inches taller. But how much weight have they put on, to match that energy-demanding height? Just one single, achingly controlled, pound. Only if she could go back in time to Rubens' era, when great thigh-bursting balloonlike shapes were the ideal for female beauty, could she safely be allowed to eat at will, and have the pleasure of seeing any of today's supermodels similarly transported back in time pitied for their scrawny inadequacy. In fact, the modern ideal of slim hips and straight legs isn't especially healthy for women. A comprehensive study at St. Thomas's Hospital in London found that health depends a great deal on where the body's fat is located. If it's found around the waist and stomach it is dangerous, for fat there is regularly broken down and circulated through the blood, where it can clog blood vessels or lead to other problems. Fat that is distributed around the thighs and hips is healthier, because this fat is rarely broken up. (A reasonable explanation for why men have more heart disease, as they are more likely than women to carry extra weight around their stomachs.)

Bathroom scales to keep track of us are relatively new, with the silvery

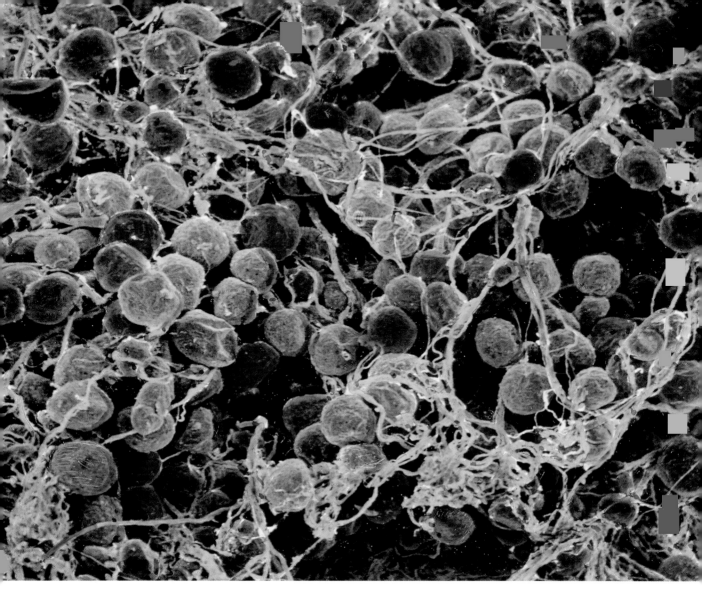

Fat cells. Each cell is a miniature balloon, filling up with liquid supplies. Thin people keep them partially empty and fat people have the cells burstingly full, but the number acquired in childhood is with you for life.

Detecto scale of 1927 apparently one of the first. Before that most people had no accurate idea what they weighed, certainly not from day to day, and so couldn't torment themselves as much. The two sexes of course torment themselves differently. When women are dissatisfied with their body they hone the critique down to detailed parts: researchers are inundated with lists of grievously imperfect waists, buttocks, feet, cheekbones, and the like that aren't right. Men are less likely to view their bodies as an assemblage of separate parts with each having to be minutely examined, and tend to worry about their overall strength or reflexes. (The only exception is that men, or at least male undergraduates, are frequently unhappy with their ears—the sole specific object about which their coed counterparts, for once, have no qualms.)

Down the drain from this girl's face go bits of clay, boiled bones, vinyl polymers, trees, alcohol, and yet more paint. All are additional constituents of a good face mask, and the result, when it's finally off, is a wonderful sense of rejuvenation, which lasts for at least four seconds till the girl looks up, to really examine her face in the mirror. She'll put on some lotions later, to get her arms and face looking really good, but for now it's going to be the unadulterated truth.

She can't see the landed microbial flyers touching down from the air, or the deluge-hiding demodex in their sweat-gland caves. But what she does see upsets her immensely: a pimple. She looks around the bathroom, poking through the glass shelf with the aspirin and breath freshener and tanning lotion to find the scrubbing brush and acne lotion— with the extra-powerful formula—she'd left out, carefully in place for such emergencies, before her brother started moving everything. A century ago there would likely have been a certain white powdered concentrate from the Bayer company mixed in there: it was a newfangled drug for family use the company was selling, called heroin. Unfortunately, it had certain problems—repeat sales were *too* good—so market withdrawal came a few years later. It was a different white powder Bayer introduced in the 1890s—aspirin—which lasted a little longer. This longevity was helped by good timing, since later FDA regulations would have kept it off the market, as too many people have stomach bleeding when they use it. (More powerful drugs such as penicillin would have been entirely impossible to introduce. In the 1940s guinea pigs were still being used for testing, and penicillin kills guinea pigs. Only the pressure of battlefield casualties in World War II allowed the drug to be rushed into use.)

The girl finds the small scrub brush and acne lotion. This time she's really going to scrape hard, getting all the infection off no matter how much it hurts, and then she'll put the lotion on, big stinging soaks of it, enough to crush, suffocate, obliterate whatever malicious bacteria—which she picked up at school? from eating chocolate?—have been constructing their career-threatening construction sites on her.

It's a common resolution, but almost always fails, for bacteria are the *least* important source of acne. The triggering cause is the sludgy butterlike sebum liquid that adolescents start pouring out—an approximate half bucket of the stuff each year—from the time they reach puberty. Sebum has no positive use at all. It doesn't guard against sunburn or kill bacteria or stop water loss. The only thing it can do is start acne. It contains fats of a sort that arriving bacteria can break down, and it's those broken fats, not the bacteria, which do the damage. The broken fats are turned into detergentlike blobs, that push out sideways from the face ducts and start digesting what's nearby. It's as unpleasant to view as to read about, whence the agony of the teen trying to hide it.

Why do our bodies do this to us? The latest theory is that it's intended as a marker of puberty: little pulsating signals, conveniently displayed out on the face, saying "I'm Fertile!" Admittedly it's a signal most teenagers could live without—discreet home-page valentines would be a lot easier—but it does give a certified advertising truth: only when you have reached puberty will that sebum pour out.

There is still a role for the bacteria that switch on the detergent blobs but that is something the daughter can't get away from, certainly not here, where although she thinks she's alone and private, isolated from all family intrusions, she's actually more closely connected to her family than ever. An ordinary family bathroom is a wonderful incubation and transfer zone—a near ideal switching center—for the family's diverse bacterial load. The most regularly fed segment of the room's infection core are the thick dangling bathroom towels. Staph and other bacteria wait on the towels, quiveringly alive for many hours. Even if the girl has insisted that no one ever rub their grubby hands on her towel she can still get it, for most families hang their towels on metal rods where the towels are close enough for the bacteria to easily bounce across from one to the other. If the hygienically optimal solution of washing all the towels more frequently is too exhausting to even think about, then simply spacing them so that they don't touch will help considerably. It's the same reason that it's wise not to have toothbrushes touch, though if the ten-year-old boy has the peculiarly ten year old's habit of running his thumb along the bristles of his brush and giving the whole counter top a good spray when he's done, then all precautions short of individual containers for brush storage will be of little avail.

The door handle starts to turn, or at least there's the sound of someone trying to turn it, and the daughter whirls around, furious that anyone could dare to intrude. She calls out, and the baby yelps, then plops back down on its pajamaed bottom. When she bangs on the inside of the bathroom fortress door for emphasis, he yelps again, thoroughly scared, and starts padding at top velocity back down the hall, hurrying desperately, till suddenly, appearing out of nowhere, reaching down for a great swooping lift, is his mother.

She's in wonderful spirits, as she carries her baby back to the master bedroom. Her boss wasn't in when she finally finished her report and phoned him, so she got to leave a message on his machine instead—one of the unsung pleasures of modern life. And how can she possibly do any more work now, when her baby son needs comforting? She triumphantly flicks off her computer and sits with the baby on the bed, holding and comforting and even passing over one of the normally rationed candies he likes, watching as his tears hesitantly stop during the intent concentration needed for unwrapping it. They lounge back together on the big clean bed as she gets out a colorful book to read aloud; they rest in this spotless room, where the windows are always left wide open for air and light and where the pillow in its crisp, freshly changed linen cover is propped comfortingly underneath them.

And where the home's final parallel family thrives.

There's an entire neo-dinosaur landscape of lumbering creatures deep inside the pillows, even in the cleanest of homes. We nourish our pillows with hours of moisture-rich exhaled air each night—a drenching half pint per night is typical—and that, combined with the skin oils and surface skin flakes we can't help but scrape loose, is enough to keep their population at levels immensely greater than the hair-follicle dwelling demodex we saw at breakfast. The demodex existed by the mere hundreds; here, on the pillow, the human family is cozily surrounded by a world—mercifully invisible to the naked eye—with hundreds of thousands of busy inhabitants.

These are *Dermatophagoides pteronyssinus*—the flesh-eating pillow mites. Unlike the cuddly rounded demodex, a microscope reveals the *Dermatophagoides* as hulking armored beasts, with eight legs and massive rhinolike necks. They're also superbly equipped for life inside the pillow—their feet even have flaring pads, like a *Star Wars* desert planet beast, to keep them from suddenly sinking in the soft filling—and despite the forbidding name and appearance, they are actually quite mild.

As it's difficult to see well in the dim light reaching their depths, they signal romantic availability not by crude bellowing calls, but by the polite release of a floating vapor. The targeted one swivels its huge neck to get a directional fix, and then, as gracefully and balletically as an armored monster is able, trundles shyly forward for the hopeful tryst that awaits.

It seems to be a near perfect life, with several generations of these bulky creatures—from gnarled grandparents to thin-walled frisky juveniles—resting, strolling, romancing, or, greatest of pleasures and definitely greatest use of time, tilting their heads up to grab the gently swirling skin flakes tumbling down. But paradise is not for our planet, and there's also one other sort of creature in the pillow: the dreaded, jaw-slobbering *Cheyletus*—a relative giant in this subvisible domain, that lives by tracking down the ordinary peaceable mites in our pillows, and eating them. Let a *Dermatophagoides* adult release a mate-luring pheromone cloud, and this *Cheyletus* will hurry along faster than the intended, to wait, jaws ready, there in the dark, till one of the hopeful suitors lumbers into reach. If the *Cheyletus* can't find suitably nutritious adults it'll simply pick off bite-size morsels of baby *Dermatophagoides*.

If this were all that happened, it wouldn't matter much that this odd world is so busily active beneath us. But the mother plumps up the pillow for her and her baby son. Any such plumping, or even any twists and turns we take on the clutched pillow at night, forces windstorm velocity air gusts into that hidden world. The air then whooshes back up, forming great arcing parabolas that rise a full three inches or even more above the pillowcase, loaded with thousands of the discreetly named "anal pellets" each *Cheyletus* has produced. They explode apart in our open air and then float. Since they

Pillow mite. Too small to see, colonies of 40,000 or more pillow mites inhabit the warmth of even the cleanest household pillows. Most are harmless scavengers, living on our scraped-loose skin, though a small number of microcarnivores—hunting these skin-eaters—rampage through their midst under our resting heads each night.

were recently inside the digestive system of an enzyme-secreting arthropod, they're not especially healthy to have floating around, especially as they're exactly the right size to get breathed in.

Adults are fairly well protected by their developed immune systems, but kids, and especially babies, can suffer, as the gut enzymes slip loose from the floating pellets or land on insufficiently blinking eyes. The baby's cells that will later be powerful histamine producers can become oversensitized when enough pellets touch and will stay that way for years. The effect is greater than that of anything else the baby encountered in the hallway: a large epidemiological study in Britain, tracing several hundred Southampton families over the years, found that one of the best predictors of getting asthma as an adolescent was living in a home with large numbers of pillow mites as a baby. It's not just a problem in the bedroom, for the haze of broken pellets floats to all the rooms, settling on baby-exposed carpets everywhere in the house. Regularly allowing the dog or cat to sleep on the bed during the day provides further supplies of warmth and nutrient breath vapor when the animals rest their heads on the pillows, thus incubating even greater numbers of pillow mites. A teenager who spends hours leaning on her pillow during her life-sustaining phone calls—her body thereby acting as a radiant heating coil for the life underneath her—will be guaranteed supremely high numbers in her room.

The results of these studies make people inquire about the price of flamethrowers. The populations are impressive, for the pillow mites have been found in virtually 100 percent of the homes studied, be it in Germany, America, or Britain. There are usually at least 10,000 mites per pillow in the most hygienic of traditional homes. If it is a house where busy professional parents only change the pillow*cases*, but somehow have forgotten to ever rinse, soak, boil, or in the faintest way wash the pillow *itself*—thereby letting the sheltered inhabitants be discreetly fruitful and multiply for weeks, months, or years on end—then the pillows they're using, and considerately providing for the rest of the family, will be home to 400,000 or more creatures. In the distressing estimate of Britain's leading pillow-mite specialist, an unwashed pillow can end up being be stuffed with up to 10 percent living or deceased *Dermatophagoides* by weight over the years. Along with cleaning one's pillows, at least occasionally, it's also good to keep the windows open sometimes. Double-glazed windows and central heating encourage the warm, moist conditions the mites like, and wherever that's kept down, their numbers fall too. Arizona and the Alps work as resorts, partly because their dry air helps kill off the asthma-production machines of such pillows.

The wife hears a call from downstairs, glances at her bedside clock to confirm the late time, and quickly gets up, one soothed baby son happy in her arms. A number of the mites come along too, clinging tightly to wife and baby alike. Habitat destruction is a continual threat. In a pillow not used for five or six months, the entire population of mites will starve. A proportion of the population valiantly travels with us all the time as a safeguard against such disasters. Most die before they're ever brought to another pillow for recolonization. But a number will survive, for the species is photophobic (averse to light) and so without quite knowing why, they do try to hunker down, tiny feet working their way down from any sun or artificial light, to clamp around our clothing fibers—wool and brushed cotton do best—till they're at least partially protected.

We accordingly are the vehicles that transport these city-state populations around from room to room in our homes, as well as carrying them to offices, schools, and one of the most fruitful switching stations: hotel rooms, with their nice, constantly reinvigorated, traveler-awaiting pillows. Here in this house representatives of the several different pillow colonies are being carried on the human family as they begin to assemble downstairs; adults and babies and juveniles and even some of the awful *Cheyletus* predators, though humbled now, and cowering away from the light as much as the others. All the movement is just a vague blur to the diverse *Dermatophagoides* holding on, as the humans collect money and jackets and candy bars and shopping lists; as the baby's bag is rechecked for extra diapers, and the dad tries not to be too impatient, holding the car keys, as the daughter comes down. Even she's been willing to hurry up, for the sake of what's coming next. The traveling mites are going to get a treat today.

This family is going to the mall.

afternoon

4

mall and lunch

Peering out from their car window, in the open parking lot, the family is a unit once again, briefly, at least until the individuals separate. Now they draw on their impressive telepathy of communication systems, including visual signals from over a dozen facial muscles for rough data transfer, as well as those invisible smaller air compressions—words!—for more detailed and precise information transmission.

Our family navigates around other visitors to the mall, careful not to cross into anyone's personal space. Women are usually polite enough, giving a large space to anyone they approach, and don't become too upset if someone comes a little closer. Men demand the largest personal space, especially men from the South, or at least the men at one American university recently, where brave social psychologists bumped a number of different students walking down a narrow corridor. The Northerners showed little effect, but the Southerners almost all had ambulance-foreboding surges of cortisol and other stress hormones in their blood when it was measured right after an encounter. That anger response is also likely to send blood to the hands, where it would provide enhanced sensitivity and strength in handling weapons. (Fear, in contrast, sends more blood to the long muscles of the legs, which is good for quick escapes. Fear also lowers the amount of blood in the skin, thereby reducing bleeding if your legs don't carry you away fast enough and you are attacked. The lack of blood in the skin also explains the famous pallor of fear.)

Luckily, if the dad makes a mistake and does come too close, a commanding, seemingly telekinetic weapon flashes out: a burbling happy smile from the baby strapped to his chest. By deep genetic primings, this usually neutralizes even the most angry stranger in the parking lot today. Face recognition structures seem to be built in to the baby's developing brain, so it locks on to other human faces, and flashes a survival-enhancing smile.

The teenage daughter is strolling ostentatiously behind, making sure that no one, and especially no one under the age of sixteen, thinks that she's somehow related to these people. But as her family strides ahead she soon needs to catch up, or at least not fall too far back. This is difficult in a crowded mall parking lot, for although we're willing to let our bubble of personal space be compressed a little, we really don't like it to be sliced through to zero. The main family groups ahead of her are safe, for if someone walks too closely toward them the whole unit can respond. First there will be a single quick visual flick-scan in the intruder's direction. If that doesn't trigger avoidance maneuvers, there are further defense displays: a flurry of blinks and seemingly quizzical head twists that usually keep potential intruders away. Monitors attached to clumsy walkers receiving such family-multiple attacks show skin sweating and heart rates rising quickly at this point.

For the girl hurrying forward alone it's harder, for now she's very far behind, almost losing sight of the family. She'll have to engage in the one path trajectory that inspires hesitation in even the most brutal of mall-eager speeders. This is to walk not just a little too close to a group of strangers, not even nonchalantly past their edges, brushing a sleeve perhaps, so that their warning blinks and head twists have to be boldly ignored from only inches away, but rather to go right ahead, desperate for speed, and walk right *through* the group of strangers.

This is something we really don't like to do. Social psychologists have filmed poor unfortunates who've had to do this, and then played back the tormented imagery. Approaching a waiting group we almost always first try a submissive posture, of bowed head and gaze firmly held downward. But as we get closer, having to ignore their startlement at seeing us not break off from the collision course, the tension gets too much, and we look up and start doing strange things with our mouths: almost always lips are tightened, mouths are pursed, and excessive head tilts of apology begin. The pulse surges up, reaching 110 on average, and just at the moment of maximum agony, maximum social isolation, right in the middle of the group being disturbed, we usually squeeze our eyes tight closed, in pathetic attempts at total escape.

A car speeds too close to the main family up ahead. A sequence of enlarging car images appear on the family's retinas, and then are cabled inward, initiating a spasm of busy nerve-cell firings in the visual movement centers of their brains. A message is hurried over to decision centers, and only then are the parents' arms finally grabbing for the kids.

Rubber molecules on the bottom of everyone's shoes crater the asphalt on the parking lot surface, as sudden g-forces distort toe bones in the deceleration. The baby's head especially jerks forward, as the father stops fast. This sends the inside of the baby's skull crashing forward, seemingly ready to scrape against his delicate brain. Luckily our brains don't just wobble inside an otherwise empty cranium, perched on the flexible support base of the brain stem. The baby's brain is floating in a slippery warm liquid—cerebrospinal fluid—and when the skull crashes forward, the liquid compresses like an airbag to keep it from impacting. If the dad's stop was exceptionally fast, there might be some bruising to the baby's brain despite this protection, but so long as it's moderate, that, too, won't be a problem. Tiny, long-stretching clearance cells are spread throughout the baby's brain, as they are inside the adults. Normally they wait in standby position, but when there's damage, mobile forms appear—a little like the macrophages we saw in the baby's lungs earlier—and in the hours to come they will wrap around the damaged bits, hauling them away. (There's some evidence that Alzheimer's, in part, can be due to these clearance cells no longer working properly.)

With the feet skidding and brains wobbling, arms need to be propelled outward to keep balance. Miniature angle detectors located in everyone's knees and shoulders measure how much the individual is tipping over, and send signals upward for the brain to do the complex trigonometry needed for correction instructions. Meanwhile, throughout the family, droplets of a long-stored chemical are pumped out from glands conveniently placed over the kidneys, and adrenaline feeds into the renal vein. In a response lasting for minutes until it breaks down muscles strengthen and brain reactions seem quicker. Such an adrenaline response is powerful, but not magically so. The surge makes you stronger, but doesn't do anything about enhancing the bones which actually support you. There have been cases where patients have stepped out of their wheelchairs in the adrenaline-charged excitement of a religious revival, only to have their still-weakened bones horribly shatter a few hours later from having carried the unexpected full body weight.

Sixty years ago suburbs were too sparse to support malls. The parking lot would probably have been a forested or empty lot then. America was a very different country, and if we could suddenly be transported back, the crowd marching around us would seem impossibly different. People didn't wear tracksuits or leisure clothes in public, but had distinct roles, revealed by their clothes. Men wore hats, which also roughly matched their social level. Despite this, incomes were much more uniform than they are now: the current figures, of chief executive officers averaging 120 times what blue collar workers earn, is historically unprecedented. (Even twenty years ago the ratio was only 35 times more.) There were fewer old people sixty years ago; there were also hardly any divorced people, for getting a divorce was strongly frowned upon. There were even fewer left-handed people than today: it was wrong to stand out in any way, and most had been forced as children to use their right hands. There were more immigrants than today, though authorities were fearful that the country would lose its identity because of them; there were fewer black people in most city stores, as official racism meant they were usually kept out. Through it all there was more trust, as polls taken then put the number of Americans who agreed that most people could be trusted at about twice the figure of today. The very trip to a city center where the shopping took place would have been a major expedition, since most people were too poor to own a car or travel far. When U.S. paratroopers made their first training jumps in World War II, they were almost always making their first airplane flights too, as very few people had flown commercially by then.

Slipping behind again, the teenage daughter has stopped to put on her dark sunglasses. Such posturing is understandable: as Diderot put it, "There is only one person in the world who walks, and that is the Sovereign. Everybody else takes up positions." It's also dangerous for her eyes, especially if the sunglasses she's behind are made of a low-price plastic. Photons sprayed out from the hydrogen bomb–making sun make the rest of the family's eye pupils contract. It's a useful reflex to block damage from that ancient light. Visible photons are blocked by the sunglasses, however cheap the lenses, but ultraviolet ones just pour on through. Since they're invisible, the girl has no way of telling that they are there, and her pupil openings won't shrink down for protection. The darker the sunglasses, the worse it is: her pupils will have *widened* in response to the dark cocoon around them, even though the ultraviolet photons are still slamming in. Only more expensive lenses, made of glass or top-grade plastic, will keep the eye-attacking ultraviolet light out. An added blast is coming at her horizontally, reflected from the car windows.

With her sleeves rolled down to heighten the mystery effect, she's receiving less ultraviolet rays on her skin than the rest of her family. In a parking lot miles long this could be wise, to help ward off skin cancer. Here though, with just a few minutes more ambling before reaching the stores, the covering ends up blocking the ultraviolet she needs for her bones. Cells called osteoblasts are crawling inside the entire family's legs, sticking calcium mineral into place. The more you walk or exercise, the faster they work, and the more they stick on. A teenager whose chief exertion of the week was rotating the bath faucet with her toe is not giving those osteoblasts much of a workout. Direct sun rays could help here, producing vitamin D as we saw on the porch. Even fifteen minutes exposure to ultraviolet can produce a lot of the vitamin. In a teenager, it would drift through the bloodstream to the intestine, to ensure that more calcium is absorbed from her food and ends up in her bones. Sleeves rolled down tight stop the process.

The color her clothes are emitting varies a little from culture to culture. In North America and Europe the brighteners added to detergents mean that a blouse we think we're seeing as white actually has a strong bluish tinge. In South America, blue doesn't carry such overtones of maximum cleanliness; instead a reddish tinge suggests cleanliness.

Car fumes spatter against the girl's protective glasses, swirling in an invisible haze around all the grouped walkers today. The heath effects of inhaling these fumes depend to some extent on how much time the family has spent living in a polluted city. Just as with the ozone gusts from the wife's laser printer, their bronchial cells will be working more efficiently than those of families that never had to become used to such air pollution. Many of the inhaled chemicals are blocked even as they start up your nose; what slips through can be further destroyed by backup enzyme systems in the blood, especially the ubiquitous glutathione. Even if a family has moved to an unspoiled suburb, the effect will carry on, to some extent, for months and even years. Any neighbor of theirs wandering in the same parking lot, who hasn't had that regular experience of urban pollution, will pull in the fumes unblocked. Long-time residents of Los Angeles carry lots of the cleansing glutathione around in their blood, even after they've moved; inhabitants of rural Canada, as blood tests show, do not.

Heat from the parking lot surface reflects upward, making the family's surface blood vessels quickly widen, pulling up to a tenth of the body's heated blood near the surface. More than 2 million perspiration holes start pumping evaporative fluids outward. With the air-conditioned car far behind, the family is a marching vapor-spray unit. The newly parked cars add to the distress, for cars are extraordinarily inefficient devices, with 80 percent of the gasoline you just used raising the temperature of the engine and exhaust system, or ultimately ending up as useless friction on the tires or car surface. The family, meanwhile, is eliminating a surprisingly large amount of heat from its heads. A brain weighs only 2.5 percent of its body's total, but the head pumps out 20 percent of the body's heat in adults and an even greater percentage in kids.

Everyone's suffering, though as usual it's the weaker sex that's suffer-

Sweat droplets on a hand. The amount seen here is what's produced after an hour's exercise.

ing more, the one which constantly needs to be reassured and consoled—the men, of course. Women are skilled at sweating: their moisture droplets come out on their skin in small, easy-to-evaporate droplets. Men, on average, pop out larger sweat globs that are more likely to drip off, producing impressive splat patterns on the ground perhaps, but doing little to cool down the mighty predators. The baby's swaddled in its belly-thick fat, but infants and young children can still grow the optimum number of sweat glands they'll need as adults. Japanese who are born and raised in the tropics end up, by one count, with 2.9 million water-releasing sweat glands, but their cousins who spend their childhoods in cooler lands make do with only 2.1 million. There's a lot of potential cooling from 800,000 extra glands. That's why people can be uncomfortable if they grow up in a cool climate but move as adults to a warm one.

The family enters the cool, air-filtered sanctum of the mall. A great deal of thought has gone into designing the entryway. The entry has to seem inviting, so people will be happy to come in, but it can't be too inviting, for then they'll linger and block it. There are likely to be benches attractively set down just inside the entrance, about as welcoming as a shopping arena can be, but look closely and you'll see that they're usually placed so that a sitter will have his back to the main traffic—a position that's psychologically all but impossible to keep for long. Tiny muscles tighten up on the family's forearms and back, forming the miniature air-slowing windbreaks we call goosebumps, as they try to orient themselves in the suddenly chilled air.

Uncomfortably hard tiles clack under the family's shoes for the first yards in, and this almost certainly makes them walk faster—about 10 percent faster, in one study—than if there had been a carpeted walkway. To be extra sure that there's no slowdown, faint clouds of ionone and other molecules are likely to be spraying out from the recessed cooling ducts further along. Ionone is easily produced—it's just the result of breaking down common carotene molecules. It gives off the delectable odor of fresh hay. There are companies that sell these chemicals in liquid vats for mall managers to use in air-cooling systems. The unembarrassed can usually confirm this use by going up to an exposed duct—perching on someone's shoulder is sometimes necessary—and taking a close-up sniff. Farther on there will be different vapors. Shoe stores are likely to spray out a liquefied leather extract to draw in passing browsers; for sports stores, wisps of floral essence work best.

As they walk, the family almost certainly follows a reflex to veer toward the right. Children do it and adults do it—whether they're left- or right-handed—and it's so powerful an instinct that stores often pay higher rents for locations at the right-hand side of the entrance where the speed-controlled temperature-dazed shoppers are most likely to be piling in. Fluorescent lights above add to the initial disorientation, for these lights exhibit a constant slight flickering, which can create detectable nerve-cell spasms inside the brains of our family. The problem can be avoided when the fluorescent lights are perfectly adjusted, but with the hundreds of lights around, and janitors who have other things to do, that's not likely to happen.

To get upstairs, the family heads toward the elevator. The mall managers may keep one elevator on the ground floor always open. People march in, and even though they wait there exactly as long as they would had it not been standing open, they almost always feel better huddling inside rather than out. The next trick is to appease restless waiting shoppers is to put mirrors on the wall of the elevator. We all tend to glance at ourselves when there's a full-length mirror nearby, be it the discreet side-glances at hair partings or shirt tucks which men are allowed, or the full-out, face-to-the-mirror, inch-by-inch makeup examination which certain Scarlett O'Hara wannabees engage in. (The observations are universal, but the admission of them isn't. In one comprehensive British poll, virtually all men said that they never looked at themselves when they passed a store window. But observers discreetly stationed at a number of mirrored posters observed a rather different truth: men were twice as likely as women to glance at themselves as they walked by, though, in mild fairness to that vainer sex, they were briefer in their mirror-assuring glances.)

A final distraction to impatient elevator waiters—though this one is expensive—is to staff an information desk across from the elevators. Up to one-third of the people coming by will then be curious enough or nervous enough

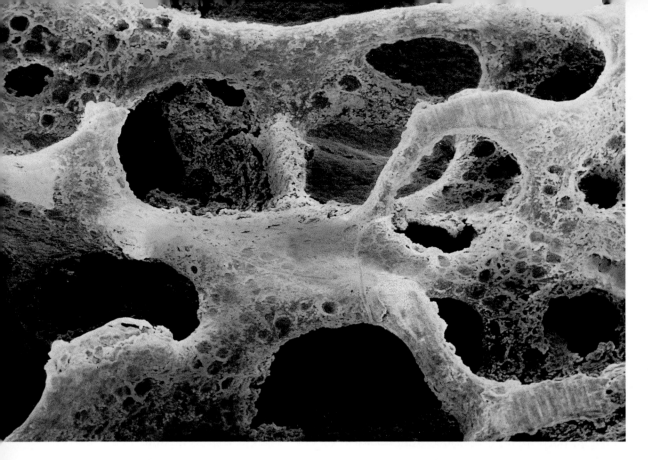

The crumbling pits of osteoporosis weaken the strength-giving columns of this bone, in contrast to the healthy, calcium-dense bone on the cover.

or just polite enough, to stop and check on location details even if they already know perfectly well where they're supposed to be going. That further reduces the buildup of people waiting for the elevators.

(Will we accept anything when we're being led around? At one airport, passengers were annoyed at how long it took to wait for their luggage. The walk to the luggage area took one minute, and the wait there took eight minutes. The solution was elegant, if disturbing when you think that most of the people who fell for it can vote: the airport staff laid out a path that incorporated arbitrary twists and turns so that it now took eight minutes to get to the luggage area. Only one minute had to be spent in front of the empty luggage carousel. Even though the total wait was still the same, there were now fewer complaints.)

The boys are fidgety here in front of the elevator. The friend reaches into his back pocket, and extracts a plastic-wrapped storage device that has been there for several weeks, and contains a mixture of pigs' fat, rubber, Vaseline, Elmer's glue, and other tasty substances. The son looks over with interest, despite the parents' disapproving glances, and as friends are nothing if not generous at age ten, he is offered a piece: it's chewing gum.

Most substances that you can put into your mouth fit into one of two categories. Either they compress and break and become a mushlike slurry you can swallow—apples, steak, and toast are notable in this category—or they don't compress, and you would be strongly advised not to put them in your mouth at all. Those are the nonfood items, such as rocks, twigs, and their like. It's very hard to get items which are in between, both destructible yet not terminally compressible. The engineers of the modern gum product, however, have managed it. Their solution is to get substances that are soft enough for chewing—that's why all the Vaseline and animal fats such as lard and beef tallow are there—pour them into a tough rubber matrix, and manipulate it in such a way that no one is going to guess what's hidden inside. Something like the Elmer's glue we saw on the stamps is used, but there are also dollops of soap, polyethylene (the stuff that makes up plastic bags), and even some soil stabilizer to keep the gum bound tight.

As the boys chomp away, Vaseline and sheep's fat drip out. It is all swallowed, and will be worked on by the liver's detoxification systems in the hours to come. Sugar oozes out too, but this is also defended against, at least in part, for teeth aren't the passive chunks we generally take them for. Their surface chemicals constantly pull in fresh minerals from saliva, and use those minerals to help toughen the regions coming under acid attack from bacteria. At the same time, your saliva does its bit to help. Saliva is not a simple watery fluid, good for spitballs and other boyhood treats. It's constantly changing through the day, as the inside of your mouth monitors what's going in, and the saliva glands readjust their chemical output to help. Here, with the boys doing their best to harm their teeth, the glands detect the need for something to destroy acid. Simple bicarbonate of soda is excellent for this purpose, and so, within a few moments of the gum chewing starting, that's what the saliva glands pump in. It binds with and neutralizes the acid that the bacteria in the mouth are producing.

Saliva glands are truly intricate chemical factories, with a blood flow

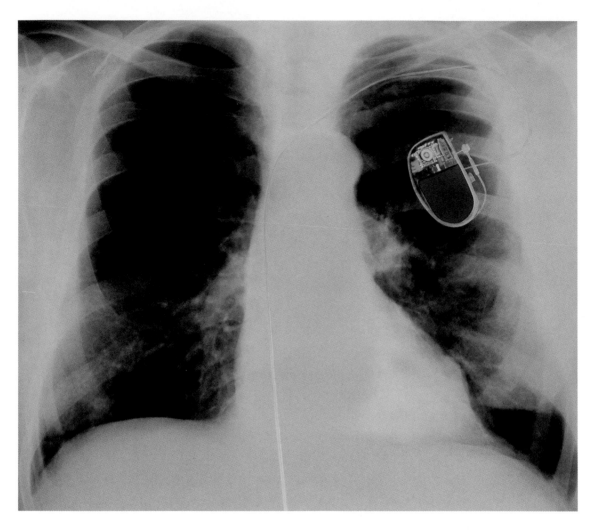

Useful and silly additions. *Left:* an electronic pacemaker, crucial for maintaining the beat of a wavering heart. *Right:* a bag of silicon implanted in a female chest wall, defying the laws of gravity.

that's ten times greater than an equal mass of actively contracting arm or leg muscle would produce. The boys' saliva glands are pumping out another chemical, called sialin. This is even more cunning, for it floats over to the teeth-hugging bacteria already in place and subverts the way they use amino acids to make energy. As a result, those bacteria start producing alkali chemicals, that neatly quench most of the threatening acid.

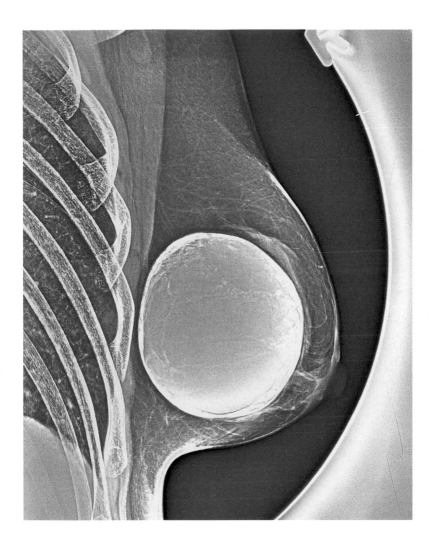

A chime rings, and the family steps forward. Even in enclosed spaces we try to keep our personal distances, and here the girl has one advantage: a single woman is almost always given more space in a crowd than anyone else. (Though as social psychologists have ungenerously observed, the more plain looking she is, the less the deferred space.) The elevator doors close, and the parents and everyone else trust that the little cable above will lift the elevator to its destination. In 1854 the original Mr. Otis stood inside an open elevator three stories up, and had visitors at a New York exhibition cut its cable with an ax. It started to fall, and everyone shrieked, but then the little retracted rollers he had invented sprang out to grip the metal tracks, stopping the elevator, and everyone applauded. A device using the same principles is on all elevators now. Even simple escalators were considered fearful devices once, which is why when Britain's first escalator was installed at Harrods in 1898, a uniformed attendant was assigned to stand at the top with a glass of brandy at hand to revivify any traveler overcome by the mechanical ascent.

The elevator box jolts up, and as it does music plays, almost unnoticeably, which is just what the American Muzak Corporation likes. The sounds they project over an estimated 400 million people worldwide each day are designed *not* to be noticed. High notes are screened out by Muzak engineers, as well as low notes and volume shifts and even most minor chords—anything that might hint at some world beyond the major-chord mush, the amiable hushed bounciness, which is all that is left. The result is a product unique in musical annals: a harmonized sound sequence *entirely without musical content*. It is even transmitted in mono—one of the last nonstereo sources around—to enhance the screened-out simplicity.

Our biorhythms fade a little twice in each day. The major tiredness collapse occurs about four or five P.M., and the other, a lesser dip, at about 11 in the morning. The Muzak that's sent out from the company's North Carolina headquarters is designed to counter these lulls. The sequences that early-morning shoppers will hear are fairly slow, but speed up toward 11 A.M., then slow and later speed up again to counter the afternoon dip, too.

It works, as Muzak corporation brochures cheerfully point out. Cows produce more milk and army staffs watching radar screens make fewer errors and cardiac patients in intensive care units recover better when they hear these counterfatigue sounds at these times. The ten year olds chewing gum, not quite realizing what is happening, will find their rate of chomping goes up slightly.

Teenagers especially dislike it, so when the owners of a 7-Eleven store in Thousand Oaks, a city near Los Angeles, found that they couldn't get rid of teenagers hanging out there, they took the gloves off and used a "Muzak Attack." The store let the warbles and glissandi and woodwind arpeggios pour happily forth. The teenagers vanished.

The family steps out of the elevator, to be met with a blast of microbe-rich air, far denser than anything they experienced at breakfast. It's supplied courtesy of the great number of nonfamily members here: all these wheezingly outpouring fellow shoppers. It's also more diverse than what the single ten-year-old friend could offer, containing a baroque bestiary of diverse, living species. There are some seriously dangerous items. About 10 percent of the country's population permanently carry around the dreaded meningitis bacterium in the backs of their throats. It staggers out as they talk, and when you walk by, there it is, hovering as a dank haze. Isolated but viable microbes for pneumonia and herpes simplex type 1—it sprays out from the liquid in any cold sore blister—and strep throat are also likely to be floating loose in an ordinary mall corridor. (You're entirely safe from the AIDS virus, though, for that one crumbles apart after only a few seconds in open air.)

The miniature windshield wipers of the family's eyelids start sweeping faster than usual, to clear a path through the dense clouds, but some of the bacteria land anyway and then it's time for serious defense. Everyone in our elevator-exiting family, even the baby, now starts pumping concentrated lysozyme chemicals into his or her tear fluid, that bursts apart the bacteria's walls. Everyone could be in more trouble from the bacteria that don't get intercepted at the eyes. Microbes are so small that they evolve in a matter of hours, while humans are so galumphily huge that we take a quarter century or so to reproduce. Without some equally small and fast parallel world operating inside us, we'd be sunk.

Enter the Memory B's to help.

Almost all the white cells we used years ago against any particular infection will have died out, but a few—the Memory B's—survive, forming a wondrous miniaturized museum. For years they travel, little counterpart families, gliding through us. One last remnant of a fever from four years ago bumps silently past the memory cell of the throat infection everyone had seven years ago. The very bodily terrain they knew changes around them: first our skin and then our muscle cells are replaced; in time, years passing, even the original stone-hard bone cells that were around when the memory cells were created will be built afresh. Only the Memory B's survive: their original roles, their very presence, soon forgotten by the humans they're wandering within.

And then, suddenly, they're needed again. The bacteria floating in this corridor have probably been let loose some time before, somewhere in the city or suburb. If anyone in our family had been infected by them, even years ago, then probably the whole family was exposed to them, and so each member will be carrying some Memory B's from that particular event. When the bacteria come in now, the old Memory B rejuvenates, and this time there's no need to wait while the whole paraphernalia of ordinary white blood cells is built up from scratch. Everything gets a head start. By the time this human family leaves the mall—before there's even time for any of them to notice what's happened—that infection is being crushed.

The only thing that makes the job harder is if too many of the people you pass have been taking antibiotics. Those kill bacteria of course, but they never kill all the bacteria in the body of the person who's taking them. A number of bacteria survive, including a few now likely to be strangely mutated: entirely resistant to the drugs their host has been taking. The genetic information that carries this resistance doesn't stay locked inside those few mutated bacteria: instead it concentrates in tough coils that are easily pushed out through the bacteria's surface, to be absorbed inside other, wholly innocent, bacteria nearby. It could be in the host's body; it could be in you. When that happens, passed to you in the public air here, not only do you have a new infection to deal with, one that your Memory B's don't have the faintest clue about, but the antibiotic your doctor might order for it is probably not going to work either. It doesn't help when doctors prescribe antibiotics with reckless abandon and start off the chain. But who, truly, feels comfortable leaving a doctor's office without a prescription for something, however useless, that might help? When whole families do it, the result is that we regularly end up walking beside people loaded with these mutation-inducing antibiotics, every day.

The herd of floating microbes that don't hit us on the first pass in these mall corridors have a good chance of getting us on a second go, and so make our immune system go through the whole rigmarole again. This is because mall managers will do almost anything to keep the air clean as long as it doesn't cost too much money. This means that the easiest solution, of switch-

Vitamin C. The monolithic slabs shown melt in the human body; large doses are avidly consumed for resistance to colds, but end up quickly floating to the bladder for disposal.

ing the ventilation system on high to get rid of all the floating junk by blowing it outside, is unfortunately out. It would cost too much to cool or heat the excess fresh air they'd have to bring in to replace it. Most malls only change about 10 percent of the air each time it passes through the huge fans hidden in the engineering units: the rest is simply shunted back down on us, having been blown uselessly around, increasingly loaded with carbon dioxide and sweat particles and wriggling hair yeasts and serious infections as the day grinds on. Instead there are filters and efforts to keep the lightbulbs wiped clean, and more use of those liquids that can be pumped through the air ducts to give the impression of fresh open air or lawns. Monday mornings tend to be the least polluted, but Saturday afternoons are the worst, as the buildup of exhaled gases bobbing along in the air around you in this too tightly sealed city can constrict blood vessels or change their flow so that headaches result. Drying the air would help, but then people would get static electricity shocks, so it's back to the aerial-soup-preserving humidity for all.

Smokers in the mall make everything worse, even if the mall forbids smoking. A little poisonous carbon monoxide still trickles from their lungs for up to an hour after their last smoke. Since this has a buoyancy almost exactly equal to ordinary air, it bobs at chest-height breathing level even after the smoker has walked on. You'd be better off in an airplane, especially if you can afford good seats, for jets have compressors connected to the pure atmosphere outside that get rid of 50 percent of the used air each time it's pumped through.

The family stops at a particularly intriguing window display; bravely breathing in as they comment. Everyone seems to be looking at the same display, but brain scans would show that they're literally seeing different things. For vision isn't a passive operation letting everything ascend, rawly unfiltered, into our minds. We'd suffer an impossible overload if that happened, which is why we regularly block out what are likely to be unimportant sights. If the teenage girl, for example, is really familiar with the fabrics here, then the visual impulses flick inside her, but her memory cells squelch some of the fabric signals, reaching over *before* they rise to her consciousness. For different family members, different visual sights are likely being suppressed, as scanning devices fitted to macaque monkeys have eerily shown.

Microcubes of dense ground-level air stream out from their middle ears—a leftover from the elevator ride up—but that's no problem. Only if there's a distant approaching thunderstorm is there likely to be the type of changed air pressure, or the distant, inaudible, ultradeep sound tremors— that creates a general, inexplicable unease.

A familiar couple appear in the distance, for one of the partners is a colleague the wife works with at the office, and because she'd rather do anything than face them now on her free day, she has no choice but to lead her family on over, and pretend that she's delighted, overjoyed, at their intrusion. Soon they are standing in odd, rigid positions; strangely garrulous and jocular, their faces twisted in muscle-tugging grimaces. Sinuous forearm extensions and a powerful pumping action—the handshake—are initiated, as the parents burble overenthusiastic greeting sounds. The kids awkwardly stiffen, knowing they're about to be questioned—with wild inaccuracy, and their mumbled corrective replies registered not at all—about grades, and favorite TV shows, and anything else the couple can think of to fill the greeting void. Even the baby waggles its yellow ducky enthusiastically, as it ponders these strange adults around it.

The handshake that formalizes this greeting is something we take for granted, but has several times become controversial. In Mussolini's Italy you could get thrown into jail if anyone saw you do it. Only the stiff-armed fascist salute was officially allowed: everything else was considered an insult to *Il Duce.* In the mid-1800s, English aristocrats were appalled at the American habit of shaking hands. One English officer observing the Confederate Army couldn't contain his distaste at the way General Lee allowed subordinate officers to shake his hand. George Washington, however, rarely shook hands in office, feeling that it lowered the dignity of a president.

Conversation begins with the colleague. When two people talk, one of them will slightly change the basic pitch of his voice to match the other. But which one? Usually it's the lower-ranking or less confident person who does the shifting; the dominant one, however casual or egalitarian he might appear, simply holds that part of his voice constant, as the other person races up or down to match. It's hard to control consciously, for it's not the whole spectrum of the voice that shifts, just this one particular part, in the region below 500 vibrations per second. This is why it reveals who thinks himself on top. When the conversational styles of a number of well-known people were ranked, based on how much they forced television interviewers to match their basic voice frequencies, Barbra Streisand and Bill Clinton came out with a quite dominant 0.80, while Elizabeth Taylor had an even more swaying 0.84. None of the Americans ranked achieved the incomparable assurance of the British politician Paddy Ashdown, which is perhaps understandable, as before entering politics Ashdown was an officer in Britain's SBS, broadly equivalent to America's Delta Force—not an occupation that tolerates submissive hesitancy. (The lowest of all individuals ranked in any country, quiveringly jumping to match whoever he was talking with, was one Daniel Quayle, who barely made it into positive figures at all, with a ranking of 0.09.)

Along with the handshake, the fixed smile has to be kept in place, which presents more of a problem, for there are definite pitfalls, each of which has to be painfully avoided. The first step is to keep the muscles around the eyes pulling hard, to avoid the giveaway of an ostensibly eager grin that fails to reach flat, uninterested eyes. The next step, even more difficult, is the struggle to keep both sides of the face smiling evenly. An ordinary smile is produced by pathways descending from the emotion-generating limbic system in our brain. The pathways are naturally symmetrical and ensure that both sides of the face pull in unison. But an artificial smile has to be generated from the more revealing motor cortex in the brain. This travels via a different network of brain-cell cabling to the centers that trigger the face muscles. The nerves that control the right side of the face frequently don't work with as much power as those controlling the left in this cabling. It's a brief imbalance, usually lasting just one-fourth or so of a second till we can stabilize and get it right. A strange gender difference pops up here. In lab tests the quarter second giveaway is usually too brief for men to notice, but women see through it almost every time. The fetish to insist on smiling at all such occasions is not universally shared. Japanese families often discourage their children from smiling, as it's generally thought to be a sign of lower intelligence and insincerity. Examination of the stiffly held smiles of certain politicians might suggest Japanese parents have a point.

"AAAA-CHOOOOO!" Everyone steps back, as the colleague sneezes, then tries to apologize, and sneezes again. The baby shrieks, utterly unprepared—it was born too late to get into the family's most recent Memory B cycle—as a gush of live nasal viruses pours over him. Cold viruses are especially well designed to travel this way, as they live best at about 3 degrees below body temperature, which is the temperature of air-cooled nasal caverns. The viruses have also evolved to be less than fatal to their human launch platforms, for otherwise we would be collapsed under the covers at home, gurgling pathetic requests for orange juice or a new cable channel, instead of helpfully staggering out of the house to sneeze them on their way to new, resource-rich nostril abodes. (That's why water-borne diseases—where the mobility of the targeted victim doesn't matter—are more often fatal than airborne ones.)

Cold viruses don't only transfer directly through aerial sneeze clouds. Surprisingly often, researchers have found, the viruses are sprayed, indirectly, onto hands, and it's those hands that carry the live infection. When you have a cold you're constantly reinfecting yourself, for although your immune system is killing many of the bacteria in your nose, you are constantly bring back fresh supplies by touching contaminated tissues or trouser pockets, and then dabbing them back into the nose for another round.

The wife isn't going to lose this excuse to escape though; she lifts the baby from the dad, and says she'll just find a restroom to feed him. Only when she goes off without taking the bottle does the colleague's wife realize, aghast, what she's intending to do: this executive woman, in our era of high-tech medicine and sterilized bottles, is actually going to breast-feed her child.

It's a wise choice. A colleague so intemperate as to sneeze all over the place at the mall on Saturday has probably been sneezing all around the office during the week. The mother will have ingested some of those viruses, processed antibodies against them, and will now send them glugging out in the breast milk. It's a marvelous mix: along with the antibodies, there are also growth chemicals the baby needs. In the weeks when the baby is finalizing its visual circuits, a retina-enhancing chemical is added to the breast milk. When the baby passes that stage, the retina chemical stops. The overall effect is impressive: the IQs of eight-year-olds in America who were breast-fed average eight points higher than the IQs of those who were bottle-fed.

Babies have evolved a number of skills to ensure they get this nutritious help. One is rather extreme: before modern hospitals, excess bleeding after labor could easily be fatal. But if a mother reaches for her baby and breast-feeds at that time, a cascade of hormones will be triggered that make her uterus contract, greatly reducing the bleeding. A breast-feeding baby moves its eyes, radarlike, to focus on just the range (about eight to twelve inches) needed to see the mother's face when feeding. If the mother's face slips from view, the baby's pulse immediately goes up, and it simply starts fast systematic side scans till it finds her again. When the mother's found again, the pulse settles back down.

At ten months there's real feeling involved in doing this, but a newborn's cortex (the higher reasoning parts of its brain) is not very developed. The smiles and eye-tracking and wiggling are controlled by its much lower brain stem regions, through instincts prewired before birth.

Into the food court, the boys are first off to select their lunches, but although they stand right beside each other, eyes similarly wide before the burger grill, their bodies react in different ways. The family's son lusts after the meat, as all ten year olds do, but his body isn't going to release insulin till after he's eaten it. That makes sense, because insulin lowers blood glucose, and after a meal there's going to be plenty of extra glucose around. As he looks at the food now, insulin levels unchanged, he doesn't feel any different from how he did a moment before. But fat people are stuck in a horribly different world. The chubby friend is quite probably leaking insulin already, just from his first look at this food, and that means his blood glucose is going down already, fast, and so he's not just hungry; he's desperate to eat.

There's a forced intake of breath as he tries to resist, but nothing about being overweight is easy. Fat children are only safe in school up to the age of five or so—kindergartners will sit as closely to a fat child as a normal-weight one—but by the age of seven, children will avoid sitting near even a cardboard cutout of a fat person. It continues. American teenagers prefer pictures of "people with facial disfigurement, a hand missing, one leg, blind, or paraplegic" to one showing a fat person. A fat person is less likely to do well on college entrance interviews, and less likely to earn a high salary than a thinner person with the same qualifications. Fat women in particular suffer, having household incomes that are $7,000 below the average.

Even when fat people know what's in store for them, it's hard to change. The chubby friend is likely to have more fat cells than the son, waiting like partly empty microballoons around his body. Though he may have been very very good and not eaten enough to load them full in the past weeks, their very

Not E.T., but the common intestinal tapeworm *T. saginata*.
Thriving in undercooked hamburgers, the head openings allow it
to dig in tight in its domain, be it the food it travels in, or the
human intestine it reaches.

number means that he suffers a greater pull of hunger now—that hunger
seems to depend in part on the sheer number of waiting fat cells someone
has. His parents might disavow all blame, saying that they had no control
over what he inherited, but that's not entirely true. Few people are born with
extra fat cells. You can't grow new ones as an adult, but you can, very easily,

as a baby. When the friend was very young, his parents, however well intentioned, were probably loading him with more food than he needed. (Some evidence that it's not genetic is that a baby adopted into an overweight household, not biologically related to the parents, is likely to end up with extra fat cells like everyone else there.) Such a bequest is an especially unkind one, as once you've put fat cells on they don't come off: the number can grow, but will never decrease.

Burgers are selected, and the friend—despite all secret vows that he is not, absolutely not, going to overeat today—somehow ends up asking for two. Napkins and glasses and little folded packets of salt need to be collected, and here another basic difference between families comes in. Which of the two boys goes off to get the items, and which one waits? One famous study at a summer camp photographed a group of adolescent girls playing tennis. Everyone would hit the ball when it came to her, but after that the chubby ones would simply stand stock still and wait. Only the girls of normal weight ran around getting in position for the next shot. The film's frames were counted. Even playing singles, the chubby ones were utterly inert about 77 percent of the time.

The boys sit down and dig in; hands almost quivering as they lift the wondrous grilled meat slabs mouthward. The table that's been selected is unlikely to have been taken at random. Food court managers can usually manipulate where we sit by making one area slightly dimmer than others. People have a reflex (it's called the "moth effect" among planners) to settle in to seats that are in the slightly dimmed area, but which face direct light. If the lighting pattern is changed, the patrons will shift to different benches so they can face what's now the brightest light.

The parents, glancing back from where they're still waiting, aren't sure the boys' burgers are the healthiest of foods, but since they are prominently advertised as being 100 percent lean beef, it can't be too bad. Can it?

To understand how fast-food hamburgers can be sold at their extraordinarily low prices, one has to venture away from this mall, to the most expensive restaurants across town. There diners are likely to be ordering exquisite Chateaubriand or other high-priced cuts. These are produced from the sort of hulking beef cattle that farmers are justifiably proud of: fleshed up on a high-protein diet of plenty of refined grains. But these grain-fed cattle also develop a layer of thick hanging fat below their chests—it's the chunk of soft tissue, hanging like a chest-front jowl that you can see on many prime steers. It would be a terrible waste to throw that huge fat chunk away.

The boys bite in. The meat that fills up most of their burgers did *not* come from any such grain-pumped cattle. That would be too expensive. Instead, it's largely supplied by scrawny, often underweight cattle, that are usually left to forage for whatever scrub they can find. (At one time it was often tropical lands—local peasants forced away—that were used for grazing, though responsible retailers have since disallowed that practice.) Unfortunately the meat from those cattle suffers from the minor problem of being nearly impossible to chew. It's too stringy. Only when it's squeezed together with the otherwise unusable yellow fat taken from the chests of the healthy big cattle does it become soft enough to eat.

The result is that kids loading up on budget-priced fast-food burgers end up subsidizing the wealthier diners. It's not the most equitable system in the world, but the people making the laws are more likely to be in the steak-eating half, and don't especially mind. To make it work you do need to get around the fact that most people wouldn't like knowing their burgers are loaded up with leftover fat wads. But that's easy. The laws have been adjusted so that a hamburger can be labeled as "lean," even when it's notably high in total fat.

Just to make it worse, fast-food burgers usually need to be bulked up with other bits of the originating cattle, because you can't make a truly filling burger with just stringy muscle and excess fat. Skin, pancreas, head muscles, gristle, and diaphragms can be included in unlimited amounts. With certain less attractive fragments—rectums, testicles, lungs, and spinal cords—proprieties are observed. Only "lesser amounts" of these can be included in a burger labeled as 100 percent lean. Whatever goes into it, a burger is immensely wasteful of water. It takes 200 liters of water to produce one pound of potatoes and about twice that to produce one pound of wheat. But it takes 45,000 liters of water to produce a pound of hamburger meat. Almost all is used for growing the feed, with only a small amount needed for the cattle to drink.

A gluey red substance drips down from the bun-squashed concoction, as the boys complete their bite. There are not a great deal of tomatoes in this ketchup—in England, for example, the legal minimum is now down to 6 percent tomato solids—but that doesn't matter. Along with its bright red distraction, we lust for it because of the detergentlike cleansing action the sugar in ketchup provides. Liquefied sugar is excellent at dissolving some of the fat sticking to the roof of the mouth. To get a bun that will be strong enough to hold all this together and still be attractively white inside, good old Plaster of Paris—the same material schoolchildren worldwide build with—is often added to the dough.

A big gulp of milk helps the bite go down. Most of the world would find this impossibly odd. The boys' very ability to digest milk marks them genetically. Only descendants of families from such areas as East Africa, the Arabian Peninsula, Europe, and parts of India—where livestock came to be used for providing milk—have this ability. Human physiology normally allows only babies to digest milk, and it was a lucky mutation, selected for in these areas and a few others, which allowed certain adults to maintain that ability.

Had the parents not been watching, the boys would have instead selected a soft drink. Carbon dioxide bubbles explode with delightful pain on tongues, and caffeine starts jolting into bloodstreams, and (especially) gobs and gobs of yet more sugar roll along in the general downpour. There are seven teaspoons in an average can of soda, which once would have made it impossibly expensive; before the Reformation sugar was a rare luxury crop. Honey was the more common sweetener. Monks produced a lot, keeping bees for the beeswax candles they needed for devotions. When monastic lands were sold off production dropped, at least locally; when slave empires began to appear, based on the harvesting of sugarcane in the tropics, supplies soared back up, and the spread of low-cost sugar began.

Caramel coloring turns the soft drink brown, which seems arbitrary, but isn't. Almost everyone judges a drink as sweeter than it is if it's colored brown. Orange juice makers get in on this notion by often using darkened glass, as did soft drink bottlers for years. But even colas served in clear plastic can still benefit from this perceptual flaw: Americans consume 126 pounds of sugar each year and without the caramel coloring to make those drinks seem sweeter than they are, even more sugar would probably have to be added.

The wife sits down, an impressive salad in hand. A century ago women were almost never allowed into restaurants, as it was considered far too unseemly. At an even earlier time, whoever was here would not have had the fork she's using. There aren't any forks in Leonardo's *Last Supper,* for the same reason that there aren't any modems in it: no one in Italian homes had any experience of them. Even as late as 1897 the Royal Navy had forbidden the use of forks as being "prejudicial to manliness."

An entire forkful of mixed vegetable fragments is lifted high, as one great mouth comes crashing down, crunching away untold billions of intricately evolved chlorophyll molecules. The first of the vegetables are propelled to the back of her throat, started on their long way down. Such vegetable intake is remarkably healthy for the eater. Vegetables are generally low-cal, for the excellent physiological reason that plants can always spread out their food reserves in tangles of roots, leaves, and spreading stems. No individual part—aside from the seeds—has to carry a dense quantity of nutrients, and so no individual part carries a lot of calories. Animals are the ones that carry their resources in the denser chunks we know as fat globules.

Vegetables are also good because they evolved in a world of direct, unblocked sunlight. Such sunlight breaks down cells, as people who've spent too long on the beach so wrinklingly demonstrate. The plants need some mechanism for building up those cells again, and for that they've evolved numerous substances, most notably the carotene molecule (which—the name is misleading—is common throughout the plant kingdom, and not just in carrots). The more a plant is exposed to sunlight, the more of this damage-fixing carotene there'll be, so when the wife swallows chunks of lettuce or spinach now, she's also swallowing carotene. It's rich in the powerful antioxidant beta-carotene. Human physiology is similar enough to plants—there are similar DNA and cell processes—that the carotene will perform a similar cell-rebuilding function in her.

The wife chews a tasty lettuce leaf next, which is about as low-cal as you can get—lettuce is 94 percent water—but still has carotene. How much depends on how dark it is. The general rule is that the more dark green chlorophyll in a leaf, the more carotene is clumped along with it. The deep green outer leaves of a lettuce can be fifty times higher than the pale inner leaves, which is why if she offers a forkful to the boys it would be foolish for them to refuse. The pathetically thin and pale lettuce fragments on their burgers have almost no carotene at all. Any dark green vegetable would be better. Broccoli is one of the best.

The next level down is peas that have been cooked from frozen. There are levels of quality to all vegetables, of course. Fresh peas are better than frozen, which are better than canned. The reason is that at harvesting time peas start metabolizing quickly. Metabolism generates heat, which destroys sugars, which creates starch, which tastes like glue. If peas are sent to a factory for freezing quickly enough you can avoid that. The peas that don't make it in time are the ones dumped into cans.

A salty chunk of chicken breast emerges from under a lettuce leaf. The chicken is easy to find, because it's so white. This is uncommon for food, which tends to be green or reddish or brown, but very rarely white. This chunk is an exception because of the sedentary lifestyle of the modern-day chicken. The flight muscles in the breast don't get used much, so there's no reason for oxygen-storing red blood cells to be soaked darkly through them. As a result, the breast comes out white. It's the same reason halibut and flounder and other deeply unadventurous hey-let's-stay-and-look-at-the-bottom-mud-some-more sea creatures also have white flesh. Only fast-swimming tuna—and fast-running chicken legs—get darker meat from all the energy-ready blood that has to be kept in place.

The bright chicken breast is also low-cal. This happens for excellent thermodynamic reasons. Chickens—and small animals generally—are so tiny that most of their bodies are quite close to the open air. They need to put what fat they have right up there, near that surface, to insulate against heat loss. Stripping off the skin means lifting off that blanket of fat. Will it be moist though? This is the great weakness of our otherwise thermodynamically perfect poultry, especially if it's stored for a long time, and so must be regularly fixed. An inspection of processing factories often reveals the surreal sight of definitely dead chickens lined up before banks of revivifying hypodermic needles—there can be six rows, with a hundred or more needles each—that tilt forward to mass inject saltwater into the chickens to keep them from drying later. Even without an inspection of the factory you can get a hint this happened by looking at the package a slice of chicken meat comes

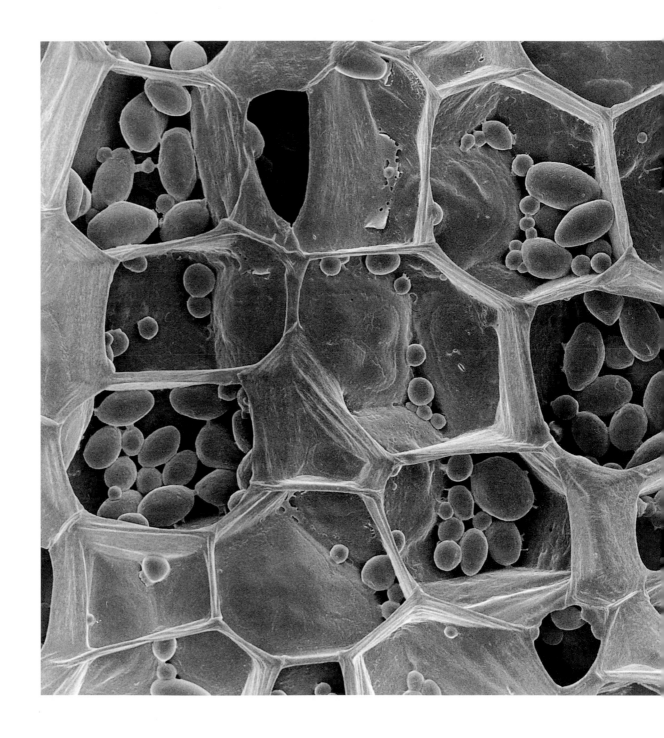

Heat a potato and the starch ovals swell like inflating footballs,
breaking down the otherwise indigestible cell walls.

in to see if the chemicals called polyphosphates are listed in the ingredients. It's a sure sign that you're paying for extra water. The hypodermics need to have some of the polyphosphates mixed in, to keep the saltwater from leaking out.

A curiously moist chicken piece gets swallowed, then the wife pauses, leaning back, to chat awhile with the boys. It's another one of those seemingly innocuous family habits, that can be of the greatest significance as it gets passed on. Overweight families, observed on video, hardly ever slow down their eating rate as they go through a meal. At Chinese restaurants in New York, average-weight diners reached for the chopsticks about 27 percent of the time in one study. Not the fat diners, though. They weren't going to be slowed down by anything: all but 2 percent grabbed for forks and spoons, to guarantee the all-crucial maximum intake speed. Their kids learn what's thought best.

Music comes out faster from the loudspeakers now, which doesn't help any efforts at moderation. Food court managers take a trick from the Muzak executives, and work carefully to speed their table-hogging customers away. In one Dallas eating area, families regularly went through their meals eleven minutes quicker when there was fast music on than when the music was slow. Listening to slow pieces of Brahms or Mozart does the reverse, which is why few except the most outrageously priced restaurants can afford it. With the more common fast music, the number of bites per minute goes up almost automatically, as hidden videos embarrassingly reveal. It's too irritating if the loudspeakers are pumping faster than 100 beats per minute—too many families then enter the food area, look around, and edge away—so as a compromise managers sometimes keep the music below 100 beats, but make sure the seats are uncomfortable. Benches with backs that are set too far away for easy leaning or are coated in slippery plastic, will do fine. On crowded weekend lunch hours managers can go further and raise the chilling air-conditioning: cool air invariably makes people feel like eating more.

The wife feels uncomfortable resting so long somehow and takes up her fork again; selecting some deep green spinach as a good way to keep her iron levels up. This isn't the best reason to eat spinach though, because it really isn't especially high in iron: the belief that it is comes from a misplaced decimal in a government report. Rather, this dangling spinach now being directed mouthward is excellent for vision, as indeed are all the other dark green vegetables. Carotene, besides repairing cells, also has the capacity to easily absorb light rays. Transferred to the omnivorous human, some is led, barely changed, to the retina of the eye. Within hours it's twisting away up there, helping trigger signals along the optic nerve to the brain.

It's too bad that no one is eating any garlic. Garlic is rich in allicin, which in the wild protects garlic plants against fungi and in the human body resists cold and flu viruses. It's capable, for example, of killing all the para-influenza 3 viruses it contacts. The onion in the salad has a related sulfurous compound. This has long been known for its effects on the mucus membranes of the eye (this is why we cry when peeling onions) but has recently been found to be equally powerful as a decongestant in the chest. These sulfur molecules are highly soluble, and the reason cutting an onion under running water helps. The irritant molecules merge with the water, and go down the drain. The chicken in the salad is rich in the amino acid cysteine, which in its variant acetylcysteine form is also good at thinning the fluids building up in the lungs of anyone suffering a cold. The old wives tale that chicken soup, rich in garlic and onions is good for your health is right.

The daughter arrives at the table, not in the best of moods, as her stomach is trying to digest itself. This is a problem all severe dieters are likely to have. The rest of this family, casually chomping down the food she craves, are lucky enough to be undergoing satisfying bouts of what is termed "retropulsion," which is the action of the stomach bottom sloshing and shearing their food. But her stomach is empty, and reduced to stripping off its own wall secretions to feed into the waiting intestine. Even this self-digestion doesn't help much. Everyone else around the table has also gradually begun slow wobblings of their intestinal muscles, as electrical signals start the intestine's toughened wall gently swinging inward and then outward, like a rope going up and down. But without having eaten any amount of food since dinner last night, she experiences painful contractions of much greater force; repeated once every three seconds for several minutes at a stretch before pausing, as the full twenty-five feet of her small intestine tries to drag along even the tiniest amounts of food that might be left in the stomach.

A dieter's torments are nearly impossible to avoid. Even the ordinary number of fat cells she's likely to have are lamentably dense. Toss a chunk of them on a fire, and they splutter madly, releasing their energy. When a teenager eats a little less, her body has no way of knowing that she's not in danger of starvation. It lowers its metabolism to make up for the change, and the dense fat-storage cells are barely affected. Only if she drops her food intake to staggeringly painful levels—overriding even the antistarvation defense—is there a chance of getting a noticeable number of them emptied.

She's also likely to poison herself, at least a little bit, if she really lowers her food levels. The dioxins everyone in the family ingested over the years from the butter and other rich sources they shared can't easily be expelled. Instead it has accumulated, locked away, fairly safely, in these out-of-the-way fat deposits. But let the teenager go on a strong enough diet, and her fat cells gush out everything they contain in a last-ditch effort to keep her from starving. The years-old dioxin comes along, reconnecting her with her family's past, as its levels rise noticeabley in her bloodstream now.

The thin plastic wrapping of a yogurt carton is torn back, and the suffering teen's spoon plunges in. If a handsome man is sitting nearby the spoon will probably just stay there: one Toronto study found that teenage girls almost always stop eating in that case, and will only pick up if the man leaves or gets distracted. (If it's a woman, and especially a chubby woman, who sits nearby, the spoon is delayed not at all.) Safely unobserved now, this daughter scoops her spoon through the container.

Since her diet allows only low-cal yogurt, she's in for a problem later. The sweet taste of artificial sweeteners makes the eater *think* she's taking in some sugar with each spoonful. The girl's blood glucose starts to go down by about 6 percent in anticipation of that change. But because no true glucose actually does come in, she'll end up stuck down there, with lower levels than originally, and before too long she'll be hungrier than when she started.

The whole idea of solving a weight problem through special diet foods reveals another curious gender difference in body perceptions. When the Pepsi company was promoting Diet Pepsi for the male market, they found that it didn't work to advertise it as having "no calories." Instead they had to

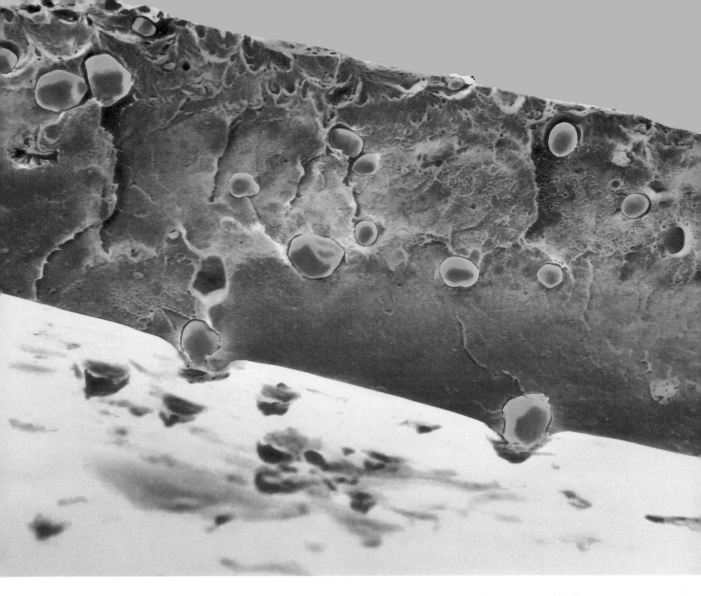

Biodegradable plastic, common in food packaging. The bright orange blobs are starch granules. Buried in the ground, the starch absorbs water and bursts the plastic open, exposing fragmented surfaces that bacteria can then digest more easily.

promote it as having "no sugar." When a man and a woman feel equally bad about their bodies, their surveys found, the man will usually assert that he just needs to exercise more; the woman, sticking to passive choices, will conclude that she needs to eat more diet food.

Some bran is sprinkled on the creamy useless yogurt. It's the sort of food dieters are convinced is good, because it certainly tastes bad enough. And although it's healthy in moderation, wheat bran is also dense with phytic acid, which can tie up much of the calcium in the yogurt. This is not especially good for anyone, let alone a nonexercising, sun-avoiding teenage female. Calcium is stiff and tough—the mortar holding the food court's bricks in place is made with it—and her osteoblast cells need a good two pounds of it so they can sculpt her bones into proper shape. Even a smaller amount available now could set her up for bone problems later. Oat bran would be better—it has hardly any of the calcium-grabbing phytic acid—and so would whole wheat bread: cooking destroys the undesired phytic acid, so only the stomach-filling safe bulk remains.

Many dieters rely on diet pills. They can work, but not in a way most users would appreciate. A typical diet pill simply mixes products that give a short-term water loss—caffeine and the irritant pesticide known as bunchu are typical here—with something really bulky, to give you the impression of being full. The bulk cattle feed known as cluster bean, grown in the southwestern United States, is commonly used for this. Once in the stomach it absorbs moisture, and—as with the stamp glues and cellulose pulp in baby-food formulas—inflates quickly in size, pressing hard against the stretch receptors there. A little bit of bran is sometimes included in the pills, although it will cost several dozen times more when consumed this way than when purchased directly.

The dieting teenager wouldn't think of drinking anything but plain water. In the waiting glass, a maelstrom of activity has been taking place. About one in every 10 million water molecules in the glass is constantly cracking apart, leaving a chunk of oxygen and hydrogen spinning off to one side, and a sliver of isolated hydrogen spinning off to the other. Without help the contents of the glass would soon disappear, in a quick-evaporating puff of gas. Luckily, elsewhere in the waiting glass a proportional number of earlier chunks are clasping back together frantically fast, to reconstitute water molecules. Dieters become dehydrated, which makes stretch receptors in the vein returning blood to her heart signal her brain strongly for fluids. Heeding the message in her brain, she drinks up.

The daughter tries to work out how many calories she's had so far. In a brain scan her frontal lobes would show up intense activity. The harder they have to work on these calculations, the more energy they will use. It doesn't help that she's trying to power up her brain despite having pretty much skipped breakfast. Starting the day without food can lower the level of the acetylcholine that carries key messages between brain cells and decreases your memory abilities hours later.

The dad's back, cheerfully carrying the mammoth-size pizza he's had to wait for. Lee Iacocca remembers, as a schoolboy in 1920s America, being beaten up when his classmates found that his mother had given him something as disgustingly foreign and un-American as pizza to eat. But so long as there's not too much fatty cheese it's an excellent food: balanced in vegetables and flour and rich in the same flooding antioxidants there were in the wife's salad and the morning's orange juice.

The family eats while clouds of carbon dioxide swirl from the cooking areas as well as from exhalations, all of it sucked into the mall's vents and sent tumbling outside.

5

separate meanderings

A half hour later and the meal's over; the older kids head out, and the parents settle back in their seats, finally alone; able to talk in quiet. Then the husband cracks his knuckles.

Cracking your knuckles doesn't sound horrible because you're violently grating human bone parts against each other. That would be a disgusting thing to do to yourself. The reason cracking your knuckles sounds horrible is because you're actually pulling human bone parts *away* from each other. Finger joints are not rigidly connected. There's lubricating fluid between them, and if you tug hard, especially between the metacarpal and the first phalanx, that fluid can't all escape from the gap. Instead, it now has to fill a larger volume. That lowers its pressure, and if a nice wrenching bone twist ensures that this happens quickly enough, then some of the water that's part of the fluid is instantly changed to a vapor state. X rays at this point show bubbles suddenly appearing. Like steam escaping from a boiling pot, they will fill up a much larger volume.

Perfect diatoms. Chunks of these marine algae help give face powder
its distinctive smooth feel.

A tenth of a second or so into the abuse, it's all still quiet. Then the enlarged vapor bubbles push the wrenched joint so far apart that other fluid in
the body, especially the fluid normally in place farther away around the joint,
comes rushing in. It's blissful for the human being doing all the tugging and
wrenching, but fatal for the vapor bubbles so produced. They can't survive
against the inrushing fluid. Each individual bubble makes only a little
crackle when it's crushed down, but since there can be very many bubbles
the result is most audible.

A small number of air bubbles remain, keeping some of the enlarged distance. It takes about twenty minutes before the gas in them finally dissolves
in the surrounding fluid, and the mighty vapor-collapse crunch can stir again.

At this point an argument might start, not necessarily about knuckle-cracking. Money, which TV programs to watch, and the kids are the most likely topics of argument in America, in that order. Once the quarrel begins, the process is surprisingly similar, regardless of the subject.

Even before any knuckle-cracking, often even before any words are exchanged at all, a curious physiological aura is passed back and forth between partners who are likely to argue. Husband and wife now enter a curious physiological state. Sitting near each other, merely knowing they're going to have to talk or share some time, their hearts start beating faster, blood pressure goes up, tiny geysers of sweat appear on their fingers, and even the speed of blood circulation in their fingertips suddenly rises. It usually can't be seen from outside, but social psychologists who've done the wiring up measurements have found that when it does occur—each partner inwardly just daring the other to start something—follow-up studies four years later show that these pretensed couples are the ones most likely to divorce. (In all cases, divorces are most likely in the third and fourth years of a marriage, when they occur at all.)

How to get in the blessed group of people who don't argue? A curiously deep division between good and bad relations was found in a study that interviewed a number of couples in-depth, and then came back four years later to see which ones were still together and happy about it, and which ones had divorced or were together but unhappy about it. In bad relations, the ones that ended up in divorce or grievously dissatisfied marriages four years later, if you asked the wife what bothered her about her partner she'd give the typical complaints which women, usually justifiably, have about men: she'd say that he didn't listen to her enough or that he didn't share his emotions or that he could be coarse in his habits. In good relations though, the ones where the couples stayed together and said they really enjoyed spending time with each other, the wife also might say yes, her husband didn't listen enough or share his emotions or he could be crude . . . but she didn't really mind. As the old saying has it, there are two marriages: his, and hers.

Barely half of American couples agree on whether their family is trying to keep a budget, and if they do agree, they often differ on which one of them is supposed to be doing it. Fifty percent of men say their wives vote the same way they do, but two-thirds of women say they voted differently. It gets worse.

Almost 75 percent of couples disagree on whether they've had a deep conversation about feelings in the past week, and about as many disagree on whether they've had an argument. Up to a third, if asked, will even—this is the sort of statistic Dave Barry likes—disagree on how frequently they've had sex that week. And nearly 1 percent, the truly befuddled, come up with different estimates about how many children they have (they may be the ones fighting over alimony and child support).

How can you tell which sort of relationship you're in? In the longer-lasting ones, both partners used the word "we" a lot when they told an interviewer those satisfyingly mythic stories about how they first met or how they decided to have kids or buy a house. But the other couples didn't: the past had been rewritten and they already were becoming two separate individuals. Even the past week was remembered differently. In a good relationship, each partner was likely to remember if the other one had done something nice—a friendly handhold, or shared laughter—recently. But in unions that were falling apart, even when one partner had done something like that recently, the other one would say that no, she had no memory of it at all. The arguments in these distressed couples can be disastrous for your health. Stress hormones pump into the bloodstream for a half hour or more after even minor run-ins, and when these are repeated enough, statistics show almost every disease rate going up. In couples that have stayed together a long time despite the arguments, women suffer most of all: the men must end up running on autopilot, for it's only the women's stress hormone levels that go up after a spat.

When marriages arranged solely for economic advantage were popular there would be fewer of these types of problems, because little emotional sharing was ever expected. When the young French aristocrat Alexis de Tocqueville visited America in the 1830s he was startled to find how offended American couples became if their partner wasn't friendly, as that was rarely a consideration in France. Romance was assumed to come from elsewhere, though if you had come to like your spouse, there might be some proprieties. One French lady informed the Seigneur of Brantôme that she always carefully assumed the top position when she was with her lover. That way, she explained, if her husband asked if she had ever let another man mount her, she could avoid hurting his feelings and quite honestly say that she hadn't.

A number of accurate predictions can be made about our modern relationships, long before the arguments and tension surges start. It helps, statistically, to have more of those background similarities we saw at breakfast: matches in age and education and looks and views. Sharing likes and dislikes in art turns out to be a good predictor of harmony; spending shared time drinking, though, is a good statistical predictor of the opposite. It also helps to not have broken up too many times before getting married. The couples that repeatedly dated, then broke up, then reconciled, in a repeated cycle of tears and hope before finally settling together, are the ones especially likely to divorce. If the harmonious life sounds boring, take heart: couples that don't feel the need to argue much have a far better sex life, enjoying two to three times the weekly average of those who do. This isn't that difficult, as the rate of those who argue is only about two times a week. (In all couples the rate is, statistically, controlled more by the wife's age than the husband's: the younger she is, the higher their average.) Combined with the fact that most Americans pray about five times a week, and many pray more often than that, this means, as the statistically deft sociologist Father Andrew Greeley has pointed out, that the average mall shopper you pass in America is more likely to have prayed that day than to have had sex.

The baby wakes up and looks around. This continued restlessness—why are the afternoon naps disappearing, but only on weekends?—puzzles the parents. The problem is the coffee that the mother drank at breakfast. Once it dissolved in her bloodstream there was nothing to stop it from slipping into her blood and then into her breast milk. This means that the baby will have received a whopping dose at its feeding just before lunch.

To make things worse, not every individual in this family can get rid of caffeine at the same rate. If the family dog had accidentally lapped some up from an abandoned coffee cup nobody would have to worry, for dogs have oxygen-insertion mechanisms powerful enough to deactivate caffeine about twice as quickly as adult humans. In two hours about half of what it might have absorbed would be gone, compared to the five hours or more for the grown-ups. Ten year olds are halfway between beagles and adults, so if the brother had sneaked some coffee at breakfast, he'd be over its effects by now, too. A baby, however, is all the way on the other side, taking seven hours to clear just half of what they intake, and so will have notable levels surviving even now. The younger the baby, the stronger the effect, which is why coffee drinking is not recommended to nursing parents who have any interest in sleep. Fetuses are even more inefficient, and whatever amount they get dumped with, crossing from the mother's bloodstream, largely stays put. By one study, most babies born in America come out with measurable caffeine levels in their blood. The average is about 1.5 to 2.0 micrograms of caffeine per milliliter of umbilical cord blood at birth, and it's two to three weeks before it's all gone.

The boy and his friend are out exploring in the mall by now. The parents were willing to let them wander unsupervised because they trust in the protecting gaze of closed-circuit cameras and security guards. They're still not as safe though as a random walker in a capital city early in this century would have been. When the young Peter Medawar was preparing to go to England for boarding school, in the 1920s, his parents told him that when he got off at Waterloo station in south London he should find some stranger, tell them he was a young schoolboy, new in the city, and ask if they could please tell him how to find his way to King's Cross station in north London. Then he was to cross the city by himself. Medawar of course had no problem, as all the strangers he encountered were reliable.

The teenage girl meanwhile has joined some friends, and they have clustered outside the jeans store. The girls are ostensibly talking to each other, but since they all know that they're just waiting for the guys to show up, they also know that no one's really listening. Instead, they're doing what teenage girls seemingly have an irrepressible reflex to do, which is, in a rush of scattered glances and dead-solid appraisals, judge how each other is dressed, and who's most popular, and so estimate who's going to have the best shot with the guys.

Bodies need to be adorned for this task, whence all the polished rocks or metal earrings, the crushed silicas and other boulder dust as foundation powder on faces. That's not to mention the dead cow skin and hooves ground

Opposite: X ray of a young woman standing up, with the colors highlighting the stress pattern in her skull. The necklace isn't floating, but resting on her neck.

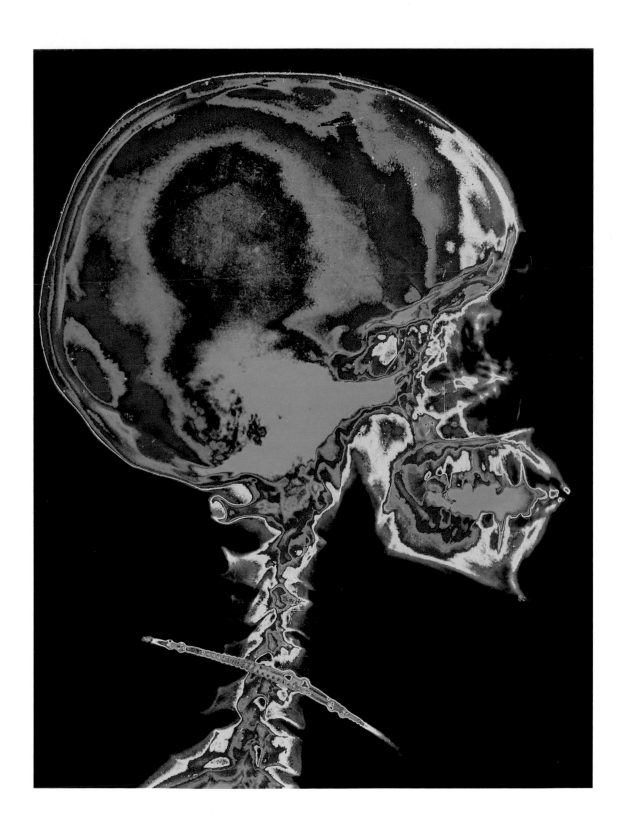

up in the polish on fingertips, and the even brighter glow in the lipstick. Cheaper brands of lipstick get their luster from mere chemical factory products, but more expensive brands get it from authentic fish scales, scraped from the eviscerated creatures and then processed at the cosmetics factories. Sometimes people have gone too far in competitive adornment. Queen Elizabeth I used white lead paint to make her face attractive. Unfortunately, lead is a poison, so it steadily ate into her flesh, and she needed to apply more and more layers before going out. In time she was using wool pads stuffed in her cheeks to mask her lost teeth, the desperately thick layers of white lead on her face, egg white over the white lead to cover the skin fissures that still showed through, and blue paint on the very top, to trace what could (if you were a courtier and your income depended on saying really nice things) be charitably described as suggestive of a young beauty's fine blue veins. Being queen though, the effects were not as distressing as they would be to others: she simply banned all mirrors from her palace so she wouldn't have to see the consequences.

Parents say that teenagers' hormones are raging, but actually they're pulsed out only a few times each day, in fast surges that last barely three to five minutes each. Stress can change the pattern. This is especially important in the autumn, when bone growth is up to two and a half times faster than at other times. There can be a vicious cycle, where after missing out on one season of this bone growth, a developing teen feels so stressed by it that her body keeps on blocking or reducing the steroid pulses that would let her catch up.

Along with the competitions though, there will also be subtle linkages among the teens. When women spontaneously tell stories about themselves, they often describe group action as succeeding; in men's stories, by contrast, it's usually a single hero, acting alone, who triumphs. There are also chemical linkages in a female group. Humans generate a tremendous number of lightweight chemicals, as we saw with the parents' immune clouds, and these steadily float loose into the surrounding air. Pregnant chemists have to be careful when they work near certain sensitive equipment, because the altered levels of steroids they're exhaling can change its calibration. Something similar seems to be the reason that girls who spend a lot of time together—school classes will sometimes be enough, though sharing a dorm is even better—

sometimes synchronize their monthly cycles. The exact chemicals being evaporated are as yet undetected, though the evidence is persuasive.

The teen girls are also likely to be keeping their voices at a precisely shared level. They take their cues, in large part, simply from how bright the light is. In one California college, turning on only a third of the fluorescent lights in a popular corridor kept the conversations down to an easy fifty decibels. With the rest of the overhead lights on, conversation rose to sixty decibels.

Racial tensions aren't likely to be much of a problem. To visiting foreigners this has been the most extreme change in America in the past generation: about 85 percent of American teens now say that they have one good friend of a different skin color . . . though they quickly go on to say that most members of their own ethnic group are more prejudiced. In Britain about half of all dark-skinned citizens originally from the Caribbean marry white Britons. By the late 1990s the number of children born to parents of different races in the U.S., though still quite low, was growing faster than the number born to same-race parents.

The guys finally arrive, and now even the pretense of female solidarity disappears. Seemingly intelligent female humans break off all conversation with each other, just so they can turn to the boys, these paragons of all satisfaction, and focus on them and smile and generally simper into their affections. Girls who had been standing straight will often start tilting their heads slightly to the side, in the universal posture of submissive interest (which also crops up in girls' high school yearbook pictures far more than it does in boys'). Occasionally there seems a violation of the simpering and neck vertebrae shifts, as when two girls suddenly start talking louder, ostensibly concentrating on each other, pretending that they're really not concerned at all with what's going on. But look closely, and they'll usually be glancing around to see that they're getting the right effect.

The boys return this attention in young male style. They grunt and laugh too loudly and interrupt each other and certainly interrupt the girls. Despite this apparent confidence, all but the closest of male friends are likely to mistrust each other, too, at this age. Teenage boys rarely look at each other's eyes as much as girls do. They stand farther from each other when they talk—which we also saw with the dad and the package deliverer in the morning—and they don't give as many of the little supportive nods and grunts that girls do. It used to be thought that stress was worst for the least popular boys. But studies of African wild dogs have shown that the dominant males in hunting packs regularly have more debilitating stress hormones in their blood than the others. It's exhausting to try to stay on top, and tension between young males of our species isn't new. In a section of the medieval Fishergate cemetery in York, spanning the eleventh to the twelfth century, twenty-nine bodies had bone injuries made by sharp instruments. Most were "injuries from edged weapons using a slicing or thrusting action, or consistent with penetration by an arrow or a crossbow bolt. . . . Some had been crippled by having their thighs hacked, some had died by thrusts in the back while lying down, some had been decapitated. . . . The victims were mainly young males."

What's really going on here is practice in selecting a mate. In the coldest of chemical views, our daughter and her friends are responding to their strong impulses to get the hydrogen bonds of one long molecule inside of them—their DNA—configured with the hydrogen bonds of the most desirable male DNA available. As they can't stick a miniature periscope inside to check out the arrangement of hydrogen bonds directly, adolescents are consigned to using indirect signs, whence the frantic attempts to give hints of maximum wealth, looks, and esteem. The rankings are surprisingly similar around the world: when thirty-seven different cultures were analyzed, women always said they were keeping men's earning power in mind more often than almost any other factor when deciding whom to settle with. Men, however, weren't so concerned with women's incomes, but instead ranked the best indirect sign of fertility—their looks—as more important.

To help matters along, the teens have powerful sex hormones floating in their bloodstreams. The boys' testosterone levels have been climbing or crashing all through the day. There are six or seven peaks daily, with the highest levels in the morning, and the lowest levels about 25 percent down, in the evenings. Even at its lowest point, though, there is plenty of testosterone for sexual purposes. Women always have a small amount of male sex

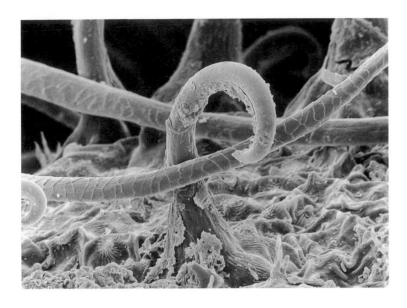

In 1948 a Swiss engineer examining burrs (*above*) which had caught on his socks came up with the idea of an artificial fastener where tough plastic hooks would grab slippery loops—what we now call "Velcro."

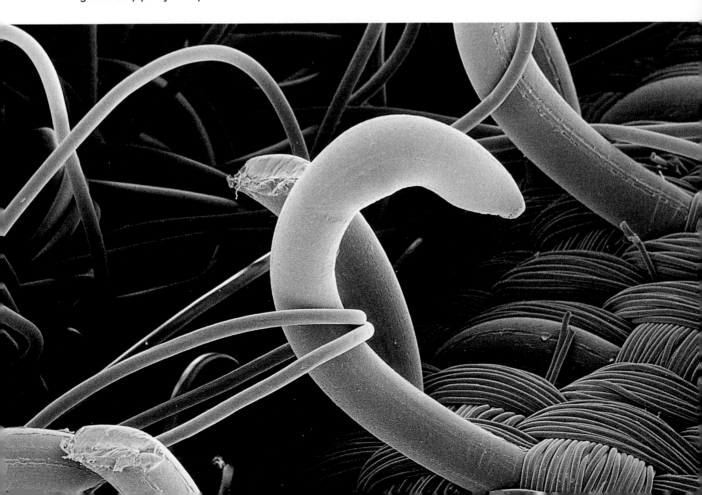

hormones in their blood, just as men have a similarly small amount of the female hormone estrogen. Among teenage girls, sexual interest generally reaches its peak just when these slight testosterone levels are at their highest—an effect that occurs, with convenient evolutionary sense, right about the times of maximum monthly fertility.

The daughter tries to keep a fixed smile on her face, as she longingly admires how the others manage to blend in, and also tries to work out which guy in particular—the shy one near the back?—she's supposed to meet. She's also trying to decide whether to remove her eyeglasses. Taking them off might seem the thing to do since girls who do that are regularly judged as more attractive than ones who leave their glasses on (an effect which, unfairly, barely occurs when boys are evaluated). But who wants only to seem more attractive? Girls who take them off are also believed dumber than ones who leave them on. Those lenses kept firmly in place mean a teenage girl's IQ will be thought to be twelve points higher than otherwise. It's an effect that lasts only so long as she stays quiet, though. The moment someone talks, she is judged by what she says, and the effect of wearing glasses vanishes. That fixed smile can hurt, too. Women are often perceived less intelligent if they smile *too* much.

First names also affect popularity. Among boys in the United States, the four most hated names in the latest survey are Myron, Reginald, Edmund, and, surpassing them all so much that it's hardly ever used anymore, Oswald. The most popular first name in America, appearing on top in surveys year after year, is (ahem), David.

Eager to look ultracool, the daughter reaches into her pocket and extracts a single long cylinder of plant fibers. To get the nicotine from that cylinder into her body isn't a simple process. First a match has to be struck—one of several hundred million in America each day. As smoking isn't allowed, it'll have to be furtive. The flame explodes, then, applied to the end of the cigarette, it makes the raw paper melt, then quickly vaporize. That ignites the densely packed tobacco inside. When a studiously casual inhalation from the teenager suctions many trillions of free-floating oxygen molecules to that tip, a great bellows roar raises the flame's temperature ferociously hotter, and that finally is enough to vaporize some of the nicotine molecules locked even deeper within the cigarette.

It also, unfortunately, is hot enough to create the tiny molecules called polycyclic hydrocarbons. Those ride into her lungs unnoticed, stuck on the top of each smoke particle like spots on a beachball. While the nicotine travels on to the brain, the polycyclic hydrocarbons fall off where they land, with the smoke of course damaging sensitive throat-lining cells as it swirls past. Teenage boys are likely to be smoking unfiltered cigarettes, and so the smoke particles are so heavy that they only reach the higher parts of the airways before the polycyclic hydrocarbons tumble off. The daughter, although aspiring to this street-tough look, too, is more likely to have a filtered brand, that lets its smaller particles go down, down, down to the very inner cavities of the lungs before dumping the polycyclics. This is why women smokers often get their first tumors deep in their lungs; male smokers usually get them higher up.

The girl coughs once, moving some of the debris along, but not really helping much. The amoebalike macrophage families in her lungs have to start hauling themselves forward, to try getting rid of the rest of the stuff. But the polycyclics are more than a match for the macrophages. If the girl stops smoking on her nineteenth birthday, she'll still be clearing her lungs of leftover polycyclic debris when she's almost thirty.

Should she be doing this at all? Everyone says not to smoke, but nicotine works on the limbic system cells in the brain, which can give the most confidence-inspiring emotional signal when properly stimulated. Teenage girls especially need that, which is why ads aimed at them work so well.

Tobacco comes loaded with nicotine, simply another alkaloid pesticide that plants evolved to defend against insects. Nicotine slows the stomach's usual movements. Dieting teenagers love this. With food staying in the stomach longer, they feel fuller, and really do have less of an appetite.

The girl looks up, for suddenly one member of the student group—the leader of the girls—has rotated a bony hinge at the side of her face, and, jaw opening wide, begun to vibrate her vocal cords in a strange fast rhythm, while simultaneously expelling huge air gulps. This has a powerfully addictive effect, and almost instantly everyone else joins in this laughter, including, a little nervously, the daughter. But she missed whatever it was that caused the laughter, and so she's feeling a little uncomfortable. Could someone have made a joke about her? She blinks, then blinks again, and turns her head. She hopes no one will see, but she's crying now.

Father and baby are sitting together on a bench in another part of the busy mall, studiously analyzing the buoyancy properties of a shiny oblate spheroid. To the baby it's truly baffling: he leans close to it but the father tugs down on the string and it suddenly disappears. Just as quickly—and there are delighted giggles now—this balloon will pop right back up. It's hard to get items that float in air this way. In a denser fluid it would be easy, and even a rock on a string would float overhead, which indeed is how the continent the father and boy are perched on keeps from sinking down to the center of the earth: it floats on the even denser magma below.

It's time for the next stage of their mall afternoon ritual, which is the sharing of the ice cream cone. This means the dad buying one from the stand beside the nearby fountain, which is messy enough while holding a stretching baby, but then he has to sit down and share it, which can be even sloppier. Strategically placed paper napkins help a little, but babies are superb sugar-hunting machines, and once they've had an initial lick of the ice cream, they want *more!*

The reason babies are so clumsy is that their brains are unfinished. The nerve fibers inside adult brains are almost always wrapped in slender jackets of fatty insulation. With these jackets in place, nerve signals travel fast, and accurate distance-judging and hand-controlling systems are built up. Babies don't have as much of the fat-dense nerve cell insulation in place yet—one reason they're so eager for the wobblingly attractive ice cream, with its thick emulsifiers and margarinelike fats, part of which will end up wrapped around those brain cells a few hours after swallowing. Sticky cholesterol helps form these nerve-wrapping insulations, with the curious result that our brain is in large part made of cholesterol.

The dad's a little tired, and yawns now. Fat from the cheese on his pizza has triggered the release of amino acids in his gut, and one of these, cholecystokinin, is especially noted for its power to increase drowsiness—a powerful cause of our general postlunch lassitude. But the baby reasserts his control by hurriedly making its tiny lungs puff out a word-resembling sound now. That brings the dad back to full alertness. In response, without any feeling of demeaning himself, he immediately contorts his chest wall and especially his throat and laryngeal muscles to pump out quick, high-frequency falsetto squeaks—baby talk.

Babies can't hear deep sounds well, partly because of their tiny ear bones, and with their incomplete brain cabling they certainly can't process the subtle shifts in sound we make in quick multisyllable talk. So they manipulate us by responding to high-frequency sounds. Babies haven't developed this skill only recently: twenty centuries ago, Roman grammarians remarked on the strange adult squeaks babies induce.

The dad could spend all day, cozy in this shared world of voice and touch. But then he sees some teenage girls whom he recognizes from his daughter's school and smiles at them. They register his attention about as much as they do the air-conditioning ducts overhead. He checks his reflection in a shop window, wondering if he really is that haggard, and then, despite his joyful child—indeed, now exacerbated by the contrast with the perfect fresh skin of his child—he begins to suffer, once again, the parent's eternal lament.

He's feeling old.

There's good reason for this, as humans seem built to hold together properly for just about long enough to produce and raise children. Decline usually starts at about twice the age of puberty, which makes the onset of middle age soon after thirty, though the exact moment has been the subject of much debate. John Donne thought the ideal age to be reincarnated at was thirty, while Aristotle pushed it a bit more and said that thirty-seven was the healthiest age. (He pushed even further and held out for age fifty-seven as the overall peak—he didn't have to wear hip-hugging blue jeans, so he could say that—on the grounds that life's wisdom should be taken into account.) Some observers are more cynical. John von Neumann, the great mathematician, observed that middle age is generally defined as occuring at age x+4, where x is the worrier's current age. A less kindly definition is that simply pondering the matter is the sign that you've arrived at middle age, for when has a truly young person worried about it?

Many of the changes are only too noticeable, such as a receding hairline or baldness in men. There's also the matter of the slightly too prominent pouches under his eyes, where saltwater-filled bags dangle in notably useless storage. (This morning's argument with his daughter might also have made that worse, by disturbing his output of vasopressin hormone, which normally helps keep that under some control.) And then there's the giveaway eye-corner wrinkles, where the connective tissue under his skin is bunching up, and all the rest. Dictionary editors might be consoled that vocabulary goes up with age, at least for college graduates, from 22,000 words at age twenty-two, to 40,000 or more by age sixty-five, but most individuals would probably be willing to trade the comprehension of abdominal isoclines (parallel gradations of stomach fat) for the satisfaction of not possessing them. It's true that the great curved mass of the omentum—the fatty sheet trundled around on the abdomen—actually contains active parts of the immune system. But even slender individuals have enough, and those who've given up on sit-ups are merely spreading out those immune units, not increasing them.

It doesn't help that this is also the period when career possibilities begin to close down. A poll of personnel officers in the London financial world found that job applicants over thirty were going to have a difficult time, while anyone over forty could just as usefully make a paper airplane out of his résumé. Being locked in your current job wouldn't be so bad if you were happy with it, but that's rarely so. Mathematicians like their careers—over 90 percent would choose them again—but they are the exception. Most professional jobs are so disliked that rarely will more than 50 percent of the people doing the work say, if interviewed in private, that they'd willingly choose the same career again. Blue collar workers rank their satisfaction with their jobs even lower. The problem, in part, is that the western notion of career goals came strongly from the religious notion of predestination, and that's a lot to load onto a decision you made on a hunch or by chance or just by simple inertia, years and years before.

If the dad wants to feel really bad, he could reflect on all the subsurface collapses he can't yet see. He's shrinking about a quarter inch by this time in the afternoon each day because the discs between his spine bones are getting squashed. For men, from age forty-five there's significantly less testosterone produced, due to reduced blood flow to the testes; for women, the production of healthy egg cells also usually diminishes by that age, with its accompanying hormonal shifts. His eyesight is probably worse than before, for cells within the lens of the eye can't have many blood vessels, as that would block our vision. Dead cells within that lens have no way to get out, so when they

Inside our eyes, dead cells stack like ziggurats to form the transparent lens. Magnification: 3,000 times.

die they stay there. Through the years their dense, useless bodies stack up, making the lens increasingly stiff and hard to focus, which is one reason people become farsighted. It doesn't help that eyeballs grow unevenly, often ending up too long from front to back. You need strong yanks from the tiny ciliary muscles to squash the stiffened wriggling glob back into shape. If someone's muscles have weakened with age, he's sunk.

His brain has begun shrinking in weight recently, too, and is now likely to have less of the full three pounds weight it had in his early twenties. And, perhaps most disturbingly of all, the very brain cells with which we're supposed to supervise these impermanent assets, are themselves increasingly popping out of existence. This raises the question of where our bits of disappearing personality and memory have crashed away to. Men especially try to avoid knowledge of such facts. The general medical knowledge of women is so much better that not only do they know more about their bodies, but they also usually know more about men's bodies: more women than men, for example, can locate the prostate gland, even though only men possess it. But avoidance is of no avail.

All our body cells have a timing mechanism, set in motion when they're first formed, that accurately determines their life span. Sometimes it's very short: the cells on the inside of the mouth last only a few days before dying and slipping off for a final flotation funeral in our saliva, down this internal Ganges to the outlet in the all-consuming stomach sea. Some of the cells are set for a little longer: the liver cells created in the baby this afternoon, from energy supplied by the salad and pizza slices, will survive inside his body till he's four or five before dying and being replaced. Memory B's, as we saw, last even longer.

Brain cells, however, are never replaced, which means that the ones you have now are some of the original 100 billion or so you were born with. They've been firing away in the wet chemical battery of your brain all that time, sloshing amid the reactive oxygen and warm water, which might not seem the ideal place to store a great number of such fragile entities. Now, one after another, they're failing. By age forty, an estimated 5 percent of the brain cells in the networks installing memories will start dying off each decade. These micro brain deaths are never a sudden flash of electricity. Instead, like a computer dimming as its battery runs down, the brain cell that is flickering out of existence at this moment took several hours to reach its end.

It sounds terrible, but a little arithmetic is reassuring. If 500 brain cells leak out of existence inside our heads each hour—an estimate that has been much debated—it adds up to 12,000 a day, or 4.4 million a year. That's 176 million in forty years, which sounds like a lot, but a ten-month-old baby has nearly 100 billion to start with, as we all did at that early age. The amount you lose in forty years then is well under $1/4$ of 1 percent of that total. If anything, getting stuck in stodgy thinking patterns with the remaining 99.75 percent of brain cells is the problem. But look at the way the baby can cable up brain circuitry in fresh patterns. Adults can too, albeit with more effort— which is just what a return to full-out play with the waiting baby, eager to have us concentrate on comprehending its wobbling gestures, will help produce now. Even the preliminary step of loosening one's necktie can sometimes help. It lowers arterial pressure, and in a number of lucky people, will reduce the eyeball distortion that blurs vision.

The wife is wandering elsewhere in the mall, untroubled by any of these biological changes. In fact she's uniquely contented, at this, the only truly free interval of her week; the one time when she's neither commuting nor working nor paying bills nor (however much she loves them) having to talk with the kids or her husband. She can do exactly what she wants. There might be a certain tinge of guilt—the universal lot of modern working women—but for a few hours, once a week, she can handle that. It's even preferred: only 15 percent of American women, in a survey by the Factory Outlet Marketing Association, wanted their husbands to come with them when they went shopping for clothes. Men are less confident when it comes to clothes hunting, and over 35 percent want their wives along when they shop. One reason for the wife's independence is the immense pleasure that comes from a successful hunt: from the same marketing association survey, 36 percent of the women polled said they would prefer finding a great clothing bargain to having great sex.

But she has a more pressing need to deal with, and looks for a sign for the ladies' room. On a warm day there's time for a casual scanning. When it's cooler, the need is more pressing. Such weather changes make your blood volume slowly decrease, and send more liquid from the blood into the kidneys and ultimately the bladder. Mall managers know that on the first days of a cold spell, the mall's rest rooms will be particularly busy. Women especially suffer, for their bladders are slightly smaller than men's (even taking into account their lower average body sizes) because of the extra space the uterus takes up. Today there's likely not to be a line, and afterward the wife won't be crowded when she checks her hair in front of the mirror before going out. This is where honesty is truly gauged, for brutally unromantic social psychologists have done some timing with stopwatches here. If someone's on a first or early date, she is likely to spend about 58 seconds grooming here. But if she is married? The average plummets to a mere 9.8 seconds.

She'll have washed her hands now, but most likely done a crummy job of it. Even if you lather on the soap and pride yourself on really rubbing your hands together, you're likely to make the same mistakes that were noticed in a now-famous surreptitious study of the handwashing techniques of Australian doctors in a neonatal unit. Right-handed doctors almost never cleaned the inside corner of their left thumb, left-handed ones missed the inside corner of the right thumbs; almost none of the doctors or nurses, no matter how often they were prompted, could remember to do the *tops* of their fingers. This is especially grievous, for it misses the snugly protected area under the fingernails, where an ecologically formidable biota comes to reside; it also misses the exposed fingertips, where samples of virtually everything that's been touched during the day will end up. (It's hard to get people to believe that they've ever been at fault here. When results of the study were announced, few doctors in the unit admitted surprise. They themselves had known they were skillful washers, almost all said it was just the other ones who were lax.)

In the first shop there's such a richness of items available that once again the wife will be led by the needs of the shop owner. There's that reflex to veer toward the right, as we've seen at the mall entrance, which is why even inside a store the most expensive items are likely to be stacked on the right-hand aisles. It's not good to let shoppers walk through the store without something to carry their selections in, for people almost always stop shopping once they've reached the limit of what they can carry. Large items are usually set out as close to the entrance as possible, so if hand baskets are available they'll be taken; in a supermarket it goes even further, and bulky food items are near the entrance so shopping carts will be selected instead of baskets.

Properly equipped, and strolling along that oddly beckoning right-hand path, a curious thing happens to how fast our wife walks. When an aisle is narrow we're likely to speed up; if it's wide we slow down. More expensive items, will oh, just by chance, end up stacked on the wider aisles where she's going to linger. They will not be stacked in just any arrangement. Most people try to scan widely, but their first focus is going to be on what's conveniently at eye level. It'll also most likely be at the middle or outer ends of aisles—what are termed the "hot spots." Items often sell twice as quickly here as elsewhere. The owners know that, and right there, most easy to notice, examine, take down, and touch and feel; this is where the items with the highest profit margins go.

Background music is a little different in this store than it was at the food court or in the elevator. The goal is slow meandering, and so, with the exception of high-gloss teenage boutiques, tunes with slower tempos are almost always chosen. Seventy beats per minute—heartbeat rate—work the best, but it's not so easy getting the chord mix right. Happy music with major chords is what customers like to listen to, but sadder music with minor chords make sales go up more. The result is likely to be a mix. Blink rates start sinking as the wistful music and mazelike aisles take effect, and soon the shopper is likely to be in that blissful autopilot realm of a hypnotic session beginning, where the great sudsy eyelid sweeps are only happening at twenty times a second or less—the level the husband sank to in his couch-dwelling TV session.

In that vulnerable, prelogical state, colors begin to have a stronger effect. Bright ones such as red or stark yellow on packages or shelf edgings, are likely to start raising blood pressure and make skin pores push out slightly more of their salt-rich perspiration water, as physiological measurements of volunteer consumers have shown. (This is why you rarely see yellow phone booths: people finish their calls too quickly.) Blue is likely to have the opposite effect from red, and shoppers, interrupted from their glaze-eyed wanderings, even seemingly intelligent ones, will often say they chose a dark blue packet because it's more trustworthy, solid, and worth more.

The result is that people select intuitively, quickly. Most items were scanned for only one-fifth of a second, and even the ones that are selected seldom receive more than twelve seconds of evaluation. Shoppers also are usually pathetically inaccurate in judging the prices of what they do take.

Hardly anyone—young shoppers are the worst here—compares what he's taking with the prices of alternative brands nearby. About 25 percent of shoppers never check any prices at all. (This is especially likely with men, particularly men shopping for clothes.)

At least 30 percent of adult women in America are still using the same brands of major cosmetics they started with as teens, and almost 7 million are using the identical brand of mascara. The continuity is so strong, and passed along in families so closely—despite their protests of individuality, daughters tend to share their mothers' specific brand preferences, especially in cosmetics—that over two dozen of the top brands from the 1930s are still selling well today.

Labels rarely have enough information on them to allow shoppers to recognize the similarities. In addition, studies show that few people read the labels for content. People simply notice how long it is, and the more information listed, the more likely the item is to be bought. Shoppers over fifty were likely to read a label all the way through so they could make their own judgments.

Shoppers who want to cut through all the puffery do have one final hope. It only applies to more expensive items—appliances and stereos and furniture and the like—but it's a good one. Labels can mislead and packaging can lie but a warranty can't. The company's actuaries insist on that, for otherwise the company could go broke. This, accordingly, is the one item marketing executives themselves often look for when they shop. It's the one statement which has to give honest an assessment of how well a product is made.

The wife moves along to the clothing section. Items the shop especially wants to sell—the sweaters or jeans or blouses with the highest profit—are likely to be laid out on large tables. It's wasteful in terms of space but it performs the all-important task of encouraging "petting" of the fabrics. People are far more likely to grip and fondle items that are out on a table. And once they touch the articles, it's hard to avoid trying them on.

Alone in her cubicle with the new jeans, she struggles to get them on.

This is usually hardest in the autumn or winter because everyone gets fatter then, usually by four pounds or more—an effect that's so regular, that airlines take it into account in making accurate fuel estimates. The wife goes to the clerk at the cash register to pay for her purchase. The idea of having an automatic cash register is an American one, developed not so much to ease matters for the consumer but more to let the owner be sure that the sales staff isn't skimming his takings.

After buying the jeans that she has succeeded in squeezing into, the wife treats herself to a small piece of chocolate. Instantly she feels better. No one knows exactly why chocolate feels this good. Certainly it has a lot of phenylethylamine in it, which is a subtle brain stimulant, but cauliflowers are also packed with phenylethylamine, and are rarely sought in moments of acute postchanging-room distress. Chocolate also has some of the chemicals found in marijuana, but probably at levels too low to have much effect. What is unique to chocolate, however, is its ability to change chemical states very quickly. This, rather than crude psychology, must be the explanation. Lifted from its cool package, a solitary chocolate segment remains haughty, aloof. Even when the tongue pokes at it in its first urgent, demanding caresses, chocolate resists, with no outer sign of change at all. But let the steamy 98-degree warm tongue lap over it a second time, and the chocolate can resist no longer: a sudden liquid flood pours off as the entire upper layer melts from within. The tongue is briefly cooled by the chemistry of this phase transition, but given the ardor—the sheer, animalistic desire—of the determined chocolate lover, the tongue soon warms again, and with that the remaining chocolate is ready to be taken, melting in a sudden flood once more.

If this impersonal chemistry fails as an explanation, there is also the matter of the theobromine in chocolate, which can lead to increased hormone secretions, and, of course, the sugar. Ordinary chocolates can be one-third or one-half straight sugar, and the sudden high from this blasting through the bloodstream, even aside from the manner of its ladling in by the tongue, is bound to have some effect. A certain fraction of the population metabolize the sugar of a true chocolate binge so efficiently that it raises their blood alcohol levels, too. It's called the "auto-brewery syndrome," and depends on the particular mix of yeast species and bacteria resident in the consumer's

Agony and the inland sea: a bladder
when full *(below)* and empty *(right)*.

intestines. In one case, a joy-inducing level of 20 mg alcohol per 100 ml of blood was produced this way. Unfortunately, this took place in Sweden, where driving laws are very strict, and led to one utterly startled chocolate junkie being ticketed for drunk driving.

Adults are even less truthful about their chocolate consumption than they are about vegetable eating. Garbagologists in Green Valley, Arizona, asked people how much chocolate they ate, and once night fell, undertook their true investigative role and looked into garbage cans to see how true the answers were. People hadn't underestimated their true count by a mere 10 percent, or so. In a society besieged by food puritans, who would dare to reveal the awful truth? The actual consumption was twenty times—2,000 percent—higher than admitted.

The boys meanwhile are in the darkened cool movie theater, undergoing agony. The popcorn they're sharing comes loaded with salt, and this draws water from the rest of the body into the bloodstream. That raises the volume of their blood, making their bodies swell slightly, Michelin-man fashion, and their blood pressure goes up. But it doesn't last long, for the kidneys get to work, pumping the excess water back out. Only this time, the fluid transfer can't go gently back to be dispersed throughout the whole body. Instead it is squirted into the waiting bladder, which begins to swell, and get rounder, and then, really bloated, triggering stretch receptors on its inner layers. Those send various awareness messages to the brain. First a small number of signals, what will be interpreted as UM, IF YOU GET A CHANCE messages, and which are still pretty easy to ignore; then, as the circumference gets pumped groaningly wider, more numerous signals, interpreted as **I STRONGLY SUGGEST YOU DO SOMETHING!!** messages to the brain. At one time it would have been made worse by the power of suggestion from water streams constantly appearing before the boys. Modern movie screens have tiny angled prisms on them to rebound light, but early ones didn't. Liquids often reflect light very well however, and patrons of early movies had to sit before a screen that was kept brightly wet by tiny streams or constant mists of water running down it. Current movie houses can be darker, with only the red glow of the emergency exit signs visible beside the screen. You can't have ordinary light sources in the signs, because they'd fail if the electricity supply went out in a fire. Instead, an indignity greater even than that of the breakfast smoke detector is suffered, for in those signs, steadily roar-decaying for the boys to ignore, there are sealed volumes of radioactive tritium—modified hydrogen atoms dating back to the universe's big bang creation itself.

Kids can take the present-day water pressure agony longer than their parents, partly because their bladder tissues are more malleable, but also because there are so many great things going on in the darkened movie house that would be terrible to miss. There's food, to begin with, enough to make the mother's single chocolate insignificant: a range of candy bars and jelly beans and caramels of course, and maybe those little peanut-butter buttons, but definitely, almost defining the movie experience, there's going to be popcorn. Aztecs enjoyed it, though without flickering screen images in accompaniment, for they too had access to corn with water residues inside that when heated, would explode out as steam, distorting the kernel into this scrumptious snack. Modern popcorn is a wonderful invention for people who make bathroom scales, as the butter dripping over it is not, usually, made of anything that came from churned milk. Often it's the far more glutinous coconut oil instead, a substance that gets its wonderful stickiness from a density of saturated fats so great it would make a meal of ordinary butter slabs seem as low fat as nibbling lettuce leaves. A single medium-size bucket of popcorn buttered with this coconut oil will, according to nutrition analysts, "contain more saturated fats than a breakfast of bacon and two eggs, a steak dinner with side dishes, and a Big Mac with a large order of fries—combined."

Sharing slobbery big handfuls of popcorn from the same bucket leads to a curious reincarnation for the bacteria we pick up—left on the nabbed-for kernels from the friend's saliva—in the process. They are destroyed when we swallow them, but that's not the final end. The raw chemicals that compose the bacterium are largely salvaged inside the body; our liver enzymes easily stripping away the few bits that are truly dangerous to keep away. The remainder flow back, pumped to the portions of our throat or elsewhere where yet another generation of these gigantic monsters are being grown. When these new bacterium get handed across during next Saturday's adventure installment—the two friends perhaps bemoaning the lack of interesting things going on in the movie—they briefly metabolize in their new home, only to be swallowed back by the body they started from, ready to be regenerated, and the great cycle starts again.

What there will be on the screen, almost certainly, is an explosion. Or several explosions. About 60 percent of the most popular films of the past ten years have featured this apparently irresistible destruction of solid objects. There's also likely to be a fight (in 62 percent of PG movies) and then, lurking somewhere around on the bright screen, there's going to be a guy named Jack. This is the most common name in movies from the past decade, by far. It's not always reserved for the hero—sometimes Jack is discreet, and settles for a bit part, letting the main character have a different name—but it's a rare film where a Jack of some sort isn't there at all. With a stunning lack of linguistic variation, the next most common name is John.

What Jack, John, and the other huge projections on the screen will do when they're not fighting or watching explosions, is say simple things. The phrase "Let's get out of here!" is exceptionally common, according to one determined English researcher who viewed over 100 of the main U.S. feature films of the last half century. It was uttered, exclaimed, whispered, or otherwise conveyed in 84 percent of them. The characters in movies also swear, though this is carefully adjusted for the intended classification level on release. Many thrillers are filmed with key swearing scenes done as written for the R movie release, and then, while everyone is still on the set and the camera is in place, those scenes are refilmed with more innocuous words. The screen shadows kill people too—there will be at least one murder in 40 percent of PG and G films—but not as frequently as they swear or fight.

There is one slightly less obvious message displayed on all screens, and you can see it in the upper-right corner, at about forty-minute intervals. The message is there to tell the projectionist that a reel change is coming up. A squiggle appears brightly on the screen when there are about twelve feet of film left, and then, seven seconds later, when the projectionist is down to two feet of film, it pops up on the screen again. Directors often draw out the end of a scene till after this changeover point, so no impor tant dialogue will be lost if the projectionist blows it. Once you've had the squiggle pointed out it's hard to miss it: the thing is big enough for the projectionist to see clearly from his distant booth. To find it just wait till there's the giveaway slight jump on the screen where the reels were changed. If the boys know how long into the movie that was, they just have to wait the same amount of time again, then look up from their life-cycling popcorn, and there it'll be.

The girl would love to escape reality in a movie, but instead is alone in a mall bathroom, dispiritedly looking at herself in a mirror, dabbing at her face with tissue. She knows you're supposed to feel better after a cry, but she doesn't, really, even though a great number of the stress chemicals that had been surging in her body were pumped out with the tears. She's also automatically helped by the tear glands opening into the bottom of her eyelids. They've been pulling in the ordinary low levels of antibodies from her bloodstream, especially the all-important immunoglobulin-A variety, which is what the baby received in its protective breast milk. The tear glands concentrate those antibodies into denser and denser agglomerations, and when the antibodies are ready the tear glands start pumping them over her eye, too. But this is no great comfort either; not after the desolation of being unpopular; so clearly an outsider even among those she considered her friends.

She tilts her head back now, the dropper from the bottle of eye lotion she bought held up at the ready. It was easy enough for her to find this bottle at the pharmacy on the way here, for it's a good product to sell. What's in the dropper is usually a generous 50 to 70 microliter pool, and most of that, once carefully squeezed down, will immediately pour down to the bottom lid, either to overflow down the face, or to be sniffed uselessly through the drainage holes leading from the nose. Our eyes can only keep about 10 microliters of extra fluid on them at once, as the manufacturers of these bottles well know. The poured-away extra is simply a quick way for them to get the bottle emptied. The little bit that sticks on the retina—there's a little polyvinyl alcohol, the stuff on the back of stamps, to help—is useful though, for it soaks down into the living eye, binds to the cells of the swollen blood vessels there, and makes them shrink.

A final tissue dab from the girl, and it's time to go. In the remaining hour till she's going to meet her parents she'll do some shopping, or maybe—for what is it ever going to matter how she looks?—just get some chocolate, yeah, lots of it. She opens the door.

And immediately bumps into a boy, the sensitive one with the (really quite slight) case of acne from the earlier group.

He's intently saying something about the other kids, but she can barely hear him: there's suddenly an incredible roaring in her ears. He must have been waiting for her, on purpose, and that means he has to be interested in her, and that means they might end up going together, and then everyone will expect that she's really involved with him, and he'll think that too, but that's terrifying because she's never slept with a guy, or really done anything with a guy. She's never—the one absolute secret, which she has guarded from her folks, and especially from everyone at school, she's never even *kissed* a guy.

Which is only understandable, being the eldest child in a family. Eldest children are almost always more restrained than others. In a study where teachers were asked to point out which were the most physically adventurous kids in a classroom, the ones they selected usually turned out to be youngest siblings; when they were asked to point out the most cautious ones, they were kids who were the oldest in their families. Eldest kids are the ones most likely to obediently take on their parents' professions, be it medicine or accountancy or living on a farm or even, as statistics back up, being an Episcopalian minister. In science, although there have been notable exceptions, first borns are usually the ones most likely to prefer long-established, traditional theories. Most of the resistance of established scientists to new theories such as special relativity or continental drift came from those who'd been the eldest in their families, too.

When it comes to sex, the same cautiousness holds. The average age for first having sex in America is now about seventeen, but it's not because everyone starts at that point. In a family of two kids, the average will likely derive from the older one starting at seventeen and a half, and the younger at sixteen and a half. If there are three kids, the youngest one will end up starting even earlier, and if the spacing between the kids is relatively wide, the difference is wider, too. Despite the daughter's pretense of social independence and utter sexual insouciance, her parents can take heart that she's unlikely, without strongly veering from the statistical average for eldest daughters in families of three kids, to start having sex before age eighteen and a half. It's the sweet-as-sugar youngest kids in big families the parents have to watch out for later. Their average age for first having sex is barely past fifteen in America now, and dropping. The combined result is that about 1 million U.S. teenagers will become pregnant this year. This sounds like a lot, but it's been higher. The peak year for teenage pregnancy was actually 1957 . . . but that was simply because the average marriage age was but nineteen.

Despite her hesitancy the girl starts walking with the boy; at first still cheek-burningly self-conscious, still embarrassed at what happened before. But gradually, as they window shop and chat, and he's gentle in all his words, she forgets that she's supposed to show off or keep him at a distance, and then—lost in their shared companionship—she just really likes it. They laugh at a hurrying family group and then at a funny window display, and suddenly it's even better, for with laughter cathecolamines start spurting inside them. These are a category of chemicals that start cascading from the brain in ordinary laughter, and act on cells in the circuits concerned with alertness and attention. The result is that the shared walkers, without quite knowing why, will suddenly feel even more closely attuned to each other.

They'll also feel happier, as several trillion of the morphinelike endorphin molecules start spraying loose within their brains. Endorphin's effect is so powerful that if the girl had been subconsciously digging her fingernails into tightly closed hands, or if he bumps into a bench edge while demonstrating a mock dance step, neither will feel any pain signal, as the endorphins will be active in their spinal cords to block it.

It's hard to tell how much time has passed—there are rarely any clocks in shopping malls, intentionally to keep shoppers isolated—but what does it matter? The couple are together on these timeless walkways. It's only natural for him to put his arm around her, and for her to lean against him, and now everything feels very very different, and the world of parents and brothers and breakfast squabbles is suddenly unimportant; immensely far away. Somehow they end up taking the turnings toward quieter corridors, no longer scared of what might happen when it's isolated enough to stop.

Walking this closely, the invisible world of sexual vapors lifting off their bodies, far stronger than their parents' immune clouds, is helping them along. The boy is spraying out the fatty chemical called androstenol from his surface blood vessels and especially from his armpits. This isn't the ammonia vapor you get from unwashed clothes. Rather, when it's concentrated enough it's usually described as having an enticing sandalwoodlike flavor. It's floating over to the chest-nestling girl at levels too low for her to consciously notice, but this doesn't mean it's having no effect. When college girls look through pictures of male students, if the level of air-filling androstenol goes up, the amount of interest they say they feel toward the man in that picture goes up, too.

The sounds of other walkers are increasingly dim, and so finally, beside an unused stock entrance door, off on the side of the upper level, they do stop and face each other, trying not to be to awkward as they entwine arms, and then, eyes closed, they tilt their faces close. The mucosal folds designed to keep food from spilling loose pucker outward, and then—after only the slightest of final life-spinning hesitations—their lips finally touch. Many cultures have resisted this strange fashion. In Japan it was abhorrent until 1945, but America's military occupation authorities encouraged it—even forcing screenwriters to include it in their scripts—on the grounds that anything encouraging young people to make their own decisions and not follow their elders (America's recent foes) was good. Nerve receptors are compressed and tugged in our couple, and data streams, many more than usual, travel at 80 mph along pathways skirting the outside of the cheek, then up the few inches into the sensorimotor sections of the brain. Bacterial transfer is still very slight at this point, for light contact only touches the outer surface of the lips, which are bacteriologically quite clean. Lips are a frontier zone between the skin's microbial lifeforms and the quite different ones inside the mouth, so although a few mutated forms manage to colonize the lips, much of the surface area is empty, as each arriving species battles the others to oblivion.

A little more pressure though, to really contact the beloved, and now the

The couple-friendly nuzzling of a kiss, viewed via heat-sensitive film.
The necks and foreheads glow hottest white; shoulders and nose are cooler,
shown in dark blue.

mucosal folds start squashing open. A low-atmospheric suction tunnel is created, linking the pair, and the first saliva streams begin cross-sloshing, whipped up by the sudden internal gale. Outer levels of bacteria are ripped loose from the teeth they're clutching to, the cementlike ligand molecules are incapable of holding them in place against this wind tunnel–like onslaught. The stored sebum from the normally subterranean follicles at the corner of the pressing lips are ripped upward, and with it, tumbling in, go great spurting jets of flying acne bacteria.

It could be enough to give anyone pause, but who can resist something that feels this trusting; this close? Desire helped by the fact that now there are yet more powerful sex chemicals hovering in the air between our delighted couple. The androstenol on the boy's body has been changing, aided by the raised temperature that kissing produces. Some of it has transformed into the even more potent androstenone molecules, and although men can barely smell it on themselves, and strongly dislike it if they ever do get a concentrated whiff from other men (they'll avoid a chair in a waiting room that has been coated with it) women in contrast like it, very much. They'll head *toward* a waiting room chair that's been dabbed with it, especially if they're given this test at the halfway point in their monthly cycle, when fertility is at its peak—and, as we saw, when the girl's blood-testosterone levels and libido would be highest, too. (There's a little androstenone in musk aftershaves—put in using a chemical process developed by none other than Wallace Carothers, the nylons inventor, which perhaps has a certain symmetry.)

Human beings aren't simple chemical machines, but at moments like this, drunk with the mix of crackling brain circuitry and androstenol clouds, we come pretty close. A practice gleaned from a certain country whose capital is Paris might even be engaged in. Mouths open slightly wider, and at this point, anyone of a squeamish disposition who has not already averted his eyes should probably do so. Tongues are extraordinarily life-dense objects, for on their roughened surfaces exists a safe refuge for innumerable microbial colonies that would otherwise be removed by ordinary chewing or saliva flow. The tongue is especially dense in the primitive anaerobic species, that normally live cowering deep underneath the surface layers, and that evolved deep in swamps and other areas where they could hope to exist away from their great nemesis—free-floating oxygen. Now, with the great lingual exploration beginning, they are scraped loose and wildly flung up. Yeasts and spirochetes and other mobile bacterium are shaken loose, too.

But readers who averted their eyes will have missed an unexpected sharing, something quite touching at this point. Until now, each of the teens has shared their separate family's general defenses against the external world's biological entities. But now, fresh biological linkings, paralleling their tentative emotional contacts will also, for the first time, intentionally be underway. Most of the anaerobic bacteria survive the impromptu aerial voyage, and hunker in their new home on the strange new tongue just fine. The giant *T. rex* of the mouth cavity, the great marauding *E. gingivalis* beast, is also likely to be making its way across, if the boy has brought it to the mall; either swept up in the general ruckus or migrating by its own power over the now extended tonguely bridge. This arrival in the girl's mouth is not any great problem, for it will simply continue its actually quite useful task of clearing up the micromeat of tooth-threatening bacteria that might already be inside her, resident on her gums. And as an example of the reciprocity this kindness entails, even as the nerve tinglings and brain contact continues, the girl is nearly certain to be loading her guy now with live colonies of *veillonellae* bacteria, which she, ultraconscious of hygiene, is likely to have nurtured at greater densities than he. The *veillonellae* take up residence in him, there amid the tumbling-down anaerobes, and diligently get to work soaking up the otherwise dangerous lactic acid, that his own, male-hygiene levels of mouth bacteria are likely to have let loose inside him.

Where there has been too much transfer, this is automatically cleared up, even as the new pair continue their delighted, boundary-crossing bliss. Saliva production goes up with the excitement of being kissed, and that means more lysozyme chemicals to break open the walls of excess bacteria, and more mucin proteins now coating the girl's mouth to stick other excess ones into harmless, dot-sized lumps. Each swallow will drain millions to the stomach for quick hydrochloric destruction, and even each gasp of pleasure will spray extra oxygen inside to neutralize any extra anaerobes still doing their free-fall gymnastics, turning them into crash-landing dying fragments. And where levels are still not right, and too many of the beloved's microbes have still made it into position? The extra saliva of this embrace will also be flowing with rich supplies of extra bicarb, and that, floating over to the attacked positions, quenches the acid the microbes produce. When the bicarb hits the acid, gusts of carbon dioxide bubble upward, tumbling to the air ducts and soon on to the world outside, yet still holding the trace of this isolated, enraptured pair.

epilogue: late night at home

Back at home, the girl contentedly perched on the soft chair across from the TV, her mouth continuing to float out carbon dioxide bubbles as she clears up any possible excesses from the afternoon's intimate transfer. The metal within her dangling bracelet acts as an inadvertent antenna, soaking up the high-speed radio waves that whirl into this room from distant stations, spinning the waves in roaring fast arcs around her wrist. As the bracelet lacks any amplifiers, all the fast-talking voices and insistent love music will quickly fade out of existence—which doesn't matter to her, as the girl is replete with wondrous reality itself. She just goes on dreamily musing, rolling over in her mind the delicious moment when he phones tomorrow and she lets her mom answer and someone calls up the stairs, in a hurried whisper, that it's a *guy* for her; she can answer, oh yes, she knows, it must be her *boyfriend.* Macrophages in her lungs are still trying to tug bagfuls of the smoke-burned polycyclic out of harm's way, and each breath out releases a few thousand of the cigarette-produced cotinine molecules, which tumble down her arm, then bounce in easy slow motion over her unheard bracelet to float on into the room. Higher up, on her face, demodex follicle mites are cautiously emerging; the excess makeup that locked them in now washed off.

The ten-year-old brother has no idea why his sister is being so nice—she even let him grab the best window seat on the way home—but he's not going to complain. She's letting him take the couch, for one, where it's great being the man of the house and they're watching his choice of video. She's made him a peanut butter and jelly sandwich, which she hasn't done in maybe a million years, and she's even brought him a second glass of milk, too. Sugar-hunting bacteria have been accumulating on his teeth, from the day's barrage of maple syrup, soft drinks, candy bars, Cracker Jacks, jelly beans, peanut-butter buttons, milk chocolates, caramels, popcorn, and that chewing gum. An evening's glass of milk is an excellent final defense against them all. One group of proteins especially abundant in milk have been keeping the bacteria from finding places to get properly attached; another chemical has been capturing some of the torn-off enamel that earlier bacteria had pulled off, and collecting it to be led back into place. He's feeling better inside as well, as his liver's detoxification systems have finally disposed of the burger's unwanted hormones, leading them safely into his bladder to join the aluminum, food additives, and even fragments of the vast eye-landing rubble from the air that had been blinked through the connecting tunnel to his nose, dissolved in his stomach, and now in part ended floating here, too.

A scary moment in the video, and the girl reaches to take a sip of his milk. The marauding *E.gingivalis* micromonster that her brother has left on the glass comes alive, dimly detecting this arriving warm flesh, and slowly, laboriously, stretching out one roiling amoebal arm to try to find it. But the girl has her own marauding specimens to leave on the glass edge, too. As she puts down the glass, the two beasts will still be a great distance apart, but these individuals are almost impossible to kill, and later this night, if the glass is left out unwashed, they will survive, slowly stumbling forward. The meeting will end either in a final slow-motion attack between these ancient ones, or, if the encounter is of a different sort, in the production of eight doubly filled cysts, which a few hours later will produce a squelching *Alien*-like expulsion, and sixteen living baby amoebae, waiting for whoever comes down earliest tomorrow, to rewind the video, and—could they?—pick up the glass, for a final lip-touching sip.

On the floor around the TV-fascinated brother and sister, the carpet is quietly digesting the day's accumulation of tumbled yeasts, spores, dandruff particles, and spilled food crumbs, as well as the final landing skin flakes, along with the dense cloud of pet saliva proteins. The dog which generated them is lying fast asleep on this active floor, nostrils only slightly blocked by the residual air freshener chemicals drifting out from the opened stick on the shelf, and absorbing the occasional radioactive radon gas oozing up from the floorboards. Ozone gusts from the upper atmosphere are still slamming against the house, but the DNA-linked ants which had been walking on the outside bricks are no longer there to be assaulted, but rather are snuggled deep in their subsurface nighttime nests. Far beyond, the expanding bubble of radio and TV waves from earth have continued moving outward, with this day's earliest broadcast offering (distant aliens are safe from cable) now itself about 8 billion miles away and going strong.

In the empty kitchen, the Formica table is slowly evaporating upward, while a few fragments of the mornings N_2O gas remain hovering shyly above the stove, not yet started on their long earth-circling voyage. Most of the flying fungi from the under-sink cupboard have landed, oblivious to the slow, nighttime ethylene gases that the apples keep on floating in painful communication to each other, as well as to the constant sizzle of radon gas, pushing up from the basement below. Over it all, the sturdy smoke detector is back to its disappointing, consistently null readings, each radioactive americium-241 spurt it beeps out registering only the faintest smoke rubble laggards.

One level up, the parents are in the bedroom, sitting at the wife's desk where a photo album is spread open to glue in—so that this time they do not get caught in a backlog—the newly processed pictures. They're feeling tired, which is understandable, as they're inhabited by brains that are now at the end of a day full of sorting input data, blocking poisons, puffing out carbon dioxide, suffering bits fading out through repair failures, and living on sugar and oxygen, all the while sloshing in wet fluid within the cranium. Percloroethylene continues gusting out from the clothes closet, but much has already been suctioned away by the micropores on the back of the now-tired geranium. The geranium is slowing its respiration rate at this late hour, after the effort of processing those vapors and then injecting them into the circulation pathway that will lead, as the parents are finally asleep later tonight, all the way down to the plant's roots. Numerous pillow mites have been returned to the bed after their venture out today, with a few live specimens from other

The inner mechanisms of a wristwatch signal the end of another day.

homes added, trying to take up new homes there, safe from the lurking *Cheyletus* predators.

Carbon dioxide is wafting in from the brain-churning children downstairs, sitting before the video, and reactive oxygen in the air is already starting one of the processes that will ultimately send the photographs' life-bursting images fading gradually away. The genetic links the family's creating will also gradually fade. By the mid-2500s, as the last of the CFCs released from this morning's kitchen are disappearing in the upper atmosphere, they and their children will only exist as tiny DNA fragments, wedged here and there in the widely separated cells of about 2^{20} or over 1 million great-great-great-great-great-great-great-great-great-great-great-great-great-great-great-great-great-great-grandchildren (less depending on inbreeding, mutation, or genetic drift).

Suddenly there's a cry, a shout almost, but different from what's been heard in this house before. Any maudlin thoughts are abandoned, as the parents hurry along the electron-scuffed trailmarks of the upstairs hall. In the final room along that hall, the baby's bedroom, their ten month old—this youngest creator of future generations—hasn't been asleep at all. Instead, he's pulled himself up, holding on to the edge of the crib for balance, concentrating intently. There had been something about that shiny helium balloon, tethered to the changing table on the other side of the room, that had made him struggle to hook his brain cells into an even more complex configuration than ever before.

And then, in the half-light, he gets it again.

The baby's excited voice shouts out once more, and the parents realize—and what greater joy in life is there?—that they're now hearing its first blurted word. They hold hands, delighted, here in the faint light of the night-light, and they step forward, one more shared journey, to hug their stupendous child.

And are even quite polite, at first, as they discuss whose name *exactly* it was their son had just said.

photo credits

Dr. Ray Clark/Mervyn Goff/MMPA AIIP ARPS/Science Photo Library, frontispiece,
22, 202

David Parker/Science Photo Library, 29

Science Photo Library, 34, 45, 167, 210

Prof. P. M. Motta, G. Macchiarelli, S. A. Nottola/Science Photo Library, 41 (top)

K. H. Kjeldsen/Science Photo Library, 41 (bottom)

Andrew Syred/Science Photo Library, 42, 69, 101, 172

David Scharf/Science Photo Library, 48, 57, 113, 151

Dr. Jeremy Burgess/Science Photo Library, 53 (top), 73, 163, 181 (both)

Dr. Tony Brain/Science Photo Library, 53 (bottom)

Clive Kocher/Science Photo Library, 60

Space Telescope Science Institute/NASA/Science Photo Library, 65

Manfred Kage/Science Photo Library, 76, 117

Natural History Museum, London, 79

CNRI/Science Photo Library, 83, 157, 187

Biophoto Associates/Science Photo Library, 86

D. Philips/Science Photo Library, 90

Princess Margaret Rose Orthopaedic Hospital/Science Photo Library, 96

Dr. Gary Settles/Science Photo Library, 108

Dr. David Gorham and Dr. Ian Hutchings/Science Photo Library, 119

Prof. P. Motta/Department of Anatomy, University *La Sapienza*, Rome/Science Photo
Library, 125, 144

Eye of Science/Science Photo Library, 130

Richard Wehr/Custom Medical Stock Photo/Science Photo Library, 141

Department of Clinical Radiology, Salisbury District Hospital/Science Photo Library,
146, 194 (both)

M. Marshall/Custom Medical Stock Photo/Science Photo Library, 147

AGFA/Science Photo Library, 177

index

Page numbers in italics indicate illustrations.

aspirin, 126
auto-brewery syndrome, 193, 195

babies:
  blink mechanism in, 55
  brains of, 20, 32, 115, 136, 156, 184, 189
  breast-fed, 155–56
  breathing of dust by, 114
  caffeine and, 175–76
  comforting, 128
  DNA repair systems of, 49
  docking position for, 30
  exploring, 88, 89, 91–93, 105
  face recognition structures of, 136
  first words of, 211
  food for, 19–21, 23, 47
  lead absorbed by, 115
  parent-controlling behavior of, 39
  pillow mites and, 130–31
  premature, lungs of, 110–11
  sweat glands of, 142
  talking to, 184–85
Babylonians, ancient, 62
Bach, Johann Sebastian, 40
Backus, Peter, 74
bacteria
  acne, 126–27, 203
  airborne, 114–15
  defenses against, 74–75
  demodex mites and, 27, 28
  in food, 82, 196–97
  kissing and, 201, 203–4
  in public spaces, 149–50
  in soil, 66
  on stamps, 100
  on teeth, 75–76, 145–46, 208
  on towels, 127

baldness, 185
balloons, 184
bathing, 119–24
beef, 158–59
beta-carotene, 161
biodegradable plastic, *167*
biorhythms, 148
birth order, 199–200
bladder, 36, 88, 189–90, *194*, 195–96
blink mechanism, 55, 90, 149, 191
body fat, 124
  cells, *125*
  hunger and, 156–58
  in middle age, 186
bone, 139, *144*
  growth of, 178
brain, 209
  aging and, 188–89
  of babies, 20, 32, 115, 136, 156, 184, 189
  of children, 85–86
  clearance cells in, 137
  during concentration, 69
  dog petting as stimulus to, 51–52
  gender differences in, 33
  of insects, 98–99
  language processing in, 83
  memory function in, 39
  nerve signals received by, *79*
  pleasure receptors of, 64
  power rating of, 30
  protection from toxins of, 36
  scans of, *83*, 85, 169
  smiling and, 154
  sound recognition in, 120
  stress and, 43
  tryptophan in, 95
  visual centers of, 38, 85

fingerprints, 88–89
fingers, 97
    joints of, 171–72
fish, 162
Fletcherizing, 62
flossing, 76
fluorescent lights, 32, 143
food, 145
    additives in, 36–37, 47, 80–81,
       208
    baby, 19–21, 23, 47
    brain activity and, 169
    children's choices of, 82
    cooking, 54–56
    digestion of, 63
    microwaving of, 73–74
    packaging of, *167*
    refrigeration of, 30–32
    shopping for, 190
    vitamins in, 37–38
    see also specific foods
forks, 161
formaldehyde, 36, 49, 100
fresh air, 56
fungi, *48*, 50
Funk, Casimir, 37–38

galactomannan, 80
gas chromatography, 103
gender differences:
    in approach, 68
    in bladder size, 190
    in body perception, 166–67
    in brain, 33
    in finger length, 97
    in heart disease, 107, 124
    in looking in mirrors, 143
    in medical knowledge, 188

    in personal space, 135
    in purchasing decisions, 77–78
    in reflexive widening of pupils, 20,
       84–85
    in school achievement, 122
    in sensory perception, 61, 81–82
    in shopping behavior, 189
    in smile perception, 154
    in sweating, 142
    in telephone answering, 102
    in treatment of babies, 105
genes:
    for acetylation, 37
    cholesterol and, 71
    hay fever and, 91
    macrophages and, 114
    of siblings, 26
glue, postage stamp, 99–100
glutathione, 140
gold, 96
goosebumps, 142
grapefruit, 101–2
grass, 72
Greeks, ancient, 44–45
Greeley, Andrew, 175
guitar string, *101*

Haber, Fritz, 51
hair:
    mites on, 27, 28
    red, 24
hamburgers, 158–60
    tapeworms in, *157*
handedness, 138, 190
handshake, 153, 154
handwashing, 190
Harrison, James, 31
hay fever, 91, 112

hearing, 61–62
    in dogs, 71
heart disease, 71, 107, 124
heat, body, 140
hemoglobin, 50
Henry, Edward, 89
hexanal, 49
hippocampus, 85
Hippocrates, 44
Holmes, Larry, 78
homework, 122
homunculus, sensory, *79*
hormones:
    in adolescence, 178, 180, 182
    aging and, 186
    female, 43, 54
    stress, *see* stress hormones
    weight and, 124
house addresses, 67–68
houseplants:
    hemoglobin-related chemical in, 50
    oxygen released by, 24
    toxins absorbed by, 49, 209
hunger, 156–58

Iacocca, Lee, 169
ice, 31
ice cream, 184
immigrants, 138
immune system, 149–50, 186
    cold viruses and, 155
    mate selection and, 24–25
    pillow mites and, 130
    of siblings, 26
    stress and, 43
incandescent bulbs, 32
incomes, disparity of, 138
insects, 66, 98–99
insulin, 95, 156

interracial marriage, 179
ionone, 142
IQ:
    of breast-fed versus bottle-fed babies,
        155
    eyeglasses and beliefs about, 182
    in mate selection, 25
    of siblings, 26
isoclines, abdominal, 186

jewelry, 176, 207
joints, 171–72
junk mail, 77–80

kahweol, 101–2
ketchup, 159–60
Khmer Rouge, 44
kidneys, 36
Kikuyu, 40
kissing, 199, 201, *202*, 203–5
knuckles, cracking, 171–73

language:
    brain areas for processing, 83
    infants and, 20
laughter, 183, 200
lead, 52, 115
Lee, Robert E., 153
Leonardo, 161
lettuce, 161–62
lightbulbs, 32
lighting:
    emergency, in movie theaters,
        196
    voice level and, 179
    see also sunlight
limbic system, 154, 183
lipstick, 178
literacy, 84

PASTRY

OFFER this Greek specialty with drinks or as a first course when giving a dinner.

Spinach and feta cheese (the white salty Greek cheese) are enclosed in layers of phylo pastry. Phylo pastry looks like sheets of thin white tissue paper and is obtainable from Greek delicatessens and large stores.

YOU WILL NEED:

1 large bunch spinach (approx. 20 sticks)
30g (1oz) butter
salt, pepper
4 shallots
30g (1oz) butter, extra
2 tablespoons flour
pinch nutmeg
¾ cup milk
125g (4oz) feta cheese
500g (1lb) phylo pastry
oil

Spinach Filling:

Wash spinach, coarsely chop leaves. Put in saucepan with butter, salt, pepper and chopped shallots. Cover, bring to boil, reduce heat, cook until spinach is tender. Drain well, chop spinach finely. Melt extra butter in pan, stir in flour and nutmeg, cook stirring 1 minute. Add milk, stir until sauce boils and thickens. Remove from heat, stir in chopped spinach and chopped feta cheese; cool.

Greek Triangles

1. Phylo pastry dries out if it is left uncovered, so deal with one sheet at a time and return remainder to packet. Cut each pastry sheet into 8cm (3in) wide strips. Brush each strip with oil. One strip of pastry makes one complete triangle.

2. Put a teaspoonful of filling on end of each pastry strip as shown. Take corner of pastry and fold over to form triangle, covering filling.

3. Lift first triangle up and over to form second triangle as shown. Continue folding over and over until you reach the end of the pastry strip. Trim edges if pastry overhangs.

4. Lower triangles a few at a time into deep hot oil. Fry until golden; drain well. The recipe makes about 90 triangles. It can of course be halved, or you can make just as many as you need, then freeze remaining pastry and filling separately.

THESE Chinese delicacies, offered as hors d'oeuvre, are encased in special spring roll wrappers available from the quick-frozen section of Chinese food stores or supermarkets. Usually in packets of 25, let the wrappers defrost in the refrigerator before use. The recipe makes about 25 Spring Rolls. They are filled with a mixture of minced pork, prawns, a touch of red pepper, green ginger, water chestnuts, mushrooms, shallots and some shredded cabbage.

YOU WILL NEED:
500g (1lb) pork mince
500g (1lb) green king prawns
1 red pepper
8 shallots
125g (4oz) mushrooms
2.5cm (1in) piece green ginger
250g (8oz) can water chestnuts
½ cabbage (preferably Chinese cabbage)
3 tablespoons dry sherry
1 tablespoon soy sauce
1 teaspoon sugar
½ teaspoon salt
455g (14½oz) packet spring roll wrappers
2 tablespoons cornflour
½ cup water
oil for deep-frying

Chinese Spring Rolls

1. Shell prawns, remove back vein, chop prawns into small pieces; chop shallots; seed and finely chop red pepper; slice mushrooms thinly, peel and grate green ginger; chop water chestnuts; shred cabbage finely.

2. Put all prepared ingredients into bowl, add pork mince, sherry, soy sauce, sugar and salt; mix well.

3. Put cornflour and water into bowl, mix well. Spoon tablespoonfuls of pork mixture evenly across one corner of spring roll wrapper, roll up in an envelope shape making sure edges have been brushed with cornflour mixture. Put into deep hot oil, fry until golden brown and cooked through, approx. 5 minutes.

PASTRY

SATURDAY lunch, Sunday brunch, or just any time at all is the right time for Sausage Rolls. They are great for a party too. The recipe makes about 24.

YOU WILL NEED:
750g (1½lb) sausage mince
1 large onion
¼ teaspoon mixed herbs
salt, pepper
4 thick slices white bread
warm water
2 x 375g (12oz) pkts puff pastry
1 egg-yolk
1 tablespoon cold water

1. Put sausage mince, peeled and grated onion, mixed herbs, salt and pepper into bowl. Cut crusts from bread, put bread in separate bowl. Pour over enough warm water to cover, let bread stand 5 minutes. Drain off water, squeeze bread gently to extract water. Add bread to sausage mince mixture; mix well. (Bread absorbs any excess fat in the sausage mince and helps to prevent meat shrinking inside pastry when cooking.)

2. With pastry at room temperature, cut each packet of puff pastry in half. Roll out each piece of pastry to 30cm (12in) square. Trim edges of each piece of pastry on three sides leaving one side untrimmed. This untrimmed side will be cut off later when rolling sausage rolls.

Sausage Rolls

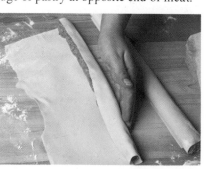

3. Fill meat mixture into large piping bag that does not have piping nozzle attached. Pipe meat along edge of pastry as shown, leaving untrimmed edge of pastry at opposite end of meat.

4. Turn edge of pastry over filling, then turn again so that filling is completely enclosed in pastry. Cut along edge of pastry with sharp knife. Repeat with remaining filling and pastry.

5. With back of knife, flatten rolls slightly at 1cm (½in) intervals. Brush rolls with combined cold water and egg-yolk. Cut rolls into 5cm (2in) pieces. Use first roll as guide for size of remaining rolls.

6. Put rolls on greased oven tray, side by side, just lightly touching as shown in picture. Bake in hot oven 10 minutes, reduce heat to moderate, cook further 15 minutes.

THIS is a favourite on menus of health food restaurants. The name comes from the Hunza Valley in the Himalayas, known for the health, vitality and long life of its residents. Their preference is for whole grains which they grow and grind themselves. This version of the pie, a high-fibre vegetarian dish, has crisp wholemeal pastry which encases a filling of spinach.

PASTRY
2 cups wholemeal plain flour
1 teaspoon vegetable salt
1 cup wheatgerm
250g (8oz) butter or vegetable margarine
¼ cup water, approx.
FILLING
1.25kg (2½lb) potatoes
2 tablespoons oil
vegetable salt
1 tablespoon kelp granules
1 small bunch spinach

Hunza Pie

1. Sift flour and salt into bowl, add husks in sifter to flour. Add wheatgerm, lightly mix into flour. Rub in butter until mixture resembles fine breadcrumbs. Add water, mix to a firm dough; a tablespoon or two more water may be needed. Turn out on to lightly floured surface, knead lightly.

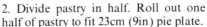

2. Divide pastry in half. Roll out one half of pastry to fit 23cm (9in) pie plate.

3. Peel potatoes, cut into quarters, boil until tender; drain. Place potatoes into bowl; mash very lightly. Add salt, kelp, oil and washed and shredded spinach; mix well. Let stand until cold.

4. Spoon spinach filling into pastry case, packing down well. Roll out remaining pastry to cover pie dish. Trim and decorate edges. Brush with water, make a few slits in top of pastry. Bake in hot oven for 15 minutes or until pastry is golden brown, reduce heat to moderate, cook further 15 minutes. Serve hot or cold.

PASTRY

THIS delicious Quiche, with its crisp pastry and creamy salmon filling, makes a perfect, light, full-of-flavour entree; or, served with salad, it is an ideal lunch or supper dish.

Salmon Quiche

PASTRY

1 cup plain flour
pinch salt
90g (3oz) butter
1 egg-yolk
1 tablespoon lemon juice

FILLING

250g (8oz) can red salmon
4 rashers bacon
1½ cups cream
3 eggs
salt, pepper
½ teaspoon paprika
2 tablespoons chopped parsley
1 tablespoon grated parmesan cheese

Pastry:

Sift flour and salt into bowl. Rub in butter until mixture resembles fine breadcrumbs. Mix to firm dough with lightly beaten egg-yolk and lemon juice; add one or two teaspoonfuls water if necessary. Turn pastry on to lightly floured surface, knead lightly.

1. Roll pastry on lightly floured surface to a circle large enough to fit base and sides of 23cm (9in) flan tin. Lift pastry gently over rolling pin, lift into flan tin.

2. Ease pastry into sides of tin and, with fingers, press into grooves of tin. Handle gently so pastry does not break.

5. Bake in moderately hot oven 10 minutes, reduce heat to moderately slow, cook further 30 to 35 minutes, or

3. Roll rolling pin over top of tin quickly and firmly; this will cut off excess pastry and leave a neat, clean edge. Refrigerate one hour.

until filling has set. Cut into wedges to serve. Serve with salad. It will serve 6 as an entree, 4 as a supper snack.

4. Put flan tin on oven tray. Drain salmon, reserving liquid. Flake salmon lightly, remove bones. Dice bacon, fry gently until crisp, remove from pan, drain well. Beat together cream, eggs, salt, pepper, paprika, parsley, parmesan cheese, and reserved salmon liquid. Arrange salmon evenly in base of pastry shell, sprinkle bacon over. Carefully, as shown, pour egg mixture over back of spoon to cover salmon and bacon.

Melton Mowbray Pie

ONE of the good foods of England, Melton Mowbray Pie is a pork pie, which is eaten cold. It is a great favourite with men. Serve it with salad; tankards of beer are traditional with it too.

HOT WATER PASTRY
3 cups plain flour
½ teaspoon salt
2 egg-yolks
125g (4oz) lard
⅔ cup water

FILLING
1 veal knuckle
4 cups water
1 large onion
salt, pepper
2kg (4lb) large lean pork chops
1 egg-yolk
1 tablespoon water, extra

1. Sift flour and salt into bowl. Make a well in centre, add egg-yolks, cover with some of the flour. Place lard and water into pan, stir over low heat until lard is melted, bring liquid to boil. Pour boiling liquid into flour all at once; mix to a firm pastry. Turn out on to lightly-floured surface; knead lightly. Cover pastry, allow to stand for 10 minutes. Knead pastry again lightly. Roll out two-thirds of pastry to line base and sides of greased deep 20cm (8in) cake tin, bring pastry to top of tin. Press pastry gently but firmly into tin; make sure there are no holes or cracks in pastry.

2. Cut veal into pieces, or ask butcher to do this. Place veal and the veal bones, water, peeled and chopped onion, salt and pepper into pan, bring to boil, reduce heat, simmer, covered for 2 hours; strain stock, skim off any fat from stock. Set aside; this makes the jellied filling for the pie. Remove bones and fat from pork, cut pork into 1cm (½in) cubes. Season pork with salt and pepper. Pack pork into pastry-lined tin, spreading out evenly. Spoon over 3 tablespoons of the stock.

3. Brush edges of pastry with combined egg-yolk and extra water. Roll out remaining pastry to cover pie. Place over meat, press edges of pastry together. Pinch edges to give decorative edge, as shown in picture. Cut a circle from centre of pastry, approximately 2.5cm (1in) wide. Brush pastry with egg-yolk mixture. Bake in hot oven for 30 minutes or until pastry is golden brown. Reduce heat to moderately slow for a further 1½ hours. If necessary, cover pastry lightly with a sheet of brown paper to stop pastry becoming too brown. As juices appear in hole in pastry top, carefully spoon out; this stops pastry becoming soft. Allow pie to cool a little in tin. Heat jellied stock if necessary, to make it liquid again; let cool. Using small funnel, pour stock into the small hole in top of pie. Do this gradually so that stock has time to settle down to the bottom of the pie; you will probably not need to use all the stock. Cover pie, refrigerate overnight. To serve, remove pie from tin, cut into wedges.

Custard Tart

A DEEP filling of creamy, velvety-textured custard in a shell of biscuit pastry makes this good-cutting Custard Tart.

PASTRY
90g (3oz) butter
¼ cup sugar
1 egg
1¼ cups plain flour
¼ cup self-raising flour

CUSTARD
3 eggs
1 teaspoon vanilla
2 tablespoons sugar
2 cups milk
nutmeg or cinnamon

1. Beat butter until creamy, add sugar, beat until just combined. Add lightly beaten egg gradually, beating well after each addition. Work in two-thirds of sifted flours with wooden spoon, then remaining flour by hand. Turn on to lightly-floured board, knead lightly until smooth. Refrigerate 30 minutes before using. Roll pastry to line greased 20cm (8in) pie plate.

2. Handle pastry carefully, making sure there are no breaks, otherwise uncooked custard will seep through. Brush base and sides of pastry with lightly beaten egg-white; this gives a light seal to the pastry — again helping to ensure that custard remains inside the pastry shell.

3. Make decorative edge on pastry with tip of lightly floured teaspoon. Don't press too hard or spoon will cut through pastry.

4. Beat eggs, vanilla and sugar together; heat milk to lukewarm, gradually stir into egg mixture. Put pie plate on to oven tray, spoon half custard mixture into pie crust. Put pie, on oven tray, into oven then carefully spoon in remaining custard. (If all custard were put in at once, it could spill while being carried to the oven.) Bake in moderate oven 50 to 55 minutes. After 15 minutes cooking time, sprinkle with nutmeg. Do not overcook, custard will firm as it cools.

Vanilla Slices

WITH a delicious filling of rich vanilla custard, these are the most popular of all slices. The slices are made with packaged puff pastry and topped with passionfruit-flavoured icing.

YOU WILL NEED:
500g (1lb) packaged puff pastry
1 cup sugar
¾ cup cornflour
½ cup custard powder
1 litre (4 cups) milk
60g (2oz) butter
2 egg-yolks
2 teaspoons vanilla
       PASSIONFRUIT ICING
1 cup icing sugar
1 teaspoon butter
1 passionfruit
1 teaspoon water, approx.

Have pastry at room temperature. Some 500g (1lb) packs of puff pastry come in two separate 250g (½lb) blocks; some come in one complete 500g (1lb) block. If using the former, roll each half separately. If using the complete 500g (1lb) block, cut pastry in half.

1. Roll each half of pastry to a 32cm (13in) square, then, with sharp knife, trim to 30cm (12in) square. Place one square of pastry on large ungreased oven tray, bake in very hot oven 5 to 10 minutes, or until well browned. Trim pastry with a sharp knife to 23cm (9in) square. Bake and trim remaining pastry in the same way. Flatten "puffy" side of both pieces of pastry with hand.

2. Line a 23cm (9in) square slab tin with aluminium foil, bringing the foil up over sides; this makes it easy to remove slice when set. Place one piece of pastry into base of tin, flattened side uppermost. Combine sugar, cornflour and custard powder in heavy-based saucepan, mix well to combine. Blend with a little of the milk until smooth, stir in remaining milk; add butter. Stir mixture constantly over heat until custard boils and thickens, reduce heat, simmer 3 minutes. Remove from heat, quickly stir in vanilla, then stir in the beaten egg-yolks. Pour hot custard immediately over pastry in tin. Place remaining pastry on top of custard so the flattened side touches the hot custard. Press pastry firmly with hand.

3. Spread evenly with Passionfruit Icing; when cool, refrigerate several hours or overnight until filling has set.

Passionfruit Icing:
Sift icing sugar into small basin, add softened butter and pulp from passionfruit. Add enough water, approximately 1 teaspoonful, to make icing of thick spreading consistency. (The amount of water needed will depend on size of passionfruit.) Beat well.

PASTRY

THESE are the little deep-fried pastries of India, filled with a spicy meat mixture. Serve them as an accompaniment to drinks with chutney for dipping. To make the chutney, heat 1 cup fruit or tomato chutney and 1 teaspoon grated green ginger; push chutney through sieve. The recipe makes approx. 36 Samosas.

PASTRY
3 cups plain flour
1 teaspoon salt
60g (2oz) butter
⅔ cup cold water
oil for deep-frying

FILLING
1 tablespoon oil
500g (1lb) minced steak or lamb
5cm (2in) piece green ginger
2 cloves garlic
1 large onion
salt, pepper
1 teaspoon garam masala
½ teaspoon turmeric
¼ teaspoon chilli powder
1 cup water

Filling:
Heat oil in frying pan, add meat, stir until light golden brown. Add peeled and grated green ginger, crushed garlic, peeled and finely chopped onion, salt, pepper, garam masala, turmeric, chilli powder; stir until onion is tender. Add water, stir until combined. Bring mixture to boil, reduce heat. Simmer uncovered for 25 to 30 minutes or until nearly all liquid has evaporated and meat mixture is very thick. Allow to become cold.

Indian Samosas

2. Turn dough out on to lightly floured surface; knead for 10 minutes or until pastry is very smooth and elastic. Place pastry into clean bowl, cover with plastic wrap. Let stand for 60 minutes. Divide pastry in half. Roll out each half to 5mm (¼in) thickness. Cut into rounds, using a 4cm (1½in) cutter. Roll out each round to a 9cm (3½in) circle. Repeat with remaining half of pastry. Cover pastry rounds with tea towel so that they do not dry out while preparing the Samosas.

1. Sift flour and salt into bowl, rub in butter until mixture resembles fine breadcrumbs. Add water all at once, mix with hand to combine pastry.

3. Hold pastry circle in palm of hand. Place two teaspoons of filling into centre of circle. Wet edges of pastry very lightly with water. Fold pastry over meat, press edges together lightly. Hold prepared pastry with filling in one hand, with other hand pinch edge of pastry with thumb and index finger, fold the piece of pinched pastry over the unpinched edge, pinching down again on the unpinched edge; repeat again around edge of pastry as shown. Repeat with remaining pastry and filling.

4. Place Samosas, a few at a time, into deep hot oil, fry until golden brown, approximately 2 minutes. Drain on absorbent paper.
NOTE: Garam masala, the mixed spice of India, is obtainable in small jars from large food stores, supermarkets or health-food stores.

FOR those with a sweet tooth, Baklava is irresistible. It is a famous Greek delicacy — layers of light golden pastry, with a filling of sugar, nuts and cinnamon, soaked in a rich honey-lemon syrup — and the perfect sweet accompaniment to after-dinner coffee. Phylo can be bought from most large food halls, or from Greek pastry shops.

YOU WILL NEED:
500g (1lb) phylo pastry
250g (8oz) butter
250g (8oz) walnut pieces
2 teaspoons cinnamon
¼ cup sugar
SYRUP
½ cup sugar
½ cup water
4 tablespoons clear honey
½ cup lemon juice

Greek Baklava

1. Melt butter; grease 28cm x 18cm (11in x 7in) lamington tin. If necessary, cut pastry roughly to size of tin. (The packaged pastry can vary in size, depending on manufacturer.) Layer half the pastry (approx. 15 sheets) one on top of the other, brushing each layer with melted butter.

2. Combine finely chopped walnuts, cinnamon and sugar, sprinkle evenly over top layer. Fold over any untrimmed edges of pastry. Continue layering remaining pastry, again brushing each layer with melted butter.

3. Cut into squares with a sharp knife, cutting right down to base; brush top pastry with butter. Bake in moderate oven approximately 45 minutes until crisp and golden brown.

4. Combine sugar, water, honey and lemon juice in pan, stir over low heat until sugar has dissolved. Bring to boil. Pour hot syrup over Baklava, leave overnight for syrup to be absorbed.

1. Filling: Place meat into pan, stir over low heat until meat is well browned. Drain off any surplus fat. Add crumbled stock cubes, water, salt, pepper and nutmeg, stir until boiling, reduce heat, cover, simmer gently 20 minutes; remove from heat. Combine extra water and flour, stir until flour mixture is smooth. Add flour mixture to meat, stir until combined. Return to heat, stir until meat boils and thickens. Add soy sauce (to give brown colour), stir until combined. Simmer, uncovered, 5 to 10 minutes; remove from heat, allow to become cold.

2. Sift flour and salt into basin. Place water and dripping into saucepan, stir until dripping melts; remove from heat. Make a well in centre of dry ingredients, add liquid, stir until combined.

3. Turn out on to lightly floured surface, knead lightly. Roll out pastry to line 8 greased pie tins. Cut excess pastry around sides of dishes using a sharp knife; slant knife, as shown, while cutting pastry. Fill centres with cold meat filling.

Australian Meat Pie

IT's Australia's own — this golden-topped pie with its deliciously savoury filling. The recipe makes eight individual pies.

FILLING	PIE BASE
750g (1½lb) minced steak	2 cups plain flour
2 beef stock cubes	½ teaspoon salt
salt, pepper	⅔ cup water
1½ cups water	60g (2oz) beef dripping
pinch nutmeg	**PIE TOP**
2 tablespoons plain flour	375g (12oz) packaged puff pastry
¼ cup water, extra	1 egg-yolk
1 teaspoon soy sauce	1 teaspoon water

4. Roll out puff pastry on lightly floured surface, cut out rounds for top of pies; use saucer as guide. Wet edges of base pastry, and gently press tops into place, trim around edges with sharp knife. Pierce centre with pointed knife. Brush tops with combined egg-yolk and water. Bake in hot oven 5 minutes or until golden brown, reduce heat to moderate, cook further 10 minutes.

1. Sift dry ingredients into bowl, rub in butter until mixture resembles coarse breadcrumbs. Mix to firm dough with lightly beaten egg-yolk, lemon juice and water, adding a little more water, if necessary. Knead lightly on floured board. Wrap in plastic food wrap, refrigerate 30 minutes.

2. Roll pastry on lightly floured surface to a circle large enough to fit base and sides of 20cm (8in) or 23cm (9in) flan tin. Lift pastry gently over rolling pin, lift into flan tin. Ease pastry into sides of tin, with fingers, press lightly into grooves. Roll rolling pin over top of tin firmly, to cut off excess pastry and neaten edges. Prick base with fork. Bake in moderately hot oven 10-15 minutes or until pale brown. Allow pastry to cool in tin.

3. When completely cold, fill base of pastry with cold custard. Arrange well-drained fruit and strawberries decoratively over custard.

4. When all fruit has been arranged, use pastry brush to brush fruit well with warm apricot glaze.

French Fruit Flan

FRUIT Flan, an elegant French dessert, has a shell of tender biscuit pastry filled with creamy custard and topped with colourful fruits covered with glistening brandied-apricot glaze. Other fruit can be used in place of the cherries, apricots and strawberries suggested here.

PASTRY
1 cup plain flour
1 tablespoon icing sugar
¼ teaspoon baking powder
pinch salt
90g (3oz) butter
1 egg-yolk
1 teaspoon lemon juice
1 teaspoon water, approx.

CUSTARD
3 tablespoons custard powder
2 tablespoons sugar
1 cup milk
½ teaspoon vanilla
½ cup cream

FRUIT TOPPING
470g (15oz) can black cherries
470g (15oz) can apricots
1 punnet strawberries

GLAZE
2 tablespoons apricot jam
1 tablespoon brandy

Custard:
Combine custard powder and sugar in saucepan, gradually add milk, stir until blended and smooth. Bring to boil, stirring constantly, add vanilla; cool. When cold, fold in lightly whipped cream.

Glaze:
Put jam and brandy in saucepan, heat gently until boiling. Push through sieve to give a smooth glaze.

BREAD, BUNS and SCONES
White Bread

THE recipe makes two loaves of beautiful bread.
You can make one to eat now, and one to freeze for later use.

YOU WILL NEED:
1.125kg (2¼lb) plain flour
3 teaspoons salt
¼ cup sugar
30g (1oz) compressed yeast
2½ cups lukewarm water
¼ cup oil
1 egg-yolk
1 tablespoon water, extra

1. Cream yeast with 1 teaspoon sugar, add 1 cup of the lukewarm water, stir until combined. Sprinkle 1 tablespoon of the flour over yeast mixture. Cover bowl, stand in warm place for 10 to 15 minutes or until frothy. Sift flour, salt and remaining sugar into large bowl. Make a well in centre of dry ingredients, add oil, remaining water and yeast mixture.

2. Mix dough well with wooden spoon. Then place one hand into mixture; mix well with hands, then gather dough up into a ball. Turn out on to floured surface, knead for 3 minutes. Place dough into large bowl, which has been brushed lightly with oil. Brush top of dough with a little oil. Cover bowl, stand in warm place for 45 minutes or until mixture has doubled in bulk.

3. Punch down dough as shown in picture. Turn out on to lightly floured surface, knead for 5 minutes. Return dough to bowl, brush top of dough with oil. Cover and stand bowl in warm place for 35 to 40 minutes or until doubled in bulk. Punch dough down again. Turn out on to lightly floured surface, knead for 3 minutes.

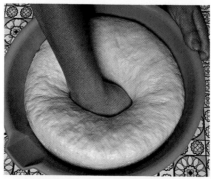

4. Divide dough into 4 equal pieces, knead each piece of dough into a ball. Place 2 balls side by side into two greased 23cm x 12cm (9in x 5in) loaf tins. Stand in warm place until dough reaches top of tins, approximately 25 to 30 minutes. Brush top of bread with combined egg-yolk and extra water. Bake in moderate oven for 40 minutes or until cooked; cool on a wire rack.

1. Cream yeast with 1 teaspoon each of the sugar and flour, add lukewarm milk, mix well. Cover, stand in warm place 10 to 15 minutes or until mixture is frothy. Sift flour, salt, sugar and spices, rub in butter, add beaten egg, sultanas and yeast mixture, beat well.

2. Cover bowl with clean cloth, stand in warm place 40 minutes or until dough doubles in bulk. Punch dough down, turn out on to floured surface, knead well until dough is smooth and elastic.

3. Cut dough into three equal pieces, cut each piece into five, making 15 buns in all. Knead each into round shape. Put buns in lightly greased 18cm x 28cm (7in x 11in) lamington tin, stand in warm place 10 to 15 minutes or until buns reach top edge of tin.

Hot Cross Buns

SUGAR and spice and all things nice — these shiny-glazed traditional buns of Easter. The recipe makes 15 buns. Of course, if you omit the crosses, the buns make good eating any time of year.

YOU WILL NEED:

4 cups plain flour	**60g (2oz) butter**
1 teaspoon salt	**¼ cup sugar**
30g (1oz) compressed yeast	**1 egg**
1½ cups milk	**½ teaspoon mixed spice**
½ cup sultanas	**½ teaspoon cinnamon**

4. Sift ½ cup plain flour, mix to paste with ⅓ cup water. Fill into small plastic bag with small hole cut across corner. Pipe crosses on each bun. Bake in hot oven 15 to 20 minutes. Remove from oven, immediately brush with glaze made by dissolving 1 tablespoon sugar and 1 teaspoon gelatine in 1 tablespoon hot water. Cool buns on wire rack.

Berlin Doughnuts

THEY'RE also called Russian Doughnuts — but whatever the name, the good taste is the same. Light-textured doughnuts, with a jam filling, are deep fried until golden, then dusted generously with icing sugar. The recipe makes about 15 doughnuts.

YOU WILL NEED:
30g (1oz) compressed yeast
¼ cup lukewarm water
60g (2oz) butter
1 cup milk
¼ cup sugar
1 teaspoon salt
2 eggs
3¾ cups plain flour
1 teaspoon grated lemon rind
1 egg-white
raspberry jam
oil for deep-frying

1. Dissolve yeast in lukewarm water. Put butter and milk in saucepan, stir over heat until butter has melted, cool to lukewarm. Beat together yeast mixture, butter-milk mixture, sugar, eggs and salt. Add sifted flour and lemon rind, beat well. Cover, let rise in warm place, until doubled in bulk (approximately 40 minutes). Turn on to floured board, knead lightly.

2. Roll dough out to approximately 1cm (½in) thick. Cut into rounds with 5cm (2in) floured cutter.

3. Brush half of rounds with lightly beaten egg-white, put 1 teaspoon of raspberry jam in centre of other rounds. Top jam rounds with remaining rounds, pinching edges together firmly. Cover, let rise in warm place until almost double.

4. Deep fry a few at a time in hot oil until golden brown, turning once. Drain on absorbent paper, dust with sifted icing sugar.

Scones

1. Sift flour and salt into basin, stir in sugar. Rub in butter with fingertips until mixture resembles fine bread-crumbs. (For a sweet scone, increase sugar to 1 tablespoon; add ½ to ¾ cup sultanas.)

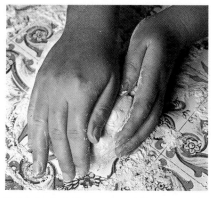

2. Make hole in centre of flour, pour in combined milk and water. Mix lightly and quickly. Turn out on to floured surface, knead lightly.

3. Pat dough out to approximately 2 cm (¾in) thickness; cut into rounds with 5cm (2in) cutter; dip cutter into flour each time before cutting. Place close together on lightly greased scone tray, or pack side by side, in rows of three, into greased 18cm x 28cm (7in x 11in) lamington tin. Brush tops with a little milk. Bake in very hot oven 10 minutes, or until golden brown. (Scones in lamington tin may take a little longer.)

IT takes only about 15 minutes to produce a basketful of lovely hot scones, featherlight, on the table. With your favourite jam, and cream, added before you serve these scones to family and friends, there's bound to be an appreciative response. Makes 12.

YOU WILL NEED:
2 cups self-raising flour
½ teaspoon salt
1 teaspoon sugar
30g (1oz) butter
½ cup milk
¼ cup water

Damper

DAMPER has become a popular item on barbecue menus. You can whip it up in minutes and bring it piping hot to the barbecue table. It does not keep well, so for best flavour we suggest you eat Damper on the same day that it is made.

YOU WILL NEED:
3 cups self-raising flour
1½ teaspoons salt
90g (3oz) butter
½ cup milk
½ cup water
extra flour

1. Sift flour and salt into bowl, rub in butter until mixture resembles fine breadcrumbs, fairly even in size.

2. Make a well in centre of dry ingredients, add combined water and milk all at once; mix lightly with sharp knife in cutting motion. Turn out on to lightly floured surface; knead lightly.

3. Knead dough into round, place on greased oven tray. Pat dough out to a 15cm (6in) circle. With sharp knife, cut two slits across dough like a cross, approximately 1cm (½in) deep. Brush top of dough with milk, sift a little extra flour over dough. Bake in hot oven for 10 minutes or until golden brown, reduce heat to moderate, cook a further 15 minutes.

BREAD, BUNS and SCONES

Bread, fresh and warm from the oven, has one of the most heartwarming aromas there is. Recipe makes two rye bread loaves. A sourdough starter is prepared first. Once it is made, a portion can be used for each fresh day's baking. The sourdough stands for two days, unrefrigerated, before use; then it can be refrigerated.

YOU WILL NEED:
4¾ cups plain flour
4 cups rye flour
2 teaspoons salt
30g (1oz) compressed yeast
1 tablespoon brown sugar
3 cups lukewarm water
¼ cup sourdough (see below)
30g (1oz) caraway seeds
2 tablespoons oil
       SOURDOUGH
15g (½oz) compressed yeast
1 teaspoon sugar
1¼ cups lukewarm water
1½ cups plain flour

Sourdough Rye Bread

1. Prepare sourdough thus: Cream yeast and sugar, add lukewarm water. Sift flour, add yeast mixture, mix until smooth; mixture will soon start to bubble as shown. Cover, stand unrefrigerated two days before using. (You will need ¼ cup sourdough for the recipe.)

2. To make the bread, cream yeast with 1 teaspoonful of the brown sugar and one teaspoonful of the plain flour. Add ½ cup of the lukewarn water, stand in warm place until mixture starts to bubble (10 to 15 minutes).

4. Turn mixture on to lightly floured surface, knead until smooth and elastic. Put into lightly oiled bowl, cover, stand in warm place until doubled in bulk, approx. 30 minutes. Punch dough down with fist. Turn on to lightly floured surface.

3. Sift flours, salt and remaining brown sugar; return husks in sifter to flour. Stir in caraway seeds. Make well in centre of dry ingredients. Combine yeast mixture, remaining lukewarm water, sourdough and oil. Add to dry ingredients, mix well. You may need an extra ¼ to ½ cup water.

5. Divide dough in two, then divide each half in two again. Knead each piece until smooth and round. Put two rounds side-by-side in two greased 23cm x 12cm (9in x 5in) loaf tins, as shown. Cover tins, stand in warm place until dough reaches edge of tins, approx. 30 minutes. Brush top of dough with water. Bake in hot oven 30 minutes or until cooked. Turn out and cool on wire rack.

Chelsea Bun

CHELSEA Bun — with its shiny glaze topping, and filling of colourful fruit and cinnamon — is a favourite with the family. It is the perfect little bun for morning or afternoon tea. Serve it warm or cold, with lots of butter.

YOU WILL NEED:
3 cups self raising flour
½ teaspoon salt
45g (1½oz) butter
1 cup milk
FILLING
60g (2oz) butter
⅓ cup brown sugar, lightly packed
½ cup sultanas
½ cup currants
60g (2oz) chopped glace cherries
60g (2oz) mixed peel
1 teaspoon cinnamon
GLAZE
1 tablespoon water
1 tablespoon sugar
1 teaspoon gelatine

1. Sift flour and salt in bowl, rub in butter lightly. Mix to firm dough with milk. Roll dough out to 30cm x 23cm (12in x 9in) oblong. Cream butter and brown sugar together, spread over dough.

3. Cut into 10 thick slices. Pack into greased 20cm (8in) sandwich tin, cut side down. Bake in moderate oven 25 to 30 minutes. Brush bun with glaze while still hot.
Glaze: Put ingredients in small saucepan, stir over low heat until sugar and gelatine have dissolved.

2. Sprinkle with fruit and cinnamon, roll up lengthwise.

79

BREAD, BUNS and SCONES
Bagels

THESE are the popular Jewish bread rolls — traditionally served warm, with cream cheese and lox (smoked salmon). But they're as nice with any usual roll filling. The recipe makes around 15.

YOU WILL NEED:
4 cups plain flour
2 teaspoons salt
23g (¾oz) compressed yeast
3 tablespoons sugar
½ cup water
½ cup milk
1 egg-yolk
3 tablespoons oil
1 egg-yolk, extra
1 tablespoon water, extra
poppy seeds or sesame seeds

1. Cream yeast with 1 tablespoon of the sugar. Add ¼ cup of the lukewarm water, stand covered in warm place until mixture bubbles, approximately 10 to 15 minutes.

2. Sift flour, salt and remaining sugar in bowl. Combine lukewarm milk, remaining lukewarm water, egg-yolk and oil. Add to dry ingredients with yeast mixture, mix to stiff dough; add up to an extra ¼ cup lukewarm water, if necessary. Turn dough out on to floured board, knead well. Put into lightly oiled bowl, cover, stand in warm place until doubled in bulk, approximately 1 hour.

4. Slide a few bagels at a time into a large saucepan of boiling water (do not let them overlap). Turn after one minute and remove with slotted spoon after boiling for one more minute.

3. Punch dough down, knead again, divide dough into 15 portions. Roll each portion into rope shape approximately 20cm (8in) long. Coil rope to make a ring, moistening ends and overlapping them, squeeze lightly to seal. Put on greased tray, allow to stand in warm place 10 minutes.

5. Put bagels into greased oven tray, brush well with combined beaten extra egg-yolk and water, sprinkle with poppy seeds or sesame seeds. Bake in hot oven 15 to 20 minutes or until golden.

80

Cream Buns

REMEMBER them from schooldays? Cream buns made from this recipe taste just as good today. Makes 12.

YOU WILL NEED:
4 cups plain flour
60g (2oz) butter
¼ cup sugar
½ cup lukewarm milk
1 cup lukewarm water
30g (1oz) compressed yeast
1 egg-yolk
1 teaspoon water, extra
Mock Cream:
Combine ⅓ cup water and 1 cup sugar, stir over heat to dissolve sugar. Bring to boil, remove from heat. When completely cold, beat 125g (4oz) butter and ½ teaspoon vanilla until white and fluffy, gradually pour in cold syrup, beating constantly.

1. Cream yeast with 1 teaspoon of the sugar. Add lukewarm milk. Let stand 10 to 15 minutes until frothy.

2. Sift flour and remaining sugar into bowl. Rub in butter until mixture resembles fine breadcrumbs. Make well in centre of dry ingredients, add yeast mixture and lukewarm water, mix to soft dough. Turn out on to floured surface. Knead 5 minutes.

3. Put dough into lightly oiled bowl. Cover and stand in warm place 1 hour or until dough has doubled in bulk. Punch dough down in bowl. Turn out on to floured surface; knead 5 minutes. Divide into twelve even portions.

4. Knead each portion of dough into a round. Put rounds on well-greased oven trays, allowing room for spreading. Set in warm place 10 minutes or until half-doubled in size. Brush with combined beaten egg-yolk and extra water. Bake in hot oven 10 minutes, reduce heat to moderate, bake further 15 minutes or until golden brown. Put buns on wire rack; when cold, slit open, fill with raspberry jam and mock cream. Dust each bun with a little sifted icing sugar.

NOTE: Two teaspoons of dry active yeast can be substituted for the compressed yeast. Sift dry yeast with flour and sugar, rub in butter, add combined lukewarm milk and water, then proceed as for recipe.

1. Divide 250g (8oz) butter in half. This butter is for making the butter pats. On a piece of aluminium foil, spread 125g (4oz) of this butter out to 15cm (6in) square, spreading as evenly as possible. Wrap aluminium foil around butter. Repeat with remaining 125g (4oz) butter as above, on another piece of foil. Refrigerate until ready to use.

Croissants

2. Sift flour and salt into bowl, add lemon rind, mix lightly. Place yeast and 1 teaspoon of the sugar into bowl, gradually add warm milk, mix until combined. Sprinkle one tablespoon of the flour over yeast mixture. Add remaining sugar to flour mixture. Place yeast mixture in warm place until frothy, approximately 10 to 15 minutes. Add yeast mixture, extra 60g (2oz) melted butter and lightly beaten egg to flour mixture; mix well. Turn out on to lightly floured surface; knead for 5 minutes. Place dough into lightly oiled bowl, cover and stand in warm place for 35 to 40 minutes or until doubled in bulk. Punch down, knead for 2 minutes. Place dough into oiled bowl, cover and stand in warm place until doubled in bulk, 20 to 25 minutes, turn dough out on to lightly floured surface, knead for 3 minutes.

YOU could be dining in Paris when you enjoy these flaky rolls. Traditionally served as a light breakfast throughout France, they are a good accompaniment to tea or coffee at any time. The recipe makes about 18. Any not eaten can be frozen for later use.

YOU WILL NEED:
250g (8oz) butter
15g (½oz) compressed yeast
1 cup lukewarm milk
4 cups plain flour
½ teaspoon grated lemon rind

3 tablespoons sugar
pinch salt
60g (2oz) butter, extra
1 egg
1 egg-yolk
1 tablespoon water, extra

3. Roll out dough to a 50cm x 18cm (20in x 7in) rectangle. Place one of the butter pats in centre of dough. Fold one side of pastry completely over butter pat. Place remaining butter pat on top of dough, directly over first butter pat, fold remaining pastry over this butter. Press dough lightly around butter pats, to seal in butter. Rest dough on table for 3 minutes.

4. Roll out dough on floured surface to a rectangle 50cm x 18cm (20in x 7in). Fold into three as shown in picture, making sure that there is no flour on top of pastry. Roll out and fold again as above. Wrap dough in plastic food wrap, then place into plastic bag; seal. Place into freezer overnight. Next day, thaw out dough, at room temperature; this will take approximately 4 hours. Repeat rolling and folding on floured surface, as above, 4 more times. Cut dough in half.

5. Roll out first half of pastry on floured surface to a 37cm (15in) square. Cut dough into 12cm (5in) squares. Brush each square of dough lightly with combined egg-yolk and extra water. Roll up each square of dough, starting at one corner, and rolling to opposite corner. Shape into horseshoe shape. Repeat with remaining squares of pastry. Place croissants on to greased baking trays. Stand in warm place until doubled in size, approximately 15 minutes. Brush with egg glaze. Bake in hot oven for 5 minutes or until golden brown. Reduce heat to moderate, cook further 10 minutes.

Indian Puris

PURIS are crisp, featherlight puffs that in India take the place of wholemeal bread; excellent with curries. Makes about 35.

YOU WILL NEED:
2 cups wholemeal plain flour
1 teaspoon salt
60g (2oz) butter
⅓ cup warm water
oil for deep-frying

1. Sift flour and salt into bowl, rub in butter until mixture resembles fine breadcrumbs. Gradually add water, mixing to a pliable dough.

2. Turn dough out on to lightly-floured surface; knead for 10 minutes, or until it is very smooth and elastic. Place into lightly oiled bowl, cover, stand in warm place for 60 minutes.

3. Roll dough out on lightly-floured surface until it is paper-thin. Cut into rounds, using a 10cm (4in) round cutter. Cover puris with cloth so that they do not dry out while you are waiting to fry them.

4. Place puris one at a time into deep hot oil. With slotted spoon or spatula, gently hold under hot oil until puri starts to puff. Then press puffed area lightly with slotted spoon so that the whole of the puri will puff. Fry until golden brown on both sides. Repeat with remaining puris.

DESSERTS

Strawberry Shortcake

THIS is probably the simplest, most delicious dessert you'll ever eat! And if you serve it as a special treat for afternoon tea, your reputation as a great cook will be firmly established!

YOU WILL NEED:
60g (2oz) butter
2 tablespoons sugar
2 egg-yolks
¾ cup plain flour
1 punnet strawberries
½ cup plum jam or strawberry jam
2 teaspoons water

1. Cream butter and sugar until light and fluffy, add egg-yolks, beat well. Work in sifted flour until well combined, knead dough on lightly floured board. Press dough into lightly greased 20cm (8in) sandwich tin, bake in moderate oven 15 to 20 minutes. Remove from tin, allow to cool slightly.

2. Reserve a few strawberries for decoration. Hull remaining strawberries, cut in halves, arrange over warm shortcake.

3. Combine jam and water, stir over low heat until boiling, push through sieve. Cool slightly, then brush generously over strawberries and shortcake. Refrigerate until set. Decorate with whipped cream and reserved strawberries; brush some of the jam glaze over strawberries for a pretty effect.

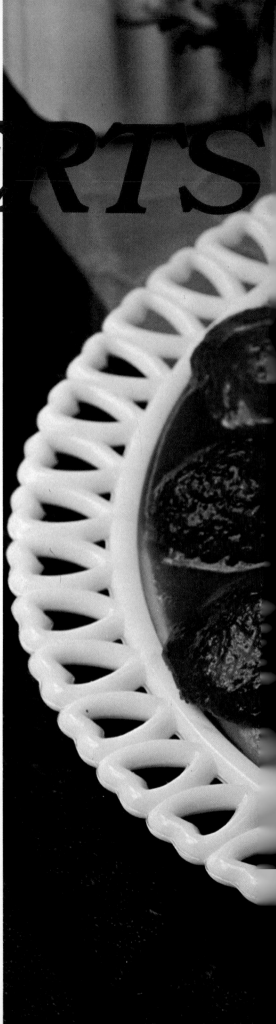

1. Sift flour, salt and icing sugar into basin; chop butter roughly, add to dry ingredients, rub in until mixture resembles coarse breadcrumbs. Add lemon juice and enough water to mix to firm dough. Refrigerate 30 minutes. Roll pastry on lightly floured surface to fit 23cm (9in) pie plate. Use rolling pin to lift pastry on to pie plate.

2. Trim and decorate edges. Prick base and sides of pastry with fork. Bake in moderately hot oven 10 to 15 minutes or until lightly browned. Allow to cool.

3. Combine sifted flours, lemon rind, lemon juice and sugar in saucepan. Add water, blend until smooth, stir over heat until mixture boils and thickens; this is important, the mixture must boil. Reduce heat, stir a further two minutes. Remove from heat, stir in butter and lightly beaten egg-yolks, stir until butter has melted; cool.

Lemon Meringue Pie

IT'S one of the world's most popular sweet pies, with a tangy filling topped by snowy meringue. Use a knife dipped in warm water to cut the pie — this ensures that the meringue cuts cleanly.

4. Spread cold lemon filling evenly into pastry case. Combine egg-whites, water and salt in small bowl of electric mixer. Beat on high speed until soft peaks form. Gradually add sugar, beat well until sugar has dissolved. Spoon on top of lemon filling, spreading meringue to edges of pie to seal; peak meringue decoratively with knife. Bake in moderate oven 5 to 10 minutes or until lightly browned. Cool, then refrigerate.

PASTRY
2 cups plain flour
pinch salt
1 tablespoon icing sugar
185g (6oz) butter
1 tablespoon lemon juice
1 to 2 tablespoons water

FILLING
4 tablespoons plain flour
4 tablespoons cornflour
2 teaspoons grated lemon rind
¾ cup lemon juice
1 cup sugar
1¼ cups water
90g (3oz) butter
4 egg-yolks

MERINGUE
4 egg-whites
2 tablespoons water
pinch salt
¾ cup castor sugar

1. Put water and butter in pan over low heat until butter is melted. Bring to boil; it is important the mixture boils. Then add sifted flour and salt all at once.

2. Stir until mixture forms a ball and leaves side of pan. Remove from heat immediately.

Cream Puffs

CHOUX pastry (pronounce it "shoo") is the basis of many delectable desserts. Cream Puffs such as these are among the most popular. Beautifully light, filled with whipped cream, who could resist them?

YOU WILL NEED:
1 cup water
75g (2½oz) butter
1 cup plain flour
pinch salt
4 eggs

3. Put mixture into small bowl of electric mixer. With wooden spoon spread mixture up sides of bowl to allow mixture to cool slightly, approx. 5 minutes.

4. Beat eggs in bowl until just combined. Beat choux pastry on lowest speed of electric mixture. Add eggs gradually, beating well after each addition. Mixture should be very thick, smooth and glossy. Drop rounded spoonfuls of mixture on to lightly greased baking trays, allowing room for spreading. Bake in hot oven 10 minutes. Reduce heat to moderate for a further 20 mins or until puffs are golden brown and firm to touch. Cooking time will depend on size of puffs. Allow approx. overall cooking time of 25 to 30 minutes for small puffs, approx. overall cooking time of 35 to 40 minutes for large puffs. When cooked, remove from oven, make a small slit in side of puffs for steam to escape; return to oven a few minutes to dry out. When cold, carefully cut puffs in half, remove any soft filling. Fill with whipped cream, sprinkle top with icing sugar.

How to Flambe Fruits

1. Put 60g (2oz) butter in flambe dish, stir until melted. Add ⅓ cup sugar. Put 5cm (2in) piece lemon rind on fork, stir sugar and butter until combined.

2. Stir sugar and butter until golden brown; watch carefully, mixture can burn at this stage.

FOR high drama at the dinner table, flambe (French for flamed) fruits take a lot of beating. They take only minutes to prepare and can be flamed sensationally right beside people at the table.

The purpose of flaming is to burn away the alcohol but keep the flavour. So the better the liquor, the better the flavour. A chafing dish is the ideal utensil for flambe foods. You can also use an electric frypan. Always pour the liquor into the hot pan from a small jug or glass, never from a bottle. If the open neck of a bottle is exposed over a dish that is flaming, there is the danger of the gases in the bottle igniting. If you have been over-generous with the alcohol and the flames rise too high, subdue them quickly by placing the lid on the pan in which the liquor is being heated. For this fruit flambe, strawberries, kiwi fruit and passionfruit are the fruits used. However, many other canned and fresh fruits are suitable. Other suggestions: pears with sliced bananas; pineapple and orange segments; canned apricots and passionfruit.

3. Add 2 tablespoons lemon juice and ½ cup orange juice. With the addition of this cold liquid, sugar in pan will turn to toffee, keep stirring until toffee dissolves. Bring to boil, boil until reduced by half.

4. Add 1 tablespoon brandy and 2 tablespoons Grand Marnier; heat gently 1 minute, do not stir. Set aflame, stir until flames die down. Boil 1 minute.

5. Add 2 punnets washed, hulled strawberries, 3 peeled, sliced kiwi fruit, pulp of 3 passionfruit. Stir until just heated through. Serves 4 to 6.

Chocolate Mousse

RICH, creamy, easy to make! This popular dessert can be made a day ahead — serves four.

YOU WILL NEED:
125g (4oz) dark chocolate
1 tablespoon brandy
4 eggs, separated
1 cup cream

1. Chop chocolate roughly, put into top of double saucepan; stir over hot water until melted. Remove from heat, cool slightly, gradually add brandy and egg yolks. Beat until mixture is smooth and thick.

2. Whip cream. Do not over-whip, or the cream will be difficult to fold in; cream should be just nicely thickened. Fold into the chocolate mixture.

3. Beat egg whites until soft peaks form. Here again, do not over-beat the whites or they will not fold so easily into the chocolate mixture.

4. Fold half the egg whites into chocolate mixture, then fold in the remaining half. (It's much easier to incorporate egg whites when you fold them into the mixture in two portions than if you add them all at once.) Spoon mixture into four individual dishes or one large dish. Refrigerate until firm. To serve, top with whipped cream and grated chocolate. (Use a vegetable peeler to grate chocolate; it gives nice, chunky pieces.)

Brandy Snaps

1. Place syrup, butter and brown sugar into saucepan, stir over low heat until butter has melted; remove from heat. Add sifted flour, ginger and salt, mix together well.

2. If you want small brandy snaps, drop teaspoonfuls of mixture on to lightly greased oven tray; for larger brandy snaps, make it heaped teaspoonfuls. Three brandy snaps will fit comfortably on to one tray; allow room for spreading. For easy handling, bake only three at a time.

YOU can make these in minutes from simple, economical ingredients — and the result is superb! Make them for dessert, or for sweet at-any-time eating. The recipe makes about eight depending on size.

YOU WILL NEED:
3 tablespoons golden syrup
90g (3oz) butter
⅓ cup brown sugar, lightly packed
½ cup plain flour
2 teaspoons ground ginger
pinch salt

3. Bake in moderate oven 5 minutes or until golden brown. Remove from oven, allow to cool on trays 1 minute. With knife, lift brandy snap from tray.

4. Roll immediately around the handle of a wooden spoon. Allow to firm and cool on spoon handle.

5. Spoon or pipe whipped cream into hollow at each end of brandy snap.

Apple Strudel

EVERYONE adores this dessert with its light, flaky pastry enclosing a filling of apples, sultanas and buttered crumbs. Cut into slices, serve with cream.

PASTRY
1½ cups plain flour
1 egg
1 tablespoon oil
⅓ cup warm water, approximately
125g (4oz) butter
60g (2oz) butter, extra

FILLING
4 large apples
½ cup castor sugar
1 teaspoon vanilla
30g (1oz) butter
¼ teaspoon nutmeg
1 teaspoon cinnamon
1 cup white breadcrumbs
1 teaspoon grated lemon rind
¾ cup sultanas
½ cup brown sugar, lightly packed

Peel, core and slice apples thinly (potato peeler will give very thin slices of apple, which are ideal). Place apple slices into bowl with sugar and vanilla; mix well. Cover bowl, and allow to stand for one hour. Melt 30g butter in pan, add breadcrumbs, stir over low heat until breadcrumbs are golden brown; cool. Mix breadcrumbs and brown sugar together. Drain off excess liquid from apples. Combine apples, nutmeg, cinnamon, lemon rind and sultanas in bowl; mix lightly.

about 100 times. Knead again for 5 minutes. The more the dough is banged down and kneaded, the lighter it will be. Form dough into ball and place into lightly oiled bowl, cover and stand in warm place for 45 minutes. Cover large table with clean cloth, rub flour over surface. Roll out dough as far as it goes.

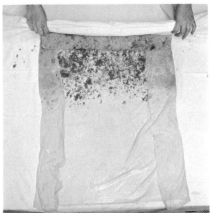

1. Sift flour into bowl, make a well in centre of dry ingredients, add egg and oil. Gradually add water, mixing to a soft dough with hands. Turn out on to lightly floured surface; knead into a ball. Now pick up dough, and throw down on lightly floured surface; do this

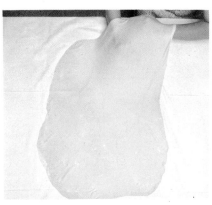

2. Flour hands, slip them under dough, then start pulling dough from centre with back of hands, rather than fingers; do this gently and carefully. Continue stretching dough until it is paper-thin and approximately 87cm (36in) square. Brush with 125g melted butter.

3. Sprinkle combined breadcrumbs and brown sugar over half the pastry. Spoon prepared apple mixture along one end of pastry about 5cm (2in) in. Fold in sides of pastry to edge of apple filling. Gather cloth in hands and carefully roll up apple strudel, pulling cloth to you as you roll. Place on large greased tray, curving gently and carefully into horseshoe shape. Brush with 60g extra melted butter. Bake in moderately hot oven 35 to 40 minutes. When cold, dust with sifted icing sugar. Serves 6.

1. Make filling: cream butter and sugar until light and fluffy. Beat egg-yolks into creamed mixture, add ground almonds and almond essence. Very gradually beat in half a cup of milk. Beat egg-whites until soft peaks form; fold half into creamed mixture, then fold in remaining half.

2. Combine rum and extra half cup of milk. Arrange 6 biscuits lengthwise in 2 rows (3 biscuits to a row) beside one another on sheet of aluminium foil or greaseproof paper. Brush liberally with rum-milk mixture.

3. Spread one-third of cream filling evenly over biscuits. Top with another layer of biscuits. Brush biscuits generously with rum-milk mixture as before. Continue with filling, biscuits and brushing, ending with a row of biscuits. Wrap in aluminium foil. Refrigerate several hours or overnight.

92

Biscotten Torte

AN easy, make-ahead dessert for six to eight people, Biscotten Torte (Biscuit Cake) is a luscious ending for a dinner or lunch party. Layers of biscuits are brushed with a rum-milk mixture and sandwiched together with a delicious almond cream.

4. Several hours before serving, arrange Torte on serving plate. Cover and decorate with whipped cream. Sprinkle top with grated chocolate or toasted flaked almonds. Refrigerate again. Cut in slices.

YOU WILL NEED:
375g (12oz) or 24 plain sweet biscuits
125g (4oz) butter
½ cup castor sugar
2 eggs, separated
125g (4oz) ground almonds
few drops almond essence
½ cup milk
½ cup milk, extra
1½ tablespoons rum
1½ cups cream
grated chocolate

Baked Rice Custard

EVERYONE will ask for "lovely rice pudding for dinner again" after you make this simple dessert. The recipe will serve four.

YOU WILL NEED:
2 tablespoons short-grain rice
2 cups water
pinch salt
3 eggs
⅓ cup sugar
1 teaspoon vanilla
2½ cups milk
¼ cup sultanas

1. Bring water and salt to the boil. Gradually add rice. Boil rapidly uncovered 10 minutes; drain well. Beat eggs, sugar and vanilla together, add rice and sultanas. Add milk gradually, stir to combine.

2. Pour into ovenproof dish. Stand in baking dish with enough water to come halfway up sides of dish. Bake in moderate oven 35 minutes.

3. Now slip a long fork under the skin that has formed on top, stir gently to distribute rice evenly. Reduce heat to moderately slow. Bake further 15 minutes, then stir with fork again. Cook further 15 to 20 minutes, or until set.

Sweet Souffles

1. Melt butter in top of double saucepan over simmering water, remove from heat, stir in sifted flour; continue stirring until mixture is smooth and free of lumps. Stir in milk and orange juice, stir until mixture is smooth.

2. Return to heat, stir over simmering water until smooth and thick. Remove from heat, stir in sugar and Grand Marnier while still hot; cool slightly. Scrape mixture into large bowl. Beat egg-yolks until fluffy, gradually stir into sauce.

3. Using clean bowl and beaters, beat egg-whites until short, moist peaks form. Don't overbeat or finished souffle will be dry.
4. With metal spoon, lightly fold half egg-whites into sauce, then fold in remaining egg-whites. Adding whites in two parts makes it easier to fold them in lightly yet thoroughly so air beaten in is not released, and there will be no white streaks.
5. Pour souffle mixture over back of metal spoon (this helps keep air in mixture) into four greased individual souffle dishes. Fill dishes to within 1cm (½in) of top. Bake on oven tray in moderate oven 25 to 30 minutes.

SOUFFLES are airy concoctions, easy to prepare from homely, basic ingredients. A souffle is simply a white sauce into which flavourings, egg-yolks, then softly beaten egg-whites are folded. It is baked to soft and shimmering perfection for a dessert that your guests will love.

LIQUEUR SOUFFLE:
4 eggs, separated
90g (3oz) butter
3 tablespoons plain flour
½ cup milk
½ cup orange juice
¼ cup sugar
¼ cup Grand Marnier or Cointreau

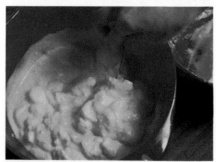

The finished souffle. Serve it at once with a bowl of whipped cream.

CHOCOLATE SOUFFLE:
Substitute 1 cup milk for the ½ cup milk and ½ cup orange juice in original recipe; sift 1 tablespoon cocoa with the flour. Stir in 125g (4oz) grated dark chocolate to the hot sauce, before adding egg-yolks and egg-whites; stir until chocolate has melted. Grand Marnier can be omitted.

STRAWBERRY SOUFFLE:
Omit orange juice from original recipe. Add 1 punnet of washed, hulled and mashed strawberries to the hot sauce, before adding egg-yolks and egg-whites.

Rum-Caramel Pineapple

THERE'S nothing quite as good as fresh fruit to end a barbecue meal. Here it is presented in a different, delicious way.
Guests spear a piece, dip it in rum, roll it in brown sugar, then they hold it over a flame until the sugar caramelizes. For the final mouth-watering touch, dip in whipped cream.

1. Choose a ripe pineapple, cut into four pieces, cutting carefully through the green top. The number of pineapples needed will depend on the number of guests.

2. Cut pineapple down into wedges inside each quarter, then run a knife along base of pineapple, under wedges, releasing them from the outside shell.

3. Take another pineapple, cut off top about quarter-way down. Use sharp knife to hollow out inside of pineapple to take a small metal bowl. (The hollowed-out pineapple pieces can be reserved and used to replenish the pineapple quarters as they empty.) Place metal bowl in centre.

4. Place hollowed-out pineapple in centre of large heatproof dish (a wooden platter is good). Arrange pineapple quarters decoratively around. (Any other fresh fruit can be added for colour — strawberries, mangoes, papaw, grapes, etc.) Arrange small bowls of rum or brandy, brown sugar and whipped cream round dish. Have a small fork and plate for each guest. When ready to serve the dessert, three-quarters fill metal bowl with methylated spirits and set aflame. If serving strawberries with the pineapple, let them soak in rum for 10 minutes; serve small bowls of rum-soaked strawberries with pineapple. One pineapple is enough for 4 people.

1. Put egg-yolks and sugar in top of double saucepan. Beat for a few minutes off heat with a rotary beater or an electric mixer until these ingredients are well combined.

2. Put mixture over simmering water; to prevent overheating, water in the bottom saucepan should not touch top saucepan. Add half marsala and half white wine, beat well; add remaining marsala and wine. (Note: Wines should be at room temperature — not chilled — when added to saucepan.)

3. Beat constantly, about 10 minutes until of thick, creamy consistency. If mixture begins to adhere to sides of saucepan, quickly remove from heat, stir vigorously with wooden spoon, especially round base. Pour into four individual glass dishes.

Zabaglione

THIS deliciously rich, foamy Italian custard can be served as a dessert by itself, with sponge finger biscuits as an accompaniment. Or it can be used as a delightful topping for fresh fruit. Strawberries, mangoes or stewed plums are ideal for serving in this way. For Zabaglione Ice-cream, make the mixture as shown, let cool, then fold in half a cup of whipped cream. Pour into freezer tray, freeze, stirring occasionally, until lightly chilled but still creamy. Quantities given here will serve four.

YOU WILL NEED:
5 egg-yolks
¼ cup sugar
½ cup marsala
¼ cup sweet or dry white wine

1. With sharp serrated knife, cut skin and white pith from oranges. Cut deep enough to allow orange flesh to show. Cut in a sawing motion around orange, as in picture.

2. Cut oranges into segments between the membranes; do this over a bowl, so that no juice is lost. Squeeze remaining portion of orange over bowl to extract remaining juice.

3. Place sugar and water into pan, stir over low heat until sugar is dissolved. Bring to boil, boil uncovered for 2 minutes. Allow to cool, then add brandy and Grand Marnier; mix well. Pour over orange segments.

Brandied Oranges

BRANDIED Oranges are an easy and elegant dessert. Make them hours, or even a day before, so the syrup flavour is absorbed.
Some people like to serve them at room temperature, thinking they have more flavour; others like to refrigerate them and serve them chilled. Top with cream or ice-cream. The recipe given here serves four.

YOU WILL NEED:
8 oranges
1½ cups sugar
1 cup water
¼ cup brandy
2 tablespoons Grand Marnier or Cointreau

Almond Peachy Pie

THE combination of flavours is delicious, and the toasted crumb topping prettily finishes off this peaches-and-cream dessert pie. It's the perfect completion to a special dinner.

ALMOND CRUST
185g (6oz) blanched almonds
1 cup coconut
¼ cup sugar
60g (2oz) butter

FILLING
1 cup sour cream

pinch salt
¾ cup icing sugar
1 teaspoon orange juice
1 teaspoon grated orange rind
1 teaspoon vanilla
822g can sliced peaches
¾ cup cream

1. Chop almonds finely or blend in electric blender. Stir in coconut and sugar. Rub butter into mixture. Reserve 3 tablespoons of crumb mixture for topping. Press remaining crumbs on to base and sides of greased 23cm (9in) flan tin. Bake in moderately hot oven 12-15 minutes or until golden brown, cool. Place reserved crumbs into small pan, stir over low heat until golden, approximately 4 minutes.

2. Combine sour cream, salt, ½ cup sifted icing sugar, orange juice, orange rind and vanilla. Pour into prepared pie shell. Arrange well-drained peach slices decoratively over top of filling.

3. Lightly whip cream and remaining sifted icing sugar. Spoon or pipe around edge of pie. Sprinkle with the toasted crumbs. Refrigerate before serving. Serves 6.

Crepes Suzette

An international favourite — and nothing could be simpler: it's just thin pancakes, heated in a rich orange sauce, then flamed with liqueur. If you wish, the flaming can be omitted and liqueur added to the sauce with the fruit juices. It's a nice do-ahead dessert, simply heat the crepes in the sauce just before serving.

PANCAKES
¾ cup plain flour
pinch salt
3 eggs
2 tablespoons oil
¾ cup milk

SAUCE
125g (4oz) butter
½ cup sugar
1½ cups orange juice
2 tablespoons lemon juice
½ cup Grand Marnier

1. Sift flour and salt into bowl, make well in centre, add whole eggs and oil; work flour in from sides, add milk a little at a time, beating until smooth. Stand 1 hour. Heat pan, grease lightly. From small jug pour 2 to 3 tablespoons of batter into pan, turn so batter coats pan evenly. Cook slowly, loosening edges with knife, until set and lightly browned underneath. Toss or turn, brown other side. Repeat with remaining batter.

2. Melt butter in pan, add sugar. Cook over low heat until sugar melts and begins to caramelize. Pour in fruit juices, stir over high heat until liquid reduces slightly and the caramelized sugar dissolves.

3. Reduce heat, add one pancake at a time to pan; swirl it around in the sauce. Then, using fork and spoon, fold pancake in half, then in half again. Repeat with remaining pancakes, adding them to pan. Allow pancakes to soak up sauce, turning them once. Pour Grand Marnier over; when warm, set aflame. Arrange pancakes on warmed plates, spoon hot sauce over.
Serves 4 to 6.

CAKES
Lamingtons

L<small>IFE</small> just wouldn't be the same without Lamingtons. Take a look at this picture then follow our recipe for the same good results.

SPONGE CAKE

3 eggs
½ cup castor sugar
¾ cup self-raising flour
¼ cup cornflour
15g (½oz) butter
3 tablespoons hot water

Sponge Cake:

Beat eggs until light. Gradually add sugar, continue beating until mixture is thick and sugar completely dissolved. Sift dry ingredients several times. Melt butter in hot water. Sift dry ingredients over egg mixture, fold in lightly; then, working quickly, fold in hot-water-and-butter. Pour into lightly greased 18cm x 28cm (7in x 11in) lamington tin. Bake in moderate oven approx. 30 minutes.

CHOCOLATE ICING

500g (1lb) icing sugar
⅓ cup cocoa
15g (½oz) butter
½ cup milk

Chocolate Icing:

Sift icing sugar and cocoa into heatproof basin, or into top half of double saucepan. Add softened butter and milk, stir with a wooden spoon to mix thoroughly. Stand over hot water, stir constantly until icing is of good coating consistency.

1. Make cake the day before cutting and icing. Thinly trim brown top and sides from cake. Cut cake into 16 even pieces.

2. Hold each cake on a fork (a two-pronged fork is best, it is less likely to break cake). Dip each cake into icing; hold over bowl a few minutes to drain off excess chocolate. If icing becomes too thick too quickly, stand it over hot water while dipping. If still too thick, add a little warmed milk or water.

3. Put cakes individually into a bowl of coconut — you'll need about 375g (12oz) coconut. Sprinkle coconut over evenly, or gently toss in the coconut. Stand on wire rack until completely dry.

1. Put eggs into small bowl of electric mixer, beat on medium to high speed until mixture is thick and creamy. Mixture will rise almost to the top of the bowl; beating time is 5 to 8 minutes. Gradually beat in sugar, beat until sugar is dissolved.

2. Sift dry ingredients several times so that all ingredients are thoroughly combined; with spatula or metal spoon, gently fold dry ingredients into egg yolk mixture. Do this lightly and quickly, so that the airy sponge mixture is not broken down, but make sure that all flour is mixed in.

3. Pour mixture evenly into two well-greased deep 20cm (8in) round cake tins. (Some champion sponge makers weigh the tins after pouring in the mixture, to make sure both tins have an equal amount).

Sponge Cake

AUSTRALIA'S most popular cake is undoubtedly the light-as-a-feather Sponge Cake, filled with cream. The top can be dusted with sifted icing sugar, or spread with passionfruit icing. Here's how to make a perfect cake every time.

YOU WILL NEED:
4 eggs
¾ cup castor sugar
⅔ cup plain flour
⅓ cup cornflour
1 teaspoon baking powder
1 cup cream
2 tablespoons passionfruit pulp (approx. 2 passionfruit)

PASSIONFRUIT ICING
1 cup icing sugar
1 teaspoon butter
2 tablespoons passionfruit pulp (approx. 2 passionfruit)
Passionfruit Icing:
Sift icing sugar into bowl, add butter and enough passionfruit pulp to mix to a stiff paste. Put bowl over simmering water, stir 1 minute or until a thin consistency, remove from heat, spread over top of cake, allow to set.

4. Bake in moderate oven 20 to 25 minutes; cake is cooked when it shrinks slightly from side of tin, as shown in picture, or when top, pressed with fingertips, springs back lightly and fingertips leave no impression. Cover a wire rack with a clean teatowel, turn cakes out of tins immediately they are cooked. Carefully invert so that tops of cakes are uppermost. When cakes are completely cold, spread one cake with whipped cream, top with passionfruit pulp. Put the second cake on top, ice with passionfruit icing.

1. Place egg-yolks in small bowl of electric mixer. Add castor sugar, beat on high speed until mixture is very thick and creamy, approximately 4 minutes.

2. Place chopped chocolate and water in top of double saucepan, stir over low heat until chocolate is just melted. Remove from heat, allow to cool slightly. Gently fold chocolate mixture into egg-yolk mixture, making sure that all chocolate is evenly distributed through egg-yolk mixture.

3. Place egg-whites into clean small bowl of electric mixer. Make sure that beaters are clean and dry. Beat egg-whites on high speed until firm (but not stiff) peaks form. Gently fold into chocolate mixture, making sure mixture is of a smooth consistency. Pour into 30cm x 25cm (12in x 10in) swiss roll tin which has been greased and had base lined with greased greaseproof paper. Bake in moderate oven for 17 minutes.
4. Remove from oven, cover cake in tin with two layers of paper towelling which have been rinsed in cold water, then wrung out. Place a clean teatowel over paper. Refrigerate 20 minutes.

Chocolate Roll

IT'S so light, so lovely — with a coffee-cream filling — this delicious dessert cake will just melt in the mouth. Note the ingredients — this cake contains no flour.

YOU WILL NEED:
4 large eggs, separated
1 cup castor sugar
125g (4oz) dark chocolate
2 tablespoons water
1 cup cream
1 teaspoon instant coffee powder
2 teaspoons sugar
¼ teaspoon vanilla
cocoa

5. Place cream, coffee, sugar and vanilla into bowl, stir until just combined. Cover bowl and put into refrigerator for 20 minutes. Remove teatowel and paper towels carefully from cake. Dust top with sifted cocoa. Carefully tip out on to large sheet of greaseproof paper. Remove lining paper. Remove cream from refrigerator, beat until firm peaks form. Spread cake with cream mixture. Hold greaseproof paper in hands, and roll up as shown in picture. Slide a flat tray under roll and refrigerate for 2 hours, before placing on to serving plate. Dust the top lightly with sifted cocoa.

BISCUITS

Italian Crostoli

ALTHOUGH they are eaten all over Italy, Crostoli are specially popular in the North. They are not too sweet and are great to serve with coffee after dinner. They will store well in an air-tight container and make an attractive small gift. The ingredients given below will make approximately 50 Crostoli.

YOU WILL NEED:
30g (1oz) butter
1 tablespoon sugar
1 egg
2 teaspoons grated lemon rind
1½ cups plain flour
1½ cups self raising flour
¾ cup milk
1 tablespoon brandy
oil for deep-frying

1. Sift flours into bowl. Combine cooled, melted butter, sugar, beaten egg and lemon rind, add to flour mixture with milk and brandy, mix to a firm dough.

2. Turn dough out on to lightly floured surface, knead into a smooth ball.

3. Cut pastry in half, roll each half out thinly, cut into strips 2cm (¾in) wide x 5cm (2in) long with knife or fluted pastry wheel. Cut 1cm (½in) slit down centre of each strip. Strips can be left plain or twisted to resemble a bow. Deep-fry in hot oil until golden brown on each side; drain well. Sift castor sugar or icing sugar over each biscuit.

1. Warm golden syrup first. Measure into a small heatproof jug (remember spoon measurements are level), stand jug in a heatproof dish or saucepan of hot water until syrup warms and softens. Cream butter and sugar until creamy, add egg-yolk, beat well. Gradually add sifted dry ingredients and warm syrup, mix well.

2. Knead mixture lightly, roll out to 3mm (⅛in) thickness on lightly floured board.

3. Cut out gingerbread man shape from cardboard, to use as guide, or buy specially shaped cutter. Cut out biscuits, lift carefully on to lightly greased oven trays. Trimmings can be used for hats as shown in picture. Press in currants for eyes, glace cherry pieces for nose. Bake in moderate oven 15 minutes; cool on trays. When cold, decorate biscuits with coloured sweets for mouth and buttons secured with a little jam, or make Royal Icing, fill it into a small plastic bag and snip off the corner so that it makes a piping bag. Pipe mouth and features on to Gingerbread Men with the Royal Icing.

Gingerbread Men

THESE Gingerbread Men are so simple the children can make them. Or, if they're very young, they can help you cut them out.

The mixture is fairly thin when rolled out and you may have to help a bit lifting the biscuits, with spatula or broad knife, on to oven trays. The special gingerbread man cutter is available at most hardware or kitchenware stores. Depending on the size of the cutter you use, the recipe below makes approximately 20 Gingerbread Men.

YOU WILL NEED:
125g (4oz) butter
½ cup sugar
1 egg-yolk
2 cups plain flour
1 teaspoon bicarbonate of soda
3 teaspoons ground ginger
2½ tablespoons golden syrup
currants
glace cherries
assorted sweets

ROYAL ICING
1¼ to 1½ cups pure icing sugar
1 egg-white
2 to 4 drops lemon juice

Sift icing sugar. Beat egg-white lightly in a small bowl, using a wooden spoon. Add icing sugar one tablespoon-ful at a time, beating well after each addition. When icing reaches desired consistency, beat in lemon juice. Amount of icing sugar required depends on size of egg-white.

1. Cover oven trays with aluminium foil. Mark 5cm (2in) circles on foil, using a scone cutter as a guide. Grease foil lightly with oil. Place almonds on separate tray, place into moderate oven for 5 minutes or until golden brown. Place sugar, water and butter into pan, stir over low heat until sugar has dissolved and butter has melted. Bring to boil, boil uncovered for 8 minutes or until mixture is dark golden brown.

2. Remove from heat immediately, add almonds all at once, stir only to combine. Do not over-stir or mixture will turn sugary.

Toffee Crisps

YOU WILL NEED:
90g (3oz) butter
1 cup castor sugar
½ cup water
185g (6oz) flaked almonds
125g (4oz) dark chocolate

EVERYONE will want the recipe for these superb biscuits — and nobody would dream they are so easy to make.

Toffee Crisps are little biscuits which, with their delicious combination of nuts, toffee and dark chocolate, need no baking. You'll find they are perfect with after-dinner coffee, and they would make a delightful gift-from-the-kitchen for birthdays or Christmas. Quantities here make approximately 18.

3. Working quickly, place tablespoonfuls of mixture on to circles, pressing out to edge of circle with back of spoon. If mixture becomes too thick, return to heat for a few seconds.

4. Place chopped chocolate in top of double saucepan, stir over simmering water until chocolate has melted; allow to cool slightly. Turn biscuits over on to flat side. Spoon a teaspoonful of chocolate on to flat side and spread out to edge. When chocolate is almost set, run a fork through the chocolate to give wavy effect.

Shortbread

MELT-in-the-mouth Shortbread is one of the easiest of recipes — and what could be more delicious when you have friends for morning coffee?

YOU WILL NEED:
250g (8oz) butter
1 teaspoon vanilla
⅓ cup castor sugar
2¼ cups plain flour
¼ cup ground rice

1. Cream butter and vanilla until light and fluffy, gradually beat in sugar, beat until very creamy.

2. Work in sifted dry ingredients. Knead well on lightly floured surface until mixture is smooth.

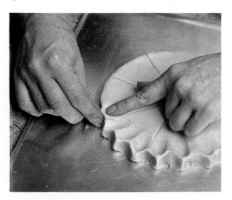

3. Press into lightly greased 18cm x 28cm (7in x 11in) lamington tin, cut into bars, prick each bar decoratively with fork. Bake in slow oven 50 to 60 minutes. Or divide mixture in two, roll each portion out to form 18cm (7in) circle, put on greased oven tray, mark into 8 wedges, pinch edges decoratively. Bake in slow oven approx. 45 minutes.

Monte Carlos

THEY'RE an old-fashioned, favourite biscuit — with a filling of jam and vanilla cream. The recipe makes about 25 biscuits.

YOU WILL NEED:
185g (6oz) butter
½ cup sugar
1 egg
1 teaspoon vanilla
1¼ cups self-raising flour
¾ cup plain flour
½ cup coconut
FILLING
60g (2oz) butter
¾ cup icing sugar
½ teaspoon vanilla
2 teaspoons milk
raspberry jam
Filling:
Cream butter and sifted icing sugar until light and fluffy, add vanilla, gradually add milk, beat well.

1. Cream butter and sugar until light and fluffy, add egg and vanilla, beat well. Add sifted dry ingredients and coconut, mix well.

2. Roll teaspoonfuls of mixture into balls. Put on lightly greased oven trays, gently press down with fork and rough up surface with back of fork. Bake in moderate oven 10 to 15 minutes or until golden brown. Remove from oven, cool on wire rack.

3. Put teaspoon of jam and teaspoon of prepared cream in centre of half the biscuits. Top with remaining halves, press together lightly.

CONFECTIONERY

Butterscotch

LOVELY buttery Butterscotch — it's one of the most popular of the old-fashioned sweets. For best results a sweets thermometer (obtainable from most large stores) should be used.

YOU WILL NEED:
2 cups sugar
⅓ cup water
⅔ cup liquid glucose
125g (4oz) butter
1 teaspoon lemon essence
½ teaspoon salt

1. Combine sugar, water and glucose in heavy saucepan, stir over low heat until sugar is dissolved, brushing down sides of saucepan frequently with wet brush. Bring to boil, reduce heat until very low (mixture will still bubble), boil to 300 deg F (150 deg C) on sweets thermometer (this will take approximately 17 to 20 minutes).

2. Mixture will be light golden brown. Remove from heat, add chopped butter and remaining ingredients, stir until well blended.

3. Pour into lightly greased 18cm x 28cm (7in x 11in) lamington tin. Mark into squares while still hot. When cold, break into pieces.

CONFECTIONERY

THIS is popular in the Middle East — as the name indicates — but almost all countries now appreciate the flavour of this lightly chewy, jellied sweet. Tartaric acid, an ingredient, is available at grocers and super-markets; rosewater at pharmacies.

YOU WILL NEED:
2 cups sugar
3 cups water
¼ teaspoon tartaric acid
¾ cup cornflour
1¾ cups icing sugar
4 drops rosewater
few drops pink food colouring

1. Put sugar and ½ cup of the water in saucepan, stir over low heat until sugar has dissolved, brushing down sides of saucepan frequently. Bring to boil, reduce heat, simmer until syrup reaches temperature of 240 deg F (115 deg C) on sweets thermometer (approximately 20 minutes). Add tartaric acid, remove from heat.

Turkish Delight

2. Combine cornflour and sifted icing sugar in bowl, add another ½ cup of the water, stir until smooth. Bring remaining water to the boil, add to cornflour mixture, stirring continually. Put into saucepan, stir over medium heat until mixture boils and thickens, add hot syrup gradually, mixing over the heat until well blended.

3. Continue to boil gently 30 minutes, without stirring. It is important to boil the mixture for this precise length of time for correct incorporation of ingredients. The mixture should be a very pale straw colour and transparent.

4. Add the rosewater and pink food colouring. Pour into greased deep 20cm (8in) square tin. Stand several hours or overnight until set. Cut into squares with wetted knife. Toss the squares in combined sifted icing sugar and cornflour (you will need about 1 cup of each). Store in air-tight container, sprinkle with a little extra combined cornflour and icing sugar.

Note: Creme de Menthe Turkish Delight is a delicious variation. Substitute 2 drops of oil of peppermint (available at pharmacies) and 1 tablespoon of creme de menthe for the rosewater and pink food colouring mentioned in the recipe.

FOLLOW these instructions for the best toffees at the fete. The recipe makes 12 toffees.

YOU WILL NEED:
3 cups sugar
1 cup water
¼ cup brown vinegar

Toffees

3. When toffee is ready, remove from heat, stand saucepan in cold water 1 minute. Remove pan from water, and allow all the bubbles to subside.

1. Place sugar, water and vinegar into saucepan, stir over low heat until sugar has dissolved; brush down sides of saucepan with brush dipped in hot water to remove any sugar from sides of pan.

2. Increase heat, boil rapidly uncovered for approximately 15 minutes or until a small amount, when dropped into cold water, will "crack." This gives a good, hard toffee. (If you prefer the "stick-jaw" or more stretchy toffee, boil for 10 to 12 minutes only or until a small amount, when dropped into cold water, forms a soft ball between the fingers.) Remove pan from heat while testing.

4. For easier handling pour toffee into heatproof jug. Then, pour into paper patty cases. (To keep good shape while toffees set, stand the paper cases in patty cake tins, as shown.) Leave 2 minutes before decorating with coconut or hundreds-and-thousands.

1. Put sugar, liquid glucose, honey, salt and water in pan, stir over low heat until sugar has dissolved. Bring to boil, cook until mixture forms a hard ball when tested in a small amount of water (252 deg F — 122 deg C — on sweets thermometer), approx. 8 minutes.

2. Beat egg-whites until firm peaks form. Pour one quarter of hot syrup in thin stream over egg-whites, beating constantly.

3. Continue beating until mixture is thick enough to hold its shape, approx. 3 to 5 minutes; picture shows consistency of egg-white mixture. Cook remaining syrup until a small amount of syrup forms brittle threads when dropped in cold water (315 deg F — 157 deg C — on sweets thermometer), approx. 5 minutes. Pour remainder of hot syrup over meringue in a thin stream, beating constantly until mixture is very thick.

Italian Nougat

As with most confectionery, use of a sweets thermometer takes the guesswork out of cooking times and temperatures when you are making nougat. However, we have given approximate cooking times too.

If you wish, you can fold in 125g (4oz) Turkish Delight, the kind you buy at the confectionery counter, when you are stirring in the almonds. It will give the pretty pink squares shown in the picture above. The quantities given in this recipe make approx. 1kg (2lb) of Italian Nougat.

YOU WILL NEED:
2 cups sugar
1 cup liquid glucose
½ cup honey
¼ teaspoon salt
¼ cup water
2 egg-whites
1 teaspoon vanilla
125g (4oz) butter
60g (2oz) whole blanched almonds

4. Add vanilla and roughly chopped butter. Beat until thick again, about 5 minutes. With wooden spoon, stir in toasted almonds. Turn mixture into greased 28cm x 18cm (11in x 7in) lamington tin, smooth top with spatula. Refrigerate until firm. Loosen edges of nougat all round, turn out in large block. With sharp knife, cut into 4cm x 2.5cm (1½ x 1in) pieces. Wrap each piece individually in cellulose paper or waxed paper. Store in refrigerator.

To Toast Almonds:
Put on oven tray, bake in moderate oven approx. 5 minutes until golden; cool.

1. Pour mixture into large bowl of electric mixer, add vanilla and lemon juice. Beat on high speed until very thick and white. Pour into two deep 20cm (8in) square cake tins which have been rinsed out with cold water. Refrigerate until set.

2. Put coconut in heavy pan. Stir with wooden spoon over moderate heat until coconut is light golden brown. Remove from pan immediately or coconut will continue to cook in heat of pan.

3. Cut marshmallow into squares with wet knife while still in the tin. Lift out with small spatula, toss in toasted coconut. Keep refrigerated.

Toasted Marshmallows

WHAT'S white, fluffy and covered in a golden drift of nutty-flavoured toasted coconut? Just the best marshmallows you've ever had the pleasure of eating, that's all! Following this step-by-step recipe, you could make them for sweet eating at home, or even bake a batch for the sweet stall at the local fete.

YOU WILL NEED:
4 tablespoons gelatine
1 cup cold water
4 cups sugar
2 cups boiling water
2 teaspoons vanilla
2 teaspoons lemon juice
250g (8oz) coconut

Sprinkle gelatine over cold water. Put sugar and boiling water into large saucepan, stir over low heat until sugar is dissolved, bring to boil. Stir in gelatine mixture. Boil steadily, uncovered, 20 minutes. Allow to cool to lukewarm.

CONFECTIONERY

APPLES-on-a-stick bring back in an instant all the fetes, fairs and shows you ever went to — and they're still a favourite. There are a few tricks to know when you make them, as explained here.

YOU WILL NEED:
10 green apples
10 butcher's skewers
4 cups sugar
1 cup water
⅓ cup liquid glucose
½ teaspoon red food colouring

Toffee Apples

1. Granny Smith apples give best results. Push butcher's skewers three-quarters way into apples at stem end. Put apples under cold running water, stand on rack until completely dry (do not rub apples with cloth).

2. Put sugar, water, glucose and food colouring into large saucepan. Stir over low heat until sugar has dissolved. Bring to boil; boil, uncovered, until small bubbles appear over the surface, then test by spooning a few drops into cold water. If ready to use, the toffee will snap and crackle when it touches the water, and harden immediately. Remove from heat.

3. Stand saucepan in a basin or sink of cold water 1 minute, to cool toffee quickly, so that bubbles subside. Remove from water; make sure there are no bubbles left in toffee before dipping apples.

4. Hold pan on side so that there is a deep pool of toffee in side of pan. Slowly dip apple into toffee, twist slowly to coat apple completely; remove apple slowly. Air-bubbles will form in toffee if apples are dipped quickly. Twirl apple round a few times before placing on greased oven tray. Repeat with remaining apples. Toffee apples are best eaten the day they are made. However, they will keep one day if, when toffee is set, they are wrapped in squares of plastic food wrap. Twist food wrap round apples at top to keep air-tight, refrigerate overnight.

Candy Popcorn

IT seems that Popcorn is a part of most people's childhood, and it's just as popular with children today. It is easy to make, and it is a great success for children's parties. Small baskets of brightly coloured popcorn are an attractive decoration for the birthday table; small packages make gifts for each young guest.

You start with a packet of popping corn. This is usually available in two sizes, 227g (around 8oz) and 454g (around 1lb). One large packet should provide enough popcorn for about eight children.

YOU WILL NEED:
½ cup unpopped popcorn
2 tablespoons oil
2 cups sugar
1 cup water
½ teaspoon food colouring

3. Put sugar, water and food colouring in very large pan, stir over low heat until sugar dissolves. Bring to boil; boil, uncovered, until small amount of toffee "cracks" when tested in cold water. Remove from heat.

4. Add popcorn to toffee. Stir constantly until toffee crystallizes and coats popcorn. Turn on to large tray to cool. Store in airtight plastic bag. For popcorn of varying colours, repeat the four steps, using a different food colouring each time.

1. Heat oil in large saucepan until very hot. Add corn, cover pan.

2. Shake pan constantly over medium heat until popping ceases. Remove from heat, turn popcorn out of pan to cool.

117

1. Put 2kg (4lb) flour into large baking dish. Spread flour out evenly. Press a large egg half way down into flour. Do this at 5cm (2in) intervals all over flour, as shown in picture, to make 12 hollows.

2. Spoon prepared marshmallow into hollows in flour bringing it right to the top. (The marshmallow does not affect the flour in any way; after the eggs are made, the flour can be repackaged and used for any purpose.)

3. The marshmallow takes 10 to 15 minutes to set firmly. At the end of this time, touch top with finger, lift out gently. Brush off any few grains of flour still adhering. Join two egg halves together. Top of marshmallow is slightly sticky, so halves cling together well.

4. Eggs can be rolled in tinted coconut or covered with chocolate, as directed in the recipe.

Marshmallow Easter Eggs

WHIP up a batch of marshmallow and let the children make their own Easter eggs. They are so easy, delicious too! The recipe makes six eggs, with directions for bright ways of covering them.

YOU WILL NEED:
1 tablespoon gelatine
¼ cup cold water
½ cup hot water
1 cup sugar
½ teaspoon vanilla
1 teaspoon lemon juice
Marshmallow:
Put cold water in bowl. Gradually stir in gelatine; let stand 5 minutes. Put hot water and sugar in large saucepan, stir over low heat until sugar has dissolved. Add gelatine mixture, stir over low heat until gelatine has dissolved. Bring to boil, boil gently uncovered, 6 minutes. Remove pan from heat, let cool to lukewarm. Put mixture into small bowl of electric mixer, add vanilla and lemon juice. Beat on high speed 5 minutes until thick and creamy and still of pouring consistency. Marshmallow can be coloured with food colouring, if

desired; add a few drops towards end of beating time.

To Cover with Coconut: Put coconut in a basin; you'll need about 2 cups coconut. Add a few drops of desired food colouring. Wet hands, shake off surplus water; use damp hands to rub colouring evenly through coconut. Coat eggs evenly with warmed, sieved jam (apricot is good), then roll in prepared coconut.

To Cover with Chocolate: Put 125g (4oz) dark chocolate into top of double saucepan, stir over simmering water until melted. Add 60g (2oz) solid white vegetable shortening, stir until melted. Remove from heat, cool to lukewarm. Press fork into marshmallow egg, dip in chocolate until evenly coated. Drain off excess chocolate, then roll in coconut (about 2 cups). Refrigerate until chocolate has set.

Buttered Brazil Nuts

THIS confectionery recipe is simplicity itself. A whole brazil nut is encased in a golden shell of toffee, with rum as one of the ingredients. Make some for your family and some as attractive gifts.

YOU WILL NEED:
3 cups sugar
1 cup water
1 tablespoon liquid glucose
30g (1oz) butter
2 tablespoons rum
250g (8oz) shelled brazil nuts

1. Dissolve sugar in water and glucose over low heat. Brush pan sides with wet brush to dissolve any sugar grains.

2. Bring to boil, boil steadily to 235 deg F (112 deg C) or when a small quantity of syrup, dropped into cold water, moulds easily with the fingers into a soft ball. Do not stir.

3. Add butter and rum, boil again without stirring until mixture is light golden brown, approximately 15 minutes. Remove from heat, drop in nuts; do not stir. Return to heat for 1 minute to reheat toffee.

4. So not to stir nuts into toffee, just tilt pan to cover nuts with toffee. Working quickly, lift out nuts one at a time, place on greased oven slide to set.

119

SOMETHING EXTRA...
Make your own Mixed Peel

DON'T throw away the rinds of oranges, lemons or grapefruit — use them to keep a supply of mixed peel, for cakes, biscuits, puddings or just for crunchy nibbling. It's easy to prepare and will keep well in a screwtop or airtight jar.

YOU WILL NEED:
rind from 1 orange
rind from 1 lemon
rind from 1 grapefruit
1½ cups sugar

1. Peel fruit, leaving the white pith on skin. Cut peel into 5mm (¼in) strips, then cut into 5mm (¼in) cubes.

2. Put chopped peel in saucepan, add enough water just to cover fruit. Bring to boil, reduce heat, simmer 10 minutes; drain. Put fruit back into saucepan, add water just to cover, bring to boil, reduce heat, simmer 10 minutes, drain again, reserve ½ cup of the liquid.

3. Put reserved liquid, ½ cup water and 1 cup of the sugar in saucepan, stir over low heat until sugar has dissolved, bring to boil. Remove from heat, pour over fruit, stand overnight.

4. Next day, put peel and liquid and remaining ½ cup sugar in saucepan, stir over low heat until sugar has dissolved; bring to the boil, reduce heat, simmer 15 minutes. Remove from heat, drain well. Cover a wire rack with greaseproof paper. Spread the peel out on this; allow to stand overnight to dry, moving the peel about occasionally with fork to separate.

1. Place water and salt into large pan, bring to boil. Gradually sprinkle cornmeal over water, stirring constantly. Make sure that there are no lumps of cornmeal.

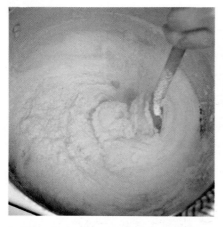

2. Turn heat down to low, continue to stir Polenta until mixture is very thick, approximately 20 minutes.

3. Leave Polenta over low heat for approximately 8 minutes, stirring occasionally. It will be ready to remove from heat when a wooden spoon will stand upright in centre of Polenta, as shown in picture, and not droop to sides of pan.

Italian Polenta

POLENTA is the bread of northern Italy, particularly around Venice. It can be kept refrigerated, and fried just when required. It can be eaten for any meal although generally it is served with a dish which contains liquid, such as a chicken casserole.

4. Spoon mixture into oiled 28cm x 18cm (11in x 7in) lamington tin. Spread mixture out evenly with a fork. Allow to become cold, then leave at room temperature for 4 hours, or let stand overnight.

5. Turn Polenta out of tin. Cut into 4cm (1½in) slices, then cut each slice in half. Heat butter and oil in large frying pan, add Polenta slices, reduce heat to low and fry gently until dark golden brown on both sides, approximately 5 minutes on each side. Place on to serving dish, sprinkle with grated parmesan cheese, if desired.
Serves 4 to 6.

YOU WILL NEED:
2 litres (8 cups) water
2 teaspoons salt
3½ cups cornmeal
90g (3oz) butter
3 tablespoons oil

Melba Toast

THIN, crunchy slices of Melba Toast, piled high in a basket, are an attractive addition to the dinner party table. Serve them with pate as a first course, as an accompaniment to the main course, or with dips when enjoying drinks among your guests.

1. Take a square loaf of unsliced bread, remove all crusts. Cut bread in half, giving two half-loaves (this way, it is easier to handle the cutting of individual slices). Now cut each loaf diagonally in half, giving four thick triangle-shaped bread pieces.

2. Place flat side down on board, as shown. Cut into wafer-thin slices. An electric knife is good for this, but any serrated or sharp knife can be used. Place triangles on ungreased baking trays. Bake in moderate oven 15 to 20 minutes, turning frequently. Melba toast will keep well for about two weeks if stored in an air-tight container.

SOMETHING EXTRA

Herb butter has many uses. Spoon it on to hot steaks or chops, so that the savoury mixture melts and forms a sauce to complement the meat.

Or put a spoonful on top of hot peas, beans or broccoli. Or spread it between slices of french bread to make a hot herbed loaf. You may think making herb butter is easy — that it doesn't need a step-by-step lesson. But we discovered a wonderfully easy way to shape the butter into a neat round log, and we wanted to share it with you.

YOU WILL NEED:
250g (8oz) butter
1 tablespoon chopped chives
1 tablespoon chopped fresh dill (or 1 teaspoon dried dill)
1 tablespoon chopped parsley
2 cloves garlic
¼ teaspoon mixed herbs
salt, pepper

1. Beat butter until light and creamy, fold in chopped chives, dill and parsley, crushed garlic, mixed herbs, salt and pepper. Spoon mixture in a rough log shape about a quarter of the way down a sheet of greaseproof paper.

Herb Butter

2. Fold paper over roll then, with ruler, push against the butter, as shown, so that mixture forms a smooth roll.

3. Roll butter in the greaseproof paper, refrigerate until firm. Cut into slices to top grilled steak, vegetables, etc.

4. You can also use the butter to make Herb Bread, which is delicious to serve with grills or at a barbecue. Slice a french loaf, cutting just to the bottom of the crust but not right through. Spread the butter on each side of each slice. Wrap in aluminium foil and bake in a moderate oven 15 to 20 minutes.

124

1. Wash lettuce well, discard tough outer leaves; pat dry, put into plastic bag and refrigerate until leaves are nicely crisp. Tear leaves into pieces, place in bowl.

2. Make the dressing. Put all dressing ingredients, except egg, in screw-top jar. To coddle egg, gently lower egg into boiling water, boil 1 minute. Remove egg from shell, add to ingredients in screw-top jar, shake well. Four finely chopped anchovy fillets can be added to the dressing, if desired.

Caesar Salad

SO many dishes are enhanced when served with a salad, and it always adds an attractively fresh look to your dinner table when you are entertaining. There are many ways of preparing salad, and as often happens with good food, the simplest recipes can often be among the best. Caesar Salad is a good example. It is simple, yet — with its topping of crunchy croutons — it has become world famous. Many restaurants claim its invention, though it is said by some people to have originated in a Mexican restaurant. The dressing can be tossed, without the egg, through the salad, then the egg can be added and tossed through separately. We think the egg mixes better when added to the dressing. Recipe serves six.

YOU WILL NEED:
2 small lettuce
30g (1oz) butter
1 clove garlic
2 slices bread
2 rashers bacon
grated parmesan cheese
chopped parsley

DRESSING
⅔ cup french dressing
1 teaspoon salt
1 coddled egg (see below)
1 teaspoon prepared mustard

3. Remove crusts from bread, cut bread into 1cm (½in) cubes. Heat butter with crushed garlic in pan, add bread cubes, cook until brown and crisp. Drain on absorbent paper. Cook chopped bacon separately until crisp, drain on absorbent paper. Add dressing to salad, toss well. Scatter croutons and bacon pieces over salad, top with chopped parsley and grated cheese.

Green Tomato Pickles

THERE'S nothing like a good flavoured pickle to add zest to food, particularly cold meats. And Green Tomato Pickle is always an outstanding favourite. It is a fast seller at fetes, too.

YOU WILL NEED:

2 kg (4lb) green tomatoes
1 kg (2lb) onions
½ medium cauliflower
1 medium cucumber
2 litres (8 cups) water
¼ cup salt

½ cup plain flour
2½ cups brown sugar, firmly packed
1½ teaspoons dry mustard
2 teaspoons turmeric
¼ teaspoon cayenne
1 teaspoon curry powder
2½ cups brown vinegar

3. Gradually add brown sugar mixture to vegetables, stir until combined. Return pan to heat, stir until mixture boils, boil for 3 minutes, remove pan from heat.

1. Chop tomatoes, peel and chop onions, chop cauliflower into flowerets, peel and chop cucumber. Put all vegetables into very large bowl, pour water over, add salt, stir until combined. Cover and stand overnight. Next day put vegetables and all liquid into very large pan. Bring to boil, boil uncovered for 2 minutes; drain. Return vegetables to pan.

2. In another saucepan place flour, brown sugar, mustard, turmeric, cayenne and curry powder, stir until combined. Gradually add vinegar, mix to a smooth paste. Stand saucepan over heat, stir until sauce boils and thickens. Reduce heat, simmer for 2 minutes, remove pan from heat.

4. Pour mixture into hot sterilized jars; seal. Makes approximately 2 litres.

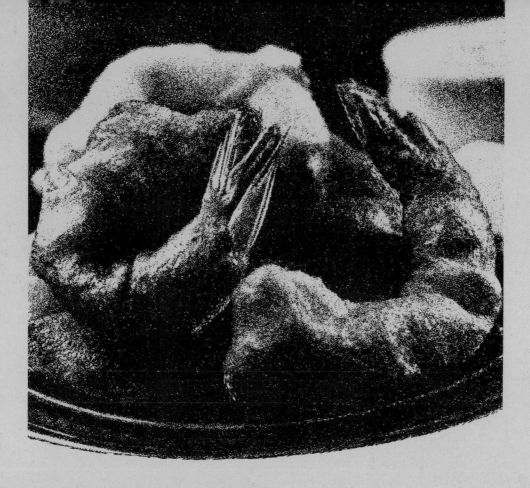

For your information...

OVEN TEMPERATURES

Electric Temperatures	Fahrenheit	Celsius
Very slow	250	120
Slow	300	150
Moderately slow	325-350	160-180
Moderate	375-400	190-200
Moderately hot	425-450	220-230
Hot	475-500	250-260
Very hot	525-550	270-290

Gas Temperatures	Fahrenheit	Celsius
Very slow	250	120
Slow	275-300	140-150
Moderately slow	325	160
Moderate	350	180
Moderately hot	375	190
Hot	400-450	200-230
Very hot	475-500	250-260

CUP MEASURES

	Metric	Imperial
1 cup flour	140g	4½oz
1 cup sugar (crystal or castor)	250g	8oz
1 cup brown sugar, firmly packed	185g	6oz
1 cup icing sugar, sifted	185g	6oz
1 cup shortening (butter, margarine, etc.)	250g	8oz
1 cup honey, golden syrup, treacle	375g	12oz
1 cup fresh breadcrumbs	60g	2oz
1 cup packet dry breadcrumbs	155g	5oz
1 cup crushed biscuit crumbs	125g	4oz
1 cup rice, uncooked	220g	7oz
1 cup mixed fruit or individual fruit such as sultanas, etc.	185g	6oz
1 cup nuts, chopped	125g	4oz
1 cup coconut, desiccated	90g	3oz

CUP AND SPOON MEASURES

Recipes in this book use this standard metric equipment approved by the Australian Standards Association:

(a) 250 millilitre cup for measuring liquids. A litre jug (capacity 4 cups) also is available.

(b) a graduated set of four cups — measuring 1 cup, half, third and quarter cup — for measuring items such as flour, sugar, etc. When measuring in these fractional cups, level off at the brim.

(c) a graduated set of four spoons: tablespoon (20 millilitre liquid capacity); teaspoon (5 millilitre); and half and quarter teaspoons.

Note: All spoon measurements are level.

Production: Philip Gore. Design: Terry Welsby.
Type set by Photoset Computer Service Pty Ltd, Sydney, Australia.
Printed by Dai Nippon Printing Co Ltd, Tokyo, Japan.

Index